REVELATIONS OF DIVINE LOVE, by Dame
Juliana of Norwich, takes its place among such great mystical
classics as those of John of the Cross and Teresa of Avila. We
do not know much about Juliana's life, but we do know of her
joyful relationship with Christ and her deep desire to *share*
that joy with every Christian. This new translation captures
beautifully her homey, simple imagery and reveals a sensitive,
holy woman whose visions of God are accessible and inspiring
to all.

Here are some other titles in the Image Spiritual Classics
Series:

THE RULE OF ST. BENEDICT, translated by Anthony C. Meisel
and M. L. del Mastro. The Rule has been an indispensable
model not only for religious and monks but for all Christians.

INTRODUCTION TO THE DEVOUT LIFE, St. Francis de Sales.
". . . among the half dozen best devotional guides of all
time."                        —*The Journal of Religious Thought*

SPIRITUAL CANTICLE, St. John of the Cross. "This book is a
gift of God to man." —E. Allison Peers

ABANDONMENT TO DIVINE PROVIDENCE, Jean Pierre de Caus-
sade. A book for all souls who truly seek God.

CLOUD OF UNKNOWING. On the Christian mystical experience.

THE IMITATION OF CHRIST, Thomas à Kempis. On the way
to perfect peace.

WAY OF PERFECTION, Teresa of Avila. A superb classic on the
practice of prayer.

# Juliana of Norwich

# REVELATIONS
# OF DIVINE LOVE

TRANSLATED,
WITH AN INTRODUCTION,
BY M. L. DEL MASTRO

IMAGE BOOKS
A Division of Doubleday & Company, Inc.
Garden City, New York
1977

Library of Congress Cataloging in Publication Data

Juliana, anchoret, 1343–1443.
Revelations of divine love.

1. Devotional literature.   I. Del Mastro, M. L.
II. Title.
BV4831.J8  1977     231'.74
ISBN 0-385-12297-7
Library of Congress Catalog Card Number 76–52004

# CONTENTS

# INTRODUCTION

The Black Death (from 1348), a large part of the Hundred Years' War (1337–1453), the Peasants' Revolt (1381), the reigns of Edward III (1327–77) and Richard II (1377–99), the defeat, abdication and execution of Richard and the usurpation of his throne by Bolingbroke as Henry IV (1399–1413), and the beginning of the reign of Henry V (1413–22) all took place within the lifetime of the woman we know as Dame Julian, or Juliana, of Norwich. Yet no hint of these momentous events appears in her book.

From her we learn nothing of the struggles for supremacy in England between king and barons, king and pope. She tells us nothing of the flourishing commercial center of the cathedral city of Norwich, nothing of the growing power of Parliament, nothing of the hardships imposed on the poor and the middle class by increased taxes and tariffs to finance royal military ambitions, nothing of growing civil unrest. She speaks of no battles, though Crécy and Neville's Cross were fought in her childhood, Wat Tyler led his rebellious peasants in an unsuccessful revolt against the poll tax and villeinage when she was thirty-eight, and she was still alive when Henry V triumphed at Agincourt (1415).

The popes, in political and economic "captivity" in Avignon since 1309, returned to Rome in 1377. Unlike her contemporary Catherine of Siena, who, by her letters, had been instrumental in returning the Papacy to Rome, Juliana does not condemn the captivity nor rejoice at the restoration of the Church to its traditional center. The Great Schism (1378–1417), following hard upon this return, tore the Church in three warring pieces. Again unlike Catherine, Juliana does not choose sides, does not deplore the situation, does not castigate those responsible for it. She ignores the entire issue.

More surprising perhaps is her silence in regard to local

corruption of the Church in its clergy and hierarchy, especially as three of her English contemporaries, John Wycliffe, William Langland, and Geoffrey Chaucer, in very different styles, attacked it vigorously.

Oxford-trained John Wycliffe (d. 1384) not only protested the dominance of a church hierarchy and scholastic reasoning in what he considered the purely personal area of the individual's practice of his faith, he set about restoring this area to what he considered its proper controller: each Christian. To this end he had Scripture translated from Latin to English. He sent preachers (later, with their followers, called Lollards and judged heretical), from village to village to expound its moral lessons. Wycliffe also wrote extensively against what he felt were abuses in organized Christian practice (masses for the dead, elaborate worship services, indulgences) and against regulations by Church authorities which curtailed Christian freedom.

Although Juliana does not cite nor even seem to see Wycliffe's points, his notion—that the gift of faith is exercised in the dialogue between man and God—is given living illustration in her work. Indeed, her book repeats portions of her dialogue with God as it extended over twenty years, while focusing on the sixteen particular revelations of her extraordinary illness. But she is not interested in proselytizing. Further, she has no quarrel with the official Church. She records the welcome presence of her curate at the scene of the revelations and her reception of the sacraments and last rites of the Church at his hands before the revelations began. Juliana is no Lollard, even unconsciously.

If Juliana does not follow Wycliffe, still less does she take the tack of William Langland, whose *Vision of Piers the Plowman* appeared in its first form in 1362—some ten years before she had experienced the sixteen revelations and thirty years before she had them written down. Langland, disappointed of a Church career by the death of a patron and his own poverty, bitterly excoriated general and particular corruption in the Church in a complex allegorical and satiric dream-vision. His targets included the perpetrators of Wycliffe's "abuses," and he focused particularly on the motives of greed and pride as their twin roots. Instead of pointing out men's failures to be human and Christian, Juliana focuses on the love of a living, loving, personal God, His sufferings, and her response to them. The anchorhold at Norwich might as well have been in China for all the notice she takes of current sins and scandals, local persons and events, or the general and particular immoralities of the failed shepherds of a spiritually starving, helpless flock.

Juliana is not callous. It is simply that, for her purposes in this book, she is not a "noticer." Her business is not to observe and comment, harshly or gently, upon the foibles and failings of those around her, as Chaucer (d. 1400) in his *Canterbury Tales* made it his, but to observe God alone, to listen to Him and make her response, and to transmit the experience to her fellow Christians.

## Juliana

Who was this extraordinarily single-minded woman?

We do not know.

We do not know her surname, nor even that her baptismal name was Julian, or Juliana. (She may have acquired the name by which we call her simply by the fact of her anchorhold's being attached to the Church of St. Julian in Norwich. We do not know.)

We know nothing of her family or its circumstances, nothing of her life within it. We do not know when, or how, she came to recognize her vocation to the life of an anchoress, or whether the decision was made before, or after, the revelations, which may have been granted her while she was still living in her mother's house or may have come to her in the anchorhold. We have the evidence of the *Ancriene Riewle* for what may have been her way of living as an anchoress, but we do not know that she knew this work, nor that she saw the vocation in the same light or with the same consequences as the author of this treatise. We do not know how she lived within the anchorhold. We have her word for it that she "could no letter" but do not know whether this indicates true illiteracy (not unlikely) or simply lack of extended formal education, whether in English or Latin. We do not know who were her friends, who her enemies. We do not know exactly when or where she was born, how or how long she lived, or the time, place or manner of her death.

Neither Juliana nor her scribe gives us the biographical details we children of the twentieth century seem to find indispensable. The omission is deliberate. Juliana did not wish attention focused on herself. Her reason is quite simple; she expresses it at the end of Chapter 8. Having recounted the circumstances surrounding the revelations and the content of what she calls the "first showing," and having noted that the revelations were intended for all, she says,

And therefore, I beg you all for God's sake, and advise you for your own profit, stop looking at the wretch to whom this revelation was shown. Intently, wisely and meekly, look at God, who because of his courteous love and unending goodness wills to show it to all of us in general, for our comfort.

It is God, not Juliana, who is to be attended to and heeded; the creature is simply his instrument. Heeding the transmitter, rather than the message and him who sends it, would be a grave and wasteful error.

A secondary motive, of which Juliana herself makes no mention, can be found in a fairly common medieval attitude toward the value of the individual and the particular in a universal context. The attitude, most clearly apparent in the work of the majority of medieval hagiographers, is that what was distinctive, individual, eccentric, unique to a particular person was, by that fact, flawed, imperfect. It marked the person's separation or distance from the ideal man or woman, the mirror of Christ the Christian was to strive to become.

The saint, who, by definition, had become such a mirror, was presumed to have eliminated such wayward, individualistic behavior and tendencies. To the extent that he had, he could be a model for his fellow Christians, who were supposed to be striving to eliminate, or at least to suppress, their own individuating tendencies and personal quirks. That was the chief function served by the hagiography—the written account of the saint's life focusing on the means by which he had left his individual self behind to become like Christ. Biographical data were used only insofar as they gave evidence of Christlike behavior, not for a "humanizing" touch. The saint, after all, was to be "divinized" as far as possible.

Thus, those who took religion seriously, and seriously strove to live its ideals, were generally trained to avoid the personal and idiosyncratic as extraneous and distracting, if not directly harmful. Benedict's *Regula* (Doubleday Image Books, 1975), the philosophical and practical foundation for most organized communal monastic life in medieval Europe for a thousand years, stresses the importance of "leveling" among the monks: all were to be equals in Christ, though rank by seniority of monastic service ordered the group. The *Rule* makes a particular point of the need for humility, describing twelve steps in the practice of this virtue which all but eliminate any attention to self.

Juliana, as far as we know, was not a member of a religious community before or after her revelations. She was an anchoress—a solitary living in a cell of two or three rooms built adjacent to a church (in many cases using the church for its fourth wall), devoting her life to prayer and meditation. Juliana also seems to have served as spiritual adviser to many who came to Norwich to her anchorhold to consult her. Margery Kempe, a religious enthusiast from nearby Lynne, mother of fourteen children, maker of pilgrimages and receiver of revelations herself, tells us in her book that she consulted Juliana about her own manner of life and her revelations. The reply she records is full of Juliana's usual good sense and great kindness, and echoes the tone and content of the *Revelations*.

Juliana, then, would not have been following Benedict's *Regula*, but, as the section quoted above suggests, she possessed to the full the spirit of humility he proposed. Attention to herself, and to the chronological details of her life for their own sakes, simply would not have occurred to her.

All this is not to say that we know nothing of Juliana but

her message. We have, in fact, a wealth of personal and circumstantial detail surrounding her reception of the revelations, which might strike us as surprising, particularly in view of the dearth of such detail concerning any other part of her life. The explanation is not difficult, in light of what has been said above, and the apparent deviation from principle is, in fact, absolute consistency.

As we have seen, for Juliana, God alone mattered. His will, his glory were all-important, and anything else was, literally, not. The revelations were given her, she realized, not just for herself but for all her fellow Christians—and not just those of her own place (England) and time (fourteenth century). Consequently they must be preserved, in writing, for that would last, and in such a way that they would be accessible and acceptable to those for whom they were intended. There must be some evidence provided for her trustworthiness, and for the credibility of what she had to say. People must not be "put off" from accepting God and this particular gift of his love because she had presented the revelations badly. They were real, not fantasy or illusion, and she must allow them to be seen so.

It is this principle and motive that determines the biographical details Juliana includes or omits from her account of the revelations.

Her scribes agreed with her in principles, motive, and practice. Consequently, they add no further biographical details of the recipient of the *Revelations*, if they had any, but leave Juliana to decide what shall and shall not be told.

To vouch for his own accuracy and trustworthiness in recording what she has told him, the scribe of the 1413 manuscript, the earliest we have, calls on Juliana herself in his Preface:

Here is a vision, shown by the goodness of God to a devout woman named Juliana, who is a recluse at Norwich and is still alive in this year of our Lord 1413. In this vision, there are a great many comforting and deeply moving words for all those who desire to be Christ's lovers.

Presumably, had he erred in repeating any of these "comforting words" or fabricated the revelations in whole or in part, the living voice of their recipient would have been raised to contradict him.

The biography that emerges from this concerted attempt to avoid biography does so reluctantly.

We learn that Juliana was born in late 1342, not because she says so but because she tells us she was "thirty and one-half years old" when the revelations were given her, on Sunday, May 8, 1373. It was, she would have us understand, a mature, responsible woman, not an impressionable child, who received the revelations.

Further, the revelations were not a generalized, euphoric, timeless "experience" but a specific event whose reality occurred on a specific day and a precise date, in a particular place, in front of independent witnesses. The revelations were so real as to be almost solid.

The witnesses were certainly real enough. Juliana does not name them and only indicates the identity of the two most important for her purposes: her mother and the curate. These two witnesses were in place before the relevations began, and remained with Juliana throughout their course.

Though none of those present could hear or see what Juliana saw and heard, all could attest to the fact that *something* was happening. At one point during the fifth revelation, Chapter 13 in the book, Juliana reports that, seeing the devil and all evil brought to nothing, "I laughed loud and long, which made those who were around me laugh too, and their laughter was a pleasure to me."

Later, after the completion of the first fifteen showings, but before the sixteenth, Juliana slept and was sent a dream of the devil, which she reports in Chapter 66. Having described the images of her dream, she continues:

This ugly showing was given me while I was asleep, as no other was. During all this time, I trusted to be saved and preserved by the mercy of God. Our courteous Lord gave me the grace of waking up, and I scarcely had any life left. The people who were with me observed me and wet my temples, and my heart began to take comfort.

And at once a little smoke came in through the door with a great deal of heat and a foul stench. I said, "Bless the Lord! Everything here is on fire!" I imagined it was a physical fire that would burn us all to death. I asked those who were with me if they smelled any stench, and they said no, they smelled nothing. I said, "Blessed be God!" because then I understood clearly that it was the fiend, who had only come to tempt me.

Further, the mother who had borne and raised her could bear witness to her habitual veracity and non-hysterical temperament, and the curate, the guide of her spirit, could give evidence of the continuance of these traits as well as of her general spiritual condition. Neither would be likely to encourage her in imaginative folly, if such were evident, nor would either connive at deception, if Juliana were attempting to practice it.

The curate, as an officer of the Church, could also, if required, speak to the doctrinal orthodoxy of the revelations, once he had learned their content. He was an excellent witness both to the character of Juliana and to the value of what she said.

Thus, Juliana provides her audience, contemporary and twentieth-century, with a set of pegs on which to fasten the revelations she has received and would pass on, into three-dimensional, historical reality. If the audience should choose not to accept her gift, it will not be on the grounds of unreality.

Nor must the revelations be left open to rejection on the grounds that they were the hallucinations of an over-stimulated, imaginative piety or of a diseased psyche. Juliana's evident balance and common sense eliminate the second possibility at once. To answer any objections along the lines of the first, Juliana provides her audience with a complete circumstantial account of the giving of the revelations. She includes not only the external details which her witnesses can corroborate, but internal psychological information as well. Since the latter was known to her alone, she could have left it unrevealed—and no doubt would have, had deceit been her object. Her candor, far from diminishing the audience's sense of her reliability, serves to increase it.

Juliana begins by reporting, in Chapter 2, the three

requests she had made of God prior to the granting of the revelations. Of these, the first is perhaps the most damaging to her credibility, on the face of it. She relates that she asked of God "a vision in which I might have more knowledge of the bodily pains of our savior, and of the compassion of our Lady and of all his true lovers who were living at that time and saw his pains."

Juliana immediately adds her reason for the request. "For I wanted to be one of them and suffer with him," amplifying somewhat further on: "I made this first petition so that after the showing I might have a truer understanding of the passion of Christ."

The case for imaginative piety run wild seems plain here: she wanted to see, and so she saw. Several elements work against it, however.

First, Juliana's request was not for a specific vision, nor even for specific personages or events, but for a sight that would have the effect of increasing her awareness of the sufferings of Christ in the passion, and her awareness of the cosufferings of Mary and all the other witnesses of the passion. She does not ask to see the passion, or any part of it, for herself, leaving it to God to choose something that will accomplish her desires.

Further, she asks this gift (as she does the second, which we shall consider in its turn) "with a condition (for it seemed to me that this was not the common object of prayer). Therefore I said, 'Lord, you know what I want. If it's your will for me to have it, let me have it. If it's not your will, good Lord, don't be displeased, for I only want what you will.'"

Further still she assures us, "I never desired any other vision or showing from God until my soul should be parted from my body. . . ." Her frankness in revealing the original request leads the audience to accept this declaration at face value.

Here is no would-be visionary, vaporing and daydreaming, but a responsible, serious, religious woman who wishes only to love her Lord better. She believes a vision will help, but is quite willing to defer to him both in the matter and manner of the vision and in its very granting.

Finally, Juliana tells us, she forgot about this request, together with the second, while she dwelt continually upon the third, where, as we shall see, dwelling could accomplish something. Apparently, having asked for two gifts she felt would be useful though not in any way essential, frills almost, Juliana submitted the decision to God, needing neither to repeat nor to dwell on her requests. Whatever God willed would come to pass, and would be for her best good. Again, Juliana's candor inclines the audience to believe her.

Juliana's second request, like her first, is, as she considers it, useful but not essential. This, too, is subjected to the condition of the first: if it is his will that she have it, she wishes it, but not otherwise. She tells us she asked for bodily illness at thirty years of age "so severe it would bring me to the point of death." Her reason for wishing a sickness so severe that she should believe herself to be dying and "have all the kinds of bodily and spiritual pain I would have had if I had actually been dying. I wanted all the terrors, the temptations of devils, and every kind of pain except the actual departure of the soul," is of a piece with the reason for her desire for a vision. She explains, "I asked all this so that by it I might be purged, by God's mercy, and afterward live more for the glory of God, because of that sickness. I also hoped it would assist me in my death, for I desired to be soon with my God and maker."

No mistaken notions of her own strength appear here. Juliana sees herself in need of purging, and envisions the illness as the most effective means of accomplishing it, as she felt a vision would be the best way for God to bring her to a fuller awareness of what he had suffered for her. Here is no self-centered, would-be saint checking her halo in advance, but a would-be lover of God who suggests to him ways to make her love him better, but does not, ever, insist upon her ways.

Coupled with the third request, which, she tells us, she asked "without any condition" and which "dwelled with me continually," the first two subsequently forgotten requests suggest not the hysteric, searching for sensation and a likely victim of her own delusions, but the eager lover desiring only to please her divine beloved, holding to nothing except his will for her. Juliana's complete submission to God is, perhaps, the surest guarantee of her freedom from illusion and delusion.

The third request was different in kind from the other two. The good asked was purely spiritual and obviously God's will, which is why Juliana could ask it "without any condition." Juliana tells us,

> Concerning my third petition, by the grace of God and the teaching of holy Church, I conceived a very great desire to receive three wounds in my life—that is to say, the wound of true contrition, the wound of natural compassion, and the wound of fullhearted longing for God.

These conditions of spirit that Juliana requested, contrition for sin, compassion for her "fellow Christians" and fullhearted longing for God, are not single experiences but habitual attitudes and behavior—virtues, in short. They are not granted once for all, but acquired by persistent, daily, sometimes painful practice. Thus Juliana's continual awareness of her third request was in itself both the granting and the receiving of it, as giving and receiving become a single reality in love.

Unlike the third, Juliana's forgetting of her first and second requests was the necessary condition for their being granted. Had she remembered asking for the illness "at the age of thirty" at the time she became ill (and she did become very ill, so that she received the last rites of the Church and all with her were sure she would die), the effect she wanted—purgation through the experience of dying—would not have been achieved. In one corner of her mind, a voice would have kept saying, "But I'm not *really* dying"—and that, in secular terms, would have spoiled the effect. A sort of charade, an imaginative *tour de force* would have resulted, with the attention focused on self, not God, yielding only increased pride.

Instead, having forgotten the request, Juliana received the illness as an unwonted, and most unwelcome, visitation—though not for the reasons one might expect. Having con-

cluded she was inevitably to die, and that soon, she remarks
in Chapter 3:

> Since I was still young, I thought it a great hardship to die,
> but not because there was anything on earth I wanted to
> live for, nor because I feared the pain, for I trusted in
> God's mercy. I would have preferred to live so that I could
> have loved God better, for a longer time, and thus, by the
> grace of God, have been able to know and love him better
> in the bliss of heaven.

Juliana's conclusion that she was about to die was based
not on emotions, or desires, but on observations and conclusions drawn from them. She says, "And I understood by my
reason, and because of the pain I was feeling, that I was
going to die. . . ." Her response to this realization is that of
a good Christian: ". . . so I assented fully, with all my heart
and will, to be at God's disposal." Her conviction that her
death was imminent (a conviction shared by those surrounding her, who sent for the curate to give her the last rites of
the Church to assist her passing from this world to the
next), lends force to what follows.

The curate held up the crucifix and bade her gaze on it,
since she had lost all power of motion and speech. Her com-
pliance is not exactly what one accustomed to the hagiographers would expect, but its ring is absolutely authentic. It
suggests something of Juliana's strength of mind, common
sense and independence of judgment, as well as her willingness to defer to the judgment of those to whom she owes
obedience. She remarks:

> It seemed to me I was all right as I was, for my eyes were
> fixed upward, gazing in the direction of the heaven into
> which I trusted I should come by the mercy of God. But
> nevertheless I assented to fix my eyes on the face of the
> crucifix, if I could do it, and so I did. It seemed to me that
> I might last longer looking straight ahead than directly up-
> ward.

Juliana's obedience brought its reward. All her senses continued to fade. She tells us:

> After this my sight began to fail, and it grew as dark
> around me in the chamber as if it had been night. I could

only see, I don't know how, the image on the cross, in daylight. . . .

After this, the other part of my body [from the waist upward] began to die, to the point where I had scarcely any feeling, and my greatest pain was shortness of breath. At that point, I was sure I was going to die.

At this point, though she still had not remembered it, Juliana's second request was fully granted. She had experienced the process of death up to the very moment when she would have completed it and died. But she was not to die—again as she had asked and then forgotten—

And then, suddenly, all my pain was taken from me, and I was as whole and healthy in every part of my body as I had ever been before.

Juliana's reaction to this sudden cessation of her illness is cautious. She recognizes the hand of God in it, but does not see herself as the recipient of a miracle, and continues to expect to die. She reports,

I marveled at this sudden change, for it seemed to me that this was a secret working of God, and not the work of nature. And yet this feeling of ease did not convince me that I should live, nor, indeed, was it a complete comfort to me. For I would have preferred to be freed from this world, and had had my heart set on it.

Here speaks a practical woman who relies on the evidence of her senses and expects only the ordinary to happen to her.

It is at this point that Juliana remembers the second part of her third, unconditional request, the gift of "natural compassion." She has been dwelling on the three parts of this request "continually," as she has testified earlier, and now, combining the desire with her own experience of dying, she asks for compassion for our Lord in his sufferings:

Then it came suddenly into my mind that I should desire the second wound as a gracious gift of our Lord, so that my body might be filled completely with the understanding and experience of his blessed passion, as I had previously prayed. I desired with compassion that his pain should be my pain, and afterward, that I should be completely filled with longing for him.

There is a difference between this prayer and the first, now forgotten, request she had made for a vision to enable her to share in the Lord's passion. Now, faced with death (as she supposes), she emphatically does not desire a vision, but the effect the vision was supposed to have. There is no time for the intermediate stage. She declares:

> But in this prayer I never desired any vision, nor any kind of showing from God—only compassion, as, it seemed to me, a soul following its natural bent might have for our Lord Jesus, who for love chose to become a mortal man. And therefore, I desired to suffer with him, living in my mortal body, as God would give me grace.

This declaration, that at the moment the vision she had once requested was about to be granted her, she not only did not remember having asked for it but did not want it, should serve to clear Juliana of any suspicion of having induced the experiences that follow out of her own desires and imagination, however well-intentioned and God-centered.

She is not a seeker after fame, is not puffed up with her own importance as a receiver of God's gifts, is not particularly aware of herself at all, except insofar as her personal responses and the reactions of the witnesses lend credibility to the revelations.

The point for Juliana is that nothing must stand between God and his children, and nothing, particularly herself, must either hamper him from giving them the gifts he wills for them, or prevent them from receiving these gifts. She is to be transparent, a medium through which God may reveal himself as he chooses to all her fellow Christians.

## The Message

God, as Juliana experiences him in the hours of revelation and the years of subsequent meditation, was a "courteous Lord," "homely" with his creatures, concerned for their welfare, and desirous of their love. This was the heart of the revelations, the truth to which Juliana bore witness in her book and her life.

Perhaps the most striking element in Juliana's report of God is her invariable reference to him as "courteous" and to the source of and reason for his deeds as his "courtesy." On the face of it, courtesy would seem incompatible with omnipotence, or at least unnecessary to it. Even we twentieth-century egalitarians expect courtesy—gentleness, respect, graciousness, politeness and ceremonious deference—to be expressed by a lesser person to his superior, and are both surprised and extraordinarily gratified when these courtesies flow in the opposite direction.

Medieval men and women, with their acute sense of social and spiritual hierarchies and of the behavior proper to persons of each relatively fixed, relatively permanent rank in dealing with persons of higher or lower ranks, might reasonably be expected to have been thunderstruck by the paradox. A "courteous Lord" who is at once God, the omnipotent creator of all that is, and a respectful pleader for the love of his creature, man, might be staggered at, even rejected, but the paradox would not go unnoticed by a medieval audience.

That the "courtesy" Juliana ascribes to God as she experienced him is not simply the "formal behavior proper to a court" incumbent on both the courtier and the king (a sort of divine *noblesse oblige*) is made clear by her insistent linking of it to the word "homely" (unassuming, unpretentious, homelike, friendly, familiar) in almost every instance.

In Chapter 7, Juliana makes an early and full declaration of this paradox. Having described the delight a servant would take in the public friendliness of his lord to him (an illustration the Lord, she says, provided for her), she continues, "And thus it is between our Lord Jesus and us, for truly, it is the greatest joy possible, as I see it, that he who is highest and mightiest, noblest and worthiest, becomes lowest and meekest, friendliest and most courteous."

The point of all this homely courtesy was even more startling for a fourteenth (and perhaps also for a twentieth) century audience. The Lord confined his omnipotence to homely courtesy in order to persuade Juliana (and all her fellow Christians) not that she ought to desire him and his love but that he, in soberest fact, desired her love.

It is in Chapters 5 and 6 that Juliana records this desire explicitly. In Chapter 5 she makes the traditional point that until man rests in God he can have no rest, no happiness, no final satisfaction, and that God wills that man love him because of this fact. Then she says, "Our Lord also showed that it is a very great pleasure to him when a simple soul comes to him nakedly, plainly and unpretentiously, for he is the habitual dwelling of the soul touched by the Holy Spirit." Where one would expect the creature to be delighted to find its natural home in its Lord, Juliana shows us the Lord delighted when the creature assents to its own best interests by coming to him. One is reminded of the parent's rejoicing in his offspring's choice of his own best good. In both cases, the more powerful being, respecting the freedom of the weaker, will not, cannot in fact, force the good, but waits and hopes for it to be chosen and rejoices when it is.

In Chapter 6 the conclusions to which this insight gives rise are elucidated. Man is beloved of God, Juliana says, and "there is no creature made who can realize how much, how sweetly and how tenderly our maker loves us. . . . Our natural will is to have God, and the good will of God is to have us, and we may never cease willing or longing for him until we have him in the fulness of joy, and then we shall will no longer. For he wills that we be occupied in knowing and loving until the time that we shall find fulfillment in heaven."

The *Revelations* are shot through with evidence supporting this description. Let us cite three examples.

In Chapter 14, Juliana reports the gratitude of God to man for his service in freedom, and the rewards of bliss he will give for every day of this service.

In Chapter 22, the love God bears man is specifically linked to Christ's passion. Juliana quotes a piece of the conversation between God and herself which makes the link clear. The snatch of dialogue is made the more poignant by the fact that Juliana believed she was on her deathbed gazing at the image of Christ on the cross at the time the revelations were made. She reports:

> Then our good Lord Jesus Christ asked me, "Are you really pleased that I suffered for you?"
>
> I said, "Yes, good Lord, thank you so much! Yes, good Lord, blessed may you be!"
>
> Then our good, kind Lord Jesus said, "If you are satisfied, I am satisfied. It is a joy, a bliss, an endless delight to me that I ever suffered the passion for you, and if I could suffer more, I would."

Again, in the same chapter, Juliana reports that we, the saved, are Christ's "bliss . . . his reward . . . his glory . . . his crown" in heaven, not because we are good, but because he has saved us, because he loves us.

The next step God takes in revealing himself and his love to Juliana, she reports, is to examine the negative relation between man and God: sin. As the positive relation, love, was examined from God's point of view, with the startling revelation discussed above as a result, so the examination of sin from God's point of view proceeds, amplifying the central truth of the whole revelation in unexpected though entirely orthodox and self-consistent ways.

To begin with, Juliana sees, in Chapter 11, that sin is not a deed, that it does not exist as a real thing, because, considering the workings of the Lord in his creatures, God does all the real deeds, which are consequently good. Chapter 13 brings the revelation that the devil is contained by God's power, works only with God's permission, and is frustrated absolutely and eternally because every bit of evil he tries to do and every bit of pain and misery he tries to cause is turned to joy and eternal glory for man and God.

In Chapter 27, Juliana repeats that sin "has no kind of substance and no part of being," adding that "it cannot be known except by the pain." The pain she sees as an agent of purgation and a cause for compassion both in God for all men and by men for their fellows. Men are to remember that they do not suffer alone, but with Christ in his passion. In Chapter 28, she sums up this view of sin, which takes no account of man's malice but views the whole affair from the divine perspective, as follows:

The careful contemplation of this will save us from grumbling and despair as we experience our pain, especially if we see that, in truth, our sin deserves it, yet his love excuses us. He does away with all our blame by his noble courtesy and regards us with compassion and pity, like innocent children, who can't be hated.

The bulk of the remaining revelations explore this paradox, arriving only at partial clarity and understanding despite Juliana's best efforts and most earnest prayer. Throughout, the Lord's love, expressed in the "homely courtesy" discussed previously is seen as motive force and power for everything that is said and done. He is revealed as father, brother, spouse and, at some length in Chapter 60, as mother of those who are to be saved. He promises that in spite of sin "all shall be well" and reveals, in part and shadow, how this will be done.

Above all, first and finally, God reveals himself to Juliana as love. This is the whole message of the revelations. It is to convey this ultimate truth, which she has experienced in the revelations and in her meditations, that Juliana has concentrated her efforts and focused her being.

## The Method

Juliana has two problems in presenting her showings to her audience. She wants first of all to make clear *what* it is that God has revealed, and then to show *how* he revealed it. Complicating the issue is Juliana's recognition, based on experience, that revelation is an ongoing process rather than a completed, or even completable, event.

The tactic she adopts to deal with these difficulties is effective. Having given, in her first chapter, a brief summary of each of the sixteen showings, a medieval practice

INTRODUCTION                    29

when the author was dealing with a multi-part subject,
Juliana proceeds chronologically to detail her experiences.
In her reporting, she first recalls what she saw and heard,
and what she thought and felt about it at the time, together with any response she made to the Lord. Then, before moving on to what happened next, she tells of any
subsequent illumination she has received on the segment of
the showing she has just related. Finally, she explains the
plain meaning of what has been shown her, for herself and
for her audience. Thus, the recounting of the revelations is
a process of "unfolding" meaning and insight from an apparently simple stimulus. It is as if Juliana, and the reader
with her, entered into the revelation through the door of
the showing and found it not only larger inside than out
but ever expanding inward to whole universes of newer,
deeper meaning, of which the end is always God.

This process of unfolding or expansion can best be understood by illustration. In Chapter 24, which relates the
tenth showing, the image itself suggests both the process of
revelation and Juliana's tactic of presentation.

The thing seen is expressed in the first sentence: "Then,
with a happy face, our Lord looked at his wounded side and
gazed into it, rejoicing." The intelligence and imagination
of the seer, Juliana, is stirred by the sight of the Lord
gazing at the wound in his side made by the soldier's spear
after his death on the cross. Her response is immediate.
She says, "With his sweet gazing he drew forth the understanding of his creature through that same wound into his
side within."

With this imaginative response made, the Lord can continue the process of revelation. Juliana continues, "And
there he showed a fair, delectable place, large enough for all
of mankind who shall be saved to rest there in peace and
love."

This sight brings another element of the passion to mind
by association, followed by another intimately connected
vision: "With this, he brought to my mind his most valuable blood and the precious water which he let pour out

completely, for love. With this sweet vision, he showed his
blissful heart cut even in two."

The process of meditative response to the vision, and the
responsive stirrings of understanding and imagination, are
detailed next. Juliana reports:

> and with the sweet rejoicing he showed my understanding
> the blessed godhead, in part (as far as he willed at that
> time), stirring the poor soul to understand it as it may be
> put into words—that is, to comprehend the endless love
> that was without beginning, is, and ever shall be.

With the recounting of the next event of the showing,
words of the Lord to Juliana, the process of explication is
seen clearly. Juliana says:

> With this, our good Lord said most blissfully, "See how I
> loved you!" It was as if he had said, "My darling, behold
> and see your Lord, your God, who is your maker and your
> endless joy! See what delight and endless bliss I have in
> your salvation. For my love, enjoy it now with me."

Nothing in the explication the second sentence offers of the
first is contradictory to it, but neither is the content of the
second sentence particularly visible in the words of the first!
If Juliana had not told us this was what the Lord meant, we
would probably not have been able to discern it for ourselves.

The Lord then speaks again, both to make clear that the
second sentence was indeed intended in the first, and to continue the unfolding of the initial sight. Juliana recalls:

> In addition, for my greater understanding, this blessed
> word was said: "See how I loved you! Behold and see that I
> loved you so much before I died for you that I chose to die
> for you, and now I have died for you, and freely and delib-
> erately have suffered all I can. Now all my bitter pain and
> all my difficult labor are turned to endless joy and bliss for
> me and for you. How should it be, now, that you should
> ask me for anything that pleases me, without my granting
> it to you with the greatest pleasure? For my delight is your
> holiness, and your endless joy and bliss with me."

Juliana completes her account of the tenth showing with
the declaration that she has done all she can to make it

clear: "This is the understanding, as simply as I can say it, of this blessed word, 'See how I loved you!'" and concludes, "Our good Lord showed this to make us glad and merry."

Other of the showings required more time, prayer and meditation to become accessible to Juliana. In Chapter 51, she presents a lengthy exposition of an extremely complex issue, the question of sin and the sinner who is chosen of God.

Again she proceeds in order, telling events and insights as they occur. In this case, however, the unfolding of the meanings, and of the meanings hidden within meanings, takes place over a period of twenty years, and Juliana is careful to preserve and present intact each of the levels of understanding to which she is led, before moving further inward in recounting her progressive penetration of the mystery.

One example may make this process clearer. Meditating upon, or "unfolding," the fourteenth showing, Juliana had asked the Lord to explain how it could be that a soul that was to be saved, and yet had sinned, should not carry the blame of that sin with it in the sight of God. In answer, the Lord showed her an example, to make visible to her the attitude of God to his servant who has sinned, and led her understanding and imagination in the usual ways.

Juliana, however, had difficulty coming to the meaning of what had been showed her. She says:

But notwithstanding all this leading forth, my wondering at the example never left me, for it seemed to me that it had been given to me as an answer to my desire. And still I could not grasp the complete understanding of it for my ease at that time.

For in the servant, who stood for Adam, as I shall explain, I saw many different properties which could in no way be applied to Adam alone. And thus at that time I was solidly fixed in unknowing, for the full understanding of this marvelous example was not given me at that time.

One further insight was given Juliana at the time: that "every showing is full of secret things." The secret things were gradually rendered more visible between the time of the

showings and the point at which Juliana recounted them to
her audience, but even at this latest date they remained mystery. She reports her present condition, and indicates the in-
completeness of her present understanding matter-of-factly:

> For this reason I now ought and have to tell three
> properties of the example about which I have been some-
> what eased. The first is what I understood of the begin-
> ning of the teaching at the time I received it. The second
> is the inward teaching that I have since understood about
> it. The third is the entire revelation from the beginning
> to the end, that is to say of this book. This our Lord God,
> of his goodness, frequently brings freely to the sight of
> my understanding.

Though she recounts the three phases of understanding
one by one, for Juliana the parts are inseparable from the
whole, and each new insight on an individual point brings
light to and is, in its turn, further illumined by the whole.
The process of unfolding continues, and will continue until,
in God's time, all is revealed.

As evidence that her trust is not misplaced, Juliana cites
the second unfolding of the meaning of the example, given
her "twenty years less three months after the time of the
showing." She is led to recall in full the example shown her
twenty years earlier, and to dwell upon each of its details.
Each separate detail then becomes, as it were, transparent,
and reveals its meanings. A first examination of the details
shows Juliana one level of meaning; a second leads her to a
deeper level; and a third further unravels complexities, while
it discovers further complications. It is as if the original revelation were a seed that germinated and grew during Juliana's
years of prayer and meditation, becoming a tree that bore
fruit and further seed, and other trees, which bore their own
fruit and still further seed, and still other trees. . . .

Revelation itself, then, is an unending process by which
God makes himself known to man. Juliana sees herself as a
part of the process of transmission, and at the same time in
process of receiving further revelation. She has written her
book because the visions were given her not for herself alone
but for all men. In Chapter 8 she insists:

All this time I was sure I was going to die, and it was somewhat of a marvel and a wonder to me, for it seemed to me this vision was shown for one who should live.

What I say of myself I say in the person of all my fellow Christians, for I was taught by the spiritual showing of our Lord that he intends it so.

But the writing of the book, while it ends Juliana's part in transmitting to her audience the progressive revelation of God to man as she has received it up to this point, does not end the process of revelation itself. God will use the book to reveal himself to each reader progressively, as the reader, following Juliana's pattern, meditates on what is revealed, prays, and responds to the revealer. "This book has been begun by God's gift and his grace," she declares as she begins Chapter 86, the last of the book, "but it has not yet been completed, as I see it."

The "completion" of the book is the response of the reader, as the completion of the showings was the response of Juliana, which we have seen active throughout her account. Both depend upon the recipient's arriving at the point of the showings—their central purpose, the single truth which contains all of the showings with their unfolding universes of truth. Juliana herself sought this single meaning in prayer for more than fifteen years after the sixteen showings were granted. She reports the result:

From the time of the showing, I desired frequently to understand what our Lord's meaning was, and more than fifteen years afterward I was answered by a spiritual understanding that said, "Do you want to understand your Lord's meaning in this experience? Understand it well: love was his meaning. Who showed it to you? Love. What did he show you? Love. Why did he show it? For love. Hold yourself in this truth and you shall understand and know more in the same vein. And you will never know or understand anything else in it forever."

Thus was I taught that love is our Lord's meaning.

The scribe of the Sloane Manuscript 2499 is no less clear. Having ended Juliana's account, he takes it upon himself to address the reader directly. Like Juliana, he seems to feel responsible for transmitting and making accessible the revelation of God to man, and to want to make sure that it is not hindered in doing God's work because the reader has missed the point or mishandled the book.

Having prayed, in conventional fashion, that the book come only to the hands of "those who will be his [God's] faithful lovers, to those who will submit to the faith of holy Church and obey the wholesome understanding and teaching of the men who lead virtuous lives, are of serious age and are profound in learning," he warns the reader:

> Beware that you do not accept one thing according to your desire and pleasure, and ignore another, for that is the behavior of a heretic. Accept everything with everything else, understanding it all truly. Everything is according to holy Scripture and is grounded in it, and Jesus our true love, light and truth will show that to all pure souls who perseveringly ask this wisdom of him with meekness.

Turning again directly to the reader, the scribe repeats Juliana's initial insight, that the revelations were meant for all. He says:

> And you to whom this book shall come, intensely and heartily thank our savior Christ Jesus for making these showings and revelations for you and to you from his endless love, mercy and goodness, for your and our safe guide and conduct to everlasting bliss.

The scribe of Sloane Manuscript 3705 amplifies this point, saying of the revelations that they have been "given to a dear lover of his [God's] and, in her, to all his dear friends and lovers, whose hearts, like hers, flame in the love of our dearest Jesus."

Though the *Revelations* can be read from beginning to end without pause, they need not be. Following Juliana's ordering is useful, in that one sees the unfolding of thought from thought as the retelling of the sixteen showings proceeds, but it is not essential to a fruitful use of the book. Juliana herself received the first fifteen showings in one day, and the sixteenth, "the conclusion to and confirmation of the preceding fifteen" on the following night, but it was not until at least twenty years had elapsed that she had them written. During this time, as we have seen, she prayed and meditated on the showings and received unfoldings of them from time to time, but not in the order of the showings themselves. The point that Juliana would make, of course, is that the book be "completed." The manner of "completion" she would undoubtedly leave to the individual man responding in terms of his own life, talents and temperament to the God who, as love, is the whole meaning and sum of the *Revelations*.

## The Mystical Experience

Juliana's experience of union with God, while personal, direct and, to that extent, unique, was not distinct from the union every Christian has with God by the fact of his baptism. The difference lies in the ways the union is experienced.

For the Christian, contact with God is made by prayer. The Scriptures, God's word, provide guidance, instruction and encouragement to do good, avoid evil and, by these means, come to final union with God after death.

For the Catholic Christian, and in Juliana's lifetime in England there was no other kind, two additional sources of divine assistance are available. The seven sacraments provide direct, if veiled, contact with God at every important juncture of living from birth to death. And the living voice of the Church's teaching authority, extending backward to the Apostles and Christ himself in an unbroken chain, offers guidance on moral and doctrinal issues as they arise in daily living.

Why, then, was Juliana's experience of her union with God so different from that of her neighbors and other contemporaries? The question can be answered in several ways.

To say simply, "Juliana was a mystic," while true, is not particularly helpful. First, it implies either a difference in kind between her and everybody else (as if she were a "petunia in an onion patch") or else a natural capacity or talent that she possessed and few others did or do (like a photographic memory).

More important, since the definition of a mystic is one who experiences union with God in an extraordinary way, to attempt to clarify the nature of the extraordinary experience of union with God by calling the experiencer a mystic is to move in a circle.

A second answer, "God willed it so," while theologically unimpeachable and, in fact, the ultimate answer to any question of this kind, does not shed much more light on the immediate issue.

It might be clearer to ask the question in three sections: Why this woman and not another? How was her experience special and different from the usual experience of union with God? How did her extraordinary experience of union with God differ from the extraordinary experiences of her contemporaries Richard Rolle, the anonymous author of the *Cloud of Unknowing*, Walter Hilton, and Margery Kempe?

Juliana herself deals with the first section of the question, why herself and not another, apparently in answer to actual or expected interpretations by which her audience could excuse itself from any need for active response to the matter revealed to her by God for their sakes. She opens Chapter 9 with a rather abrupt denial that her virtue had anything to do with God's revealing himself to her, or that the revelations either were themselves a sign that she was more pleasing to God than anyone else, or excused her from the ordinary practice of virtue.

Juliana is quite clear in her insistence both on her role as mediator of the revelation to her fellow Christians for whom it was intended, and on the necessity of response to the revelation by an increase of love of God. It's not receiving the revelation that makes the saint, or saves the sinner, but responding to whatever is revealed. The revelation, so far as Juliana was concerned, was simply another means by which God might reach the soul and the soul might reach God.

As to why she, not another, was chosen to see and speak, Juliana does not inquire. In her discussion of how one ought to pray, however, she indicates some dispositions that may have made her receptive and the revelations, in the human sense, possible.

Perhaps the most important of these is the awareness that, as Augustine of Hippo had put it some thousand years previously in his *Confessions*, "Thou hast made us for thyself, O God, and our hearts are restless until they rest in thee" (Book 1, § 1).

For Juliana the insight came in the revelation recorded in Chapter 5, that all created things ought to be seen as "a little thing, the size of a hazelnut, lying in the palm of my hand," which would "fall into nothingness" but for the power of God, who "made it," "loves it" and "keeps it" in existence.

Awareness that God is all in all and that created things are nothing but for him leaves one nothing to be proud of. Such an insight can lead to despair, unless it is accompanied by faith that the omnipotent God is also loving. For Juliana, it was, and the next insight she reports seems to be a description of her own dispositions from the beginning:

Our Lord also showed that it is a very great pleasure to him when a simple soul comes to him nakedly, plainly and unpretentiously, for he is the natural dwelling of the soul touched by the Holy Spirit. This is what I understand from this showing, at any rate.

The prayer that follows illustrates the response of the soul to the double insight into God's power and love:

God, of your goodness, give me yourself, for you are enough for me. I can ask for nothing less that is completely to your honor, and if I do ask anything less, I shall always be in want. Only in you I have all.

When one has once realized these essential truths, the manner of praying must change. Juliana reports in Chapter 6 the simplification of her prayer, leading more and more to the extraordinary awareness of and response to union with God, which has been defined as the prayer of the mystic.

Summarizing examples of the kinds of "means" used commonly in prayer—motives, as it were, that men offer God to grant their petitions—Juliana concludes that any man can think of, can be reduced to God's goodness, which, she says, is the "highest prayer."

The knowledge, the awareness, that one is "in truth" "enclosed" in God is usually considered as part of the reward of the life after death. Juliana, describing her awareness of this state in her present life, begins to answer the second aspect of the original question: How was her experience special? She says:

For as the body is clad in the clothes, and the flesh in the skin, and the bones in the flesh, and the heart in the whole, so are we, soul and body, clad and enclosed in the goodness of God. Yes, and more intimately than this, for all these may waste and wear away, but the goodness of God is ever whole, and closer to us than any comparison can show.

Awareness of the union of her soul with God was accompanied by the insight that God wanted her love and wanted to love her. The usual stress in Christian teaching is that the Christian must love God and desire him above all. That that love and desire are reciprocated and, more than that, by a God who needs nothing and no one, broke on Juliana with some force, and she is most anxious to make this glorious revelation absolutely clear to an audience that probably does not expect it. She declares:

Our soul is so specially loved by him who is the highest that it goes far beyond the ability of any creature to realize it. That is to say, there is no creature made who can realize how much, how sweetly and how tenderly our maker loves us. And therefore we may, with his grace and his help, stand in spirit, gazing with endless wonder at this lofty, unmeasurable love beyond human scope that Almighty God has for us of his goodness. And therefore we may ask our lover, with reverence, all that we will.

Juliana completes her account of this startling truth by placing it in the context of life after death:

Our natural will is to have God, and the good will of God is to have us, and we may never cease willing or longing for him until we have him in the fulness of joy, and then we shall will no longer. For he wills that we be occu-

pied in knowing and loving until the time that we shall
find fulfillment in heaven.

And that is the reason this lesson of love was shown,
with all that shall follow, as you shall see.

The "knowing and loving" with which we are to "be oc-
upied" on earth can be defined as simple meditation, but
or Juliana the experience goes far beyond what ordinary
Christians come to. This is not because Juliana has done any-
hing special, but because God has taken the initiative as, in
uliana's (and the orthodox theological) view, he always
loes. She remarks, in Chapter 10:

We are now so blind and so unwise that we never seek
God until he, of his goodness, shows himself to us. And
when we see anything of him, through his graciousness, we
are stirred by the same grace to seek with great desire to
see him more blissfully.

The "stirring" of which Juliana speaks is, like all the work-
ngs of God, accomplished in each person according to his
alents, sensibilities, life circumstances, and intellectual,
noral and emotional powers—in short, according to his
node of being. In Juliana the "stirrings" operated on three
evels, which she is careful to distinguish. In Chapter 9 she
ays:

All his revelation was shown in three ways, that is to say,
by what I saw with my eyes, by words formed in my understanding and by spiritual insight.

What she saw with her eyes she reports clearly, exactly,
with vivid, homely imagery. It consisted chiefly of the sufferings of Jesus during his crucifixion. The description of the
bleeding of the head of Jesus which occurs in Chapter 7
shows us Juliana's ability to observe and convey what she has
seen.

Great drops of blood poured down from under the garland
like pellets, just as if they had come out of the veins. In
coming out of the head, the drops were brown-red, for the
blood was very thick, but in spreading out, the blood was
bright red. When the blood came to the brows, it vanished,
but notwithstanding, the bleeding continued, until many
things had been seen and understood; nevertheless, the

fairness and lifelikeness continued to have the same beauty
and loveliness.

The fairness and lifelikeness is like nothing but itself.
The plenteousness of the bleeding is like drops of water
that fall from the eaves of the house after a great rainstorm; they fall so thick no man can count them with his
human powers. As they spread over the forehead, the drops
of blood were like herring scales in their roundness.

These three images came to me at that time. The drops
were round like pellets in coming out of the head, and like
herring scales in spreading out on the forehead; in their unnumberable plenty, they were like raindrops falling from
the eaves.

While bodily sight was going on, Juliana was also experiencing spiritual insight as to the meaning and implica-
tions of what she was seeing. It is her account of what she
saw with her eyes and of the words in her understanding
—the alternate and sometimes simultaneous means by which
the showings were conveyed to her—that keeps the chronological thread of narrative unbroken and provides a context
for the spiritual insight and "unfolding" of truth which are
the point of the revelations.

Juliana's response to the threefold showings was always the
same: an increase of love. She expresses it in Chapter 10:

Thus I saw him and sought him, I had him and I wanted
him. . . .

Her next sentence refers not to the visions, which she considers accidental in the scholastic sense, that is, not essential
but to the response any man should make to any "stirrings"
of God in his soul: "And this is, and should be, the way we
commonly work in this, as I see it."

That one of the means God might use to "stir" her fellow
Christians might be her book is never far from Juliana's
mind. She says, as we have noticed, that the revelations
were given her not for herself alone but for all her fellow
Christians; she sees the revelations as a process of the unfolding of truth and the flowering of love not only in herself but in all who receive them.

In common with many another who has experienced that

extraordinary awareness of union with God called mystical, Juliana found it generally difficult, and occasionally impossible, to reduce the experience to words. Unlike the Apostle Paul, who was referring to the experience for other purposes and hence contented himself with ". . . caught up into paradise and heard things which must not and cannot be put into human language" (2 Corinthians 12:2–4), Juliana was concerned about communication. She felt it her responsibility to say as clearly as possible what she had experienced and learned, for the sake of those for whom the showings had been made: all her fellow Christians. The only solution she could see lay with God. She would do what she could, and trust God to "fill in" for each reader as he or she had need.

Having described in Chapter 9 the three means of "stirring" that God used to reveal himself to her—bodily sight, words and spiritual insight—she adds:

> The spiritual insight I neither can nor may show as openly and fully as I would like to, but I trust in our Lord God Almighty that he shall, of his goodness and for your love, make you understand it more spiritually and sweetly than I can or may tell it.

In Chapter 26, reporting the understanding she was given that God is indeed all in all for every creature, Juliana is overwhelmed by the illumination and almost stammers in the overflowing of divine love that floods her being. She begins by declaring her understanding that the soul "shall never have rest until it comes to him, knowing that he is the fulness of joy, familiarly and courteously blissful, and life itself." Then she continues:

> Our Lord Jesus frequently said, "I am it! I am the one! I am that which is highest! I am what you love! I am what delights you! I am the one you serve! I am what you long for! I am what you desire! I am what you intend! I am all! I am what holy Church preaches and teaches you! I am the one who has shown myself to you here."

The number of the words exceeded my wit, all my understanding and all my powers, and as I see it, this is the highest point, for in these words is comprehended— I cannot tell; but the joy I saw in the showing of them goes beyond anything heart may will and soul may desire. That is why the words are not repeated here. But let every man, according to the grace God gives him in understanding and loving, receive them as our Lord intends them.

In her preoccupation with communicating to the people for whom it was intended the revelation the Lord was giving her, Juliana did not lose sight of the necessity of fitting her experience into the teachings of the Church. In the first place, she had been taught, and firmly believed, that the Church was the extension in time of Jesus' divine ministry on earth. The Church, for Juliana and her contemporaries, was both the repository of revelation and the living, interpretive voice speaking with divine authority. Any teaching that contradicted Church teaching was, by that fact, not truth but error. If Juliana found herself walking a road not sanctioned by orthodox Church teaching, she would have identified "the fiend" as the author of her experiences and rejected them. Consequently, when she finds her experiences, illuminations and insights on uncharted or dubious grounds, she is most careful to affirm her belief in the Church's teaching and her loyalty to her faith.

In Chapter 9, as she ends her comments on the first showing, she explains that she speaks "of those who shall be saved, for at this time God showed me no others." Then immediately, lest she seem to deny the doctrine of hell's existence, or the possibility of men's going there, both tenets of the Church based on revelation, she declares:

But in all things I believe as holy Church believes, preaches and teaches. For the faith of holy Church which I had beforehand understood and, as I hope by the grace of God, deliberately kept in use and custom, stood continuously in my sight. I chose and intended never to receive anything that might be contrary to it. With this intention I beheld all this blessed showing as one in God's meaning.

The discussion of evil, and the reconciliation of the fact of human wickedness and Church teachings on hell and damnation with the Lord's assurance that "all shall be well" taxed Juliana considerably. The illumination she received enabled er to effect a reconciliation of sorts between the two by ranscendence, as she reports in Chapter 32. The only solution Juliana is given is that both elements in the paradox are rue in a way that is beyond her comprehension. She is to believe both and not fuss about *how* both can be true.

Concerning all this, I had no other answer in any showing from our Lord God but this: "What is impossible to you is not impossible to me. I shall save my word in all things, and I shall make all things well."

Thus was I taught by the grace of God that I should steadfastly hold myself in the faith as I had before understood it, and that I should seriously believe that all manner of things would be well, as our Lord at that same time had showed me.

In Chapter 30 Juliana confronts the limits of human understanding in dealing with divine truth and distinguishes carefully between those truths the knowledge and understanding of which are necessary for salvation, and those which are not. The first, every man of good will can apprehend, taught by Holy Church from without and counseled by the Holy Spirit from within. In this area all is light, and, says Juliana, "The more fully we take from this source with reverence and meekness, the more thanks we earn from him, and the more success we gain for ourselves. Thus we can say, rejoicing, that our part is our Lord."

As for the truths that are not necessary for salvation, such as the example quoted above, man must not indulge in idle, speculative curiosity. It is enough that Juliana knows *that* the elements in the paradox can be reconciled; she need not know *how*. Her statement on these truths bears repetition in full, challenging, as it does (though not by name), the metaphysicians and schoolmen with their practice of debating abstruse theological and philosophical questions having no bearing on practical questions of Christian living and salvation.

The second part of truth is hidden and barred from us— that is to say, everything that is unrelated to our salvation. These are our Lord's secret purposes. It belongs to the royal lordship of God that he have his secret purposes in peace; to his servants belong obedience and reverence, not full knowledge of his purposes.

Our Lord has pity and compassion on us, because there are some of us who so busy ourselves in his secret purposes. I am sure if we knew how very greatly we would please him and ease ourselves by abandoning this curiosity, we would do so. The saints who are in heaven will to know nothing but what our Lord wills to show them. Their charity and desire are also ruled according to the will of our Lord. We ought, like them, to will in this way; then we would will and desire nothing but the will of our Lord, as they do, for we are all one, as God sees things.

In Chapter 33 Juliana again faces paradox, this time concerning damnation. She tells us she wished to see hell and purgatory, not to test the teachings of the Church but that she might live better. Then, when no further illumination was forthcoming, she followed the instructions she reported in the previous chapter, putting the elements of the paradox side by side and vigorously affirming all of them. She declares:

Although this was a revelation of goodness and made little mention of evil, I was still not drawn by it from any point of faith that holy Church teaches me to believe. I saw the passion of Christ in several different showings— the first, the second, the fifth and the eighth—as I have said before. I had in part a sense of the sorrow of our Lady and of his true friends who saw him in pain, but I did not see properly specified the Jews, who did him to death, despite the fact that I knew in my faith that they were accursed and damned without end, except for the ones who were converted by grace.

I was strengthened and taught in general to keep myself in the faith at every point, and in all that I had understood before. I hoped that, with the mercy and grace of God, I was doing so, and in my intentions I desired and prayed that I might continue to, until the end of my life.

In the matter of God's secrets, of course, it is God who is always master. Juliana remarks at the end of Chapter 33, "For I saw in truth that our Lord means us to understand

hat the more we busy ourselves to know his secrets, in that
r anything else, the further away we shall be from knowing
1em." It is God who reveals, not man who discovers. That
: not to say man must be passive; Juliana has stressed
hroughout, both by precept and by practice, the need for
1e soul's response to complete the process of revelation, or
ather, to allow it to continue. That she has not changed
er mind, that what she condemns is idle curiosity and not
enuine response, is made clear in the next chapter.

Referring to the Great Deed by which God will make all
o be well, she reiterates that its secrets are to remain hidden
until the time he chooses to show them to us clearly."
he other secrets, however, those which are necessary for
alvation, shall not remain hidden, either by God's will or
y man's blindness, "for he wills that we grasp that it is his
vill that we should know them." Juliana goes on:

> They are secrets to us not only because he wills that they
> be hidden from us but because of our blindness and igno-
> rance. On these he has great pity, and therefore he wills to
> make them more open to us himself, so that we may know
> him, love him and cling to him. For all that it is expedient
> for us to grasp and know, our Lord will most courteously
> show us—and that showing is this revelation with all the
> preaching and teaching of holy Church.

An examination of the whole of the *Revelations* will make
lear, as no discussion of them could, the development of
loctrine that has taken place in the six hundred or so years
etween the original showings and the present time. Prob-
ems that troubled Juliana have found some degree of solu-
ion, paradoxes have been given some formulation. Never-
heless, the point remains. God is in charge of the process of
evelation, though he chooses to depend on human response
o make the process work. What he wishes to reveal, he re-
eals; what he wills to remain hidden remains hidden.

At the end of Chapter 7, Juliana outlines the elements in
his paradoxical relationship between the action of God and
he response of man in the process of revelation. Having seen
he bleeding of the head under the garland of thorns, and
ecognized in it a sign of the great courtesy and familiarity of

God approaching his own creatures in love, she notes that God wills that men "believe, choose and trust him, enjoy and delight in him, comforting and solacing ourselves as best we can with his grace and his help until the time we see it in reality." Then she states the paradox. God takes the initiative, but faith and love play a necessary part not only at the time of revelation but throughout life.

But this marvelous familiarity no man may experience in this present life unless he does so through a special showing of our Lord, or through great fulness of grace given him inwardly by the Holy Spirit. But faith and belief, with charity, deserve their reward, and thus it is attained by grace. For in faith, with hope and charity, our life is grounded.

The showing, made to whomever God wills, plainly teaches the same thing, open and declared, and shows many secret points belonging to our faith, which are good for us to know.

And when the showing, which is given at a single time, has passed away and is hidden, then the faith, by the grace of the Holy Spirit, preserves it to the end of our lives. Thus the showing is not other than the faith, neither less nor more, as can be seen in our Lord's teaching on the same matter, about when each shall come to its end.

The fine balance between the actions of grace and free will is here perfectly maintained. Such precision, expected in a theologian, strikes one as unusual in Juliana, who has declared herself in Chapter 2 "a simple, uneducated creature." Yet it is characteristic of her. A natural balance of mind, evident throughout her work, operates here to present a complex issue clearly and simply, without blurring over the difficulties.

Juliana was not the only person in fourteenth- and fifteenth-century England to experience union with God in the extraordinary way we have come to call mystical, nor was she the only mystic to record her experience. Since the experience characteristic of the mystic is an extraordinary awareness of personal union with God, the same God, one might expect Juliana's account to tally in some respects with the accounts her contemporary mystics have left. Since each person's

nion with God is a unique experience, given the uniqueness
f the individual, we should further expect her account to
ear the stamp of her individuality, to be one of a kind. Both
xpectations are met in the *Revelations*. Answering the third
ection of our original question, how do Juliana's experiences
iffer from those of Richard Rolle, the anonymous author
f the *Cloud of Unknowing*, Walter Hilton, and Margery
Kempe, we shall also note what similarities occur.

Richard Rolle (c. 1300–49), the unknown author of the
*Cloud of Unknowing*, who wrote around 1370, Walter Hil-
on (d. 1396), and Margery Kempe (c. 1373–after 1436)
ad in common with Juliana of Norwich a confirmation in
heir experience of the Apostle John's insight "God is love.
He who abides in love abides in God and God in him" (1
ohn 4:16). Each experienced God as love in his own way,
nd each responded as his temperament, talent, training and
ife circumstances dictated, but the God was the same and so
vas the love. In all cases, the heart of the mystical experience
vas a heightened awareness of this identity, and an in-
ensified union with him. The differences are not so much a
natter of God's telling different things to different people, as
f God's revealing his infinite being to finite persons, each of
vhom apprehends him as best he may, given his particular
trengths and limits.

In the case of Richard Rolle, the experience of union with
God as love took physical as well as psychological form. In
Chapter 14 of his *Incendium amoris* (*The Fire of Love*)
(1343), the best known of his works, Rolle reports that he
as "found that to love Christ above all else will involve
hree things: warmth and song and sweetness" (Clifton
Wolters, trans., *The Fire of Love by Richard Rolle*, pp.
88–89).

The identification is not simply metaphorical. Rolle explains:

> I call it *fervour* when the mind is truly ablaze with eternal
> love and the heart similarly feels itself burning with a love
> that is not imaginary but real. For a heart set on fire pro-
> duces a feeling of fiery love.
> I call it *song* when there is in the soul, overflowing and

ardent, a sweet feeling of heavenly praise; when thought turns into song; when the mind is in thrall to sweetest harmony.

This twofold awareness is not achieved by doing nothing, but through the utmost devotion; and from these two there springs the third, for unspeakable *sweetness* is present too. Fervour and song bring marvelous delight to a soul, just as they themselves can be the product of very great sweetness. (pp. 89–90)

Rolle's description of his own reception of these three gifts, occurring in the next chapter (15), makes the physical component clear. He says, concerning the first gift,

I was sitting in a certain chapel, delighting in the sweetness of prayer or meditation, when suddenly I felt within myself an unusually pleasant heat. (p. 93)

In his Prologue, Rolle is more specific in reporting his physical sensations. He says:

I cannot tell you how surprised I was the first time I felt my heart begin to warm. It was real warmth, too, not imaginary, and it felt as if it were actually on fire. I was astonished at the way the heat surged up, and how this new sensation brought great and unexpected comfort. I had to keep feeling my breast to make sure there was no physical reason for it. (p. 45)

Of the second and third gifts, song and sweetness, Rolle reports that he both heard heavenly music and was himself moved to inward song, which resulted in sweetness. Some nine months after his first experience of inward fire, he says:

I knew the infusion and understanding of heavenly, spiritual sounds, sounds which pertain to the song of eternal praise, and to the sweetness of unheard melody. . . . I heard above my head it seemed, the joyful ring of psalmody, or perhaps I should say, the singing. In my prayer I was reaching out to heaven with heartfelt longing when I became aware, in a way I cannot explain, of a symphony of song, and in myself I sensed a corresponding harmony at once wholly delectable and heavenly, which persisted in my mind. Then and there my thinking itself turned into melodious song, and my meditation became a poem, and my very prayers and psalms took up the same sound. The effect of this inner sweetness was that I began to sing what previously I had spoken; only I sang inwardly, and that for my Creator. (p. 93)

In this account, so different from Juliana's, we can see one familiar thing: the inability of the recipient to reduce his experience to words—in this case, the way in which Rolle apprehended his music. The rest of the chapter includes further familiar material. Rolle declares his unworthiness to have received these gifts, so far beyond human imagining:

Meantime wonder seized me that I should be caught up into such joy while I was still an exile, and that God should give me gifts, the like of which I did not know I could ask for, and such that I thought that not even the most holy could have received in this life. (p. 93)

He acknowledges their source in God who gives them freely where he will, saying,

from which I deduce that they are not given for merit, but freely to whomsoever Christ wills. (p. 93)

Finally, he notes the role of human response and readiness in the divine granting of such gifts. He declares:

All the same I fancy that no one will receive them [the gifts] unless he has a special love for the Name of Jesus, and so honours it that he never lets it out of his mind, except in sleep. (pp. 93–94)

Rolle's account is not a chronological one. Biographical data appear, but more as an illustration of some lesson being taught than as an ordering framework or a proof of historicity.

The structure of *Incendium amoris* is not linear but, as Wolters observes, circular. "The book goes on in great circular sweeps, saying much the same thing each time, yet adding a little here, a little there, catching it up in the next swinging movement" (pp. 9–10). The work seems to consist of a series of discourses on the spiritual life, and on the means a person should employ to ready himself for union with God. The order is, to some extent, random, with the first section of the book focusing on the process of wholehearted turning to God, the central autobiographical section illustrating that

process by example, and the final section dealing with the
various difficulties one might meet in persevering in the con-
version effected.

Rolle's teaching seems to be the result of his own meditation, as to some extent Juliana's is. But where Juliana is ab-
sorbed in the progressive unfolding of the meaning inherent
in the sixteen showings granted her that May day in 1373,
Rolle meditates upon Scripture, much in the manner of a
medieval commentator. The direction—the love of God—is
the same; the routes are very different.

Rolle's purpose in writing, and his intended audience, may
have had as much to do with his structural peculiarities as his
temperament. His declared intention was unabashedly didactic. He wanted to revive the pursuit of the one thing necessary, the love of God, in all men. He addresses, he says, not
the professionals of religion, the theologians and philosophers, but the amateurs, who starve, amid professional jar-
gon, for real nourishment.

> I offer, therefore, this book for the attention, not of the
> philosophers and sages of this world, not of great theolo-
> gians bogged down in their interminable questionings, but
> of the simple and unlearned, who are seeking rather to love
> God than to amass knowledge. For he is not known by ar-
> gument, but by what we do and how we love. I think that
> while the matters contained in such questionings are the
> most demanding of all intellectually, they are much less
> important when the love of Christ is under consideration.
> Anyhow, they are impossible to understand! So I have not
> written for the experts, unless they have forgotten and put
> behind them all those things that belong to the world; un-
> less now they are eager to surrender to a longing for God.
> (pp. 46–47)

As we have seen, Juliana, too, warned against idle prying
into the secrets of God but included herself in the warning:
"I am sure if we knew how very greatly we would please him
and ease ourselves by abandoning this curiosity, we would do
so" (Chapter 30). Rolle stands apart from his audience, ex-
cludes the pryers (of whom he plainly disapproves), and includes himself among the lovers, of whom he approves. His

ance is that of the teacher in possession of truth he must
inculcate in eager, if unready, pupils; Juliana's is that of the
intermediary, privileged to transmit a message of love from
God to his creatures, her brothers and sisters.

Rolle declares this sense of mission in the last lines of the
Prologue (p. 47), where he explains his choice of a title for
he book:

And so, because I would stir up by these means [an ascet-
ical program involving humility, poverty, prayer and meditation, which will prepare them to experience divine love]
every man to love God, and because I am trying to make
plain the ardent nature of love and how it is supernatural,
the title selected for this book will be *The Fire of Love*.

About the author of the *Cloud of Unknowing* we know
less than we do about Juliana, though they must have been
roughly contemporaries. The *Cloud* was written, scholars
conclude, around 1370, about the time Juliana was receiving
the sixteen showings that were to become the center and
source of her growing relationship with God.

The points of similarity between the *Cloud* and Juliana's
book lie in content rather than in intention, audience, point
of view or tone. The God revealed here is loving, in communication with his creatures, desirous of their salvation and
of particular union with them. He makes the approaches and,
provided the person chosen is ready to receive them and recognizes them, fills his beloved with his presence. Always God
takes the initiative and the beloved responds; God establishes
the "timetable" for his beloved's experiences and growth in
holiness. And the experience is beyond reduction to words, as
the God experienced is beyond human intellectual comprehension.

The author of the *Cloud* is careful from the outset to be
most explicit on these last points. In his first chapter he declares, in a discussion of the four stages of the spiritual life—
Common, Special, Singular and Perfect—that it is God who
calls his chosen ones from stage to stage, by kindling in them
desire and longing for closer and closer union with him. The
chosen one responds, and the quality of the response deter-

mines the kind of gift God is able to finish giving. As the au
thor explains in Chapter 2,

> For now, if you wish to keep growing you must nourish i
> your heart the lively longing for God. Though this lovin₃
> desire is certainly God's gift, it is up to you to nurture it
> But mark this. God is a jealous lover. He is at work in you
> spirit and will tolerate no meddlers. The only other one h
> needs is you. And all he asks of you is that you fix you
> love on him and let him alone. (William Johnston, *Th*
> *Cloud of Unknowing*, p. 47.)

Although the author maintains throughout his book his as
sertion of Chapter 2, "Our Lord is always ready. He await
only your cooperation" (p. 47), he does not suggest that Goc
is at man's beck and call. In fact, although God is in on
sense absolutely accessible to the loving, humble, responsiv
person, he is in another sense absolutely inaccessible to th
same person. This is because he is God, of course, and abso
lutely beyond human encompassing.

The *Cloud*'s author describes the experience in Chapter ₃
and clarifies his description in Chapter 4. Speaking of th
person trying consciously to respond to God with wha
Juliana called "fullhearted longing" (Chapter 2), he urge
perseverance and then says:

> For in the beginning it is usual to feel nothing but a kind
> of darkness about your mind, or as it were, a *cloud of un*
> *knowing*. You will seem to know nothing and to feel noth-
> ing except a naked intent toward God in the depths of
> your being. Try as you might, this darkness and this cloud
> will remain between you and your God. You will feel frus-
> trated, for your mind will be unable to grasp him, and your
> heart will not relish the delight of his love. (pp. 48–49)

That is not to say that God cannot be known at all. On the
contrary, as the author explains in Chapter 4, the soul "transformed by his redeeming grace is enabled to embrace him by
love" (p. 50). It is the faculty by which God is comprehended that people most often mistake, with disastrous results. The author goes on:

> He whom neither men nor angels can grasp by knowledge
> can be embraced by love. For the intellect of both men and

angels is too small to comprehend God as he is in himself. (p. 50)

To an audience used to considering the intellect as the chief faculty for knowing, he explains further:

> Try to understand this point. Rational creatures such as men and angels possess two principal faculties, a knowing power and a loving power. No one can fully comprehend the uncreated God with his knowledge; but each one, in a different way, can grasp him fully through love. Truly this is the unending miracle of love: that one loving person, through his love, can embrace God, whose being fills and transcends the entire creation. (p. 50)

It is worth noting that the author never explains either why or how this can be so. He simply affirms that it is so.

Though the God revealed by Juliana and the *Cloud*'s author is the same, and though the humanly apprehended aspect of this God is similar in each work, everything else is different. As is evident in the passages just quoted, the author of the *Cloud* is a master in the spiritual life, instructing an audience, singular or plural, seeking to learn how to achieve union with God in a special way; the author's intention to instruct is indicated in the full title of the book: *A Book on Contemplation called THE CLOUD OF UNKNOWING in which cloud a soul is united with God*. What is promised here is not the record of one person's experience of union with God, but a book *about* this particular kind of union, examining it as a phenomenon, apart from the discussants.

In the Foreword, the author indicates very clearly the qualities he demands in anyone who would be his audience, his pupil. He charges "whoever you are possessing this book . . . whether this book belongs to you, whether you are keeping it for someone else, whether you are taking it to someone, or borrowing it, you are not to read it, write or speak of it, nor allow another to do so, unless you really believe he is a person deeply committed to follow Christ perfectly" (p. 43). He continues:

> I have in mind a person who, over and above the good works of the active life, has resolved to follow Christ (as far as is humanly possible with God's grace) into

the inmost depths of contemplation. Do your best to determine if he is one who has first been faithful for some time to the demands of the active life. (p. 43)

The reason for this stringent limitation of his potential pupils by the author is simple. To anyone without the qualities and determinations he has outlined, the book will mean nothing, the treasure will be wasted.

A preselected audience of pupils does not end the demands of this teacher. He also prescribes the manner in which each pupil shall approach the book, and like a good pedagogue, explains the reason for his demand:

warn them (as I warn you) to take the time to read it thoroughly. For it is very possible that certain chapters do not stand by themselves but require the explanation given in other chapters to complete their meaning. I fear lest a person read only some parts and quickly fall into error. To avoid a blunder like this, I beg you and anyone else reading this book, for love's sake, to do as I ask. (pp. 43–44)

The treatment of the individual present reader, the holder of the book who is to be pupil, as one who will be a teacher in his turn, or at least an instructor as far as this book is concerned, establishes the relationship between the "I" and the "you," the master and the pupil, throughout the book.

The master is master by virtue of longer and more extensive experience in the matter at hand—the art of contemplation, responding to God's particular grace of closer union—but not by any innate superiority. As he is quick to declare, in Chapter 33,

I will not go into any other techniques right now. If you master these, I believe you will be more qualified to teach me than I am to teach you. For although all I have said about their efficacy is quite true, I am far from being very skilled in them. And so I sincerely hope that you will help me by becoming proficient in them yourself. (p. 89)

Having traveled the route he is pointing out to his pupil, however, he is in position to point out dangers and pitfalls, and to suggest to the neophyte ways of avoiding useless digressions and of making the swiftest progress, subject always to the controlling hand of God.

What is the novice to do about the "cloud of unknowing" between himself and God? Three things.

First, he must await God's good pleasure, and prepare himself. "But learn to be at home in this darkness. Return to it as often as you can, letting your spirit cry out to him whom you love," the master advises in Chapter 3, explaining,

> For if, in this life, you hope to feel and see God as he is in himself it must be within this darkness and this cloud. But if you strive to fix your love on him forgetting all else, which is the work of contemplation I have urged you to begin, I am confident that God in his goodness will bring you to a deep experience of himself. (p. 49)

What the author tells the pupil to "strive for" is forgetfulness of self and all creation. It is his second task. Having described man's limitations in apprehending God as a "cloud of unknowing" set between himself and God, the master urges the novice, in Chapter 5, deliberately to construct a second "cloud," a "cloud of forgetting," between himself and all creation, including his own pious thoughts. If he is ever to come *into* the "cloud of unknowing," that is, into the inapprehensible but real presence of God, there to work, responding as he can to God's grace, for complete union, he must, says the author, construct such a cloud. He continues:

> Every time I say "all creatures," I refer not only to every created thing but also to all their circumstances and activities. I make no exception. You are to concern yourself with no creature whether material or spiritual nor with their situation and doings whether good or ill. To put it briefly, during this work you must abandon them all beneath the *cloud of forgetting*. (p. 53)

The reason for this stricture lies in the easily distracted nature of man. Explains the author,

> For although at certain times and in certain circumstances it is necessary and useful to dwell on the particular situation and activity of people and things, during this work it is almost useless. Thinking and remembering are forms of spiritual understanding in which the eye of the spirit is opened and closed upon things as the eye of a marksman is on his target. But I tell you that everything you dwell upon

during this work becomes an obstacle to union with God. For if your mind is cluttered with these concerns there is no room for him. (pp. 53–54)

The third thing the neophyte is to do is based upon a previous observation of the author: God cannot be known by the intellect but can be known by love. The preparatory explanation, which opens Chapter 6, serves also to explain further the necessity of putting the "cloud of forgetting" even between a man and his own religious thoughts.

He begins with a reprise of the "cloud of unknowing" and the ineffectiveness of intellect in apprehending God.

Now you say, "How shall I proceed to think of God as he is in himself?" To this I can only reply, "I do not know." With this question you bring me into the very darkness and *cloud of unknowing* that I want you to enter. A man may know completely and ponder thoroughly every created thing and its works, yes, and God's works too, but not God himself. Thought cannot comprehend God. (p. 54)

What, then, is to be done? The author replies:

And so I prefer to abandon all I can know, choosing rather to love him whom I cannot know. Though we cannot know him we can love him. By love he may be touched and embraced, never by thought. Of course, we do well at times to ponder God's majesty or kindness for the insight these meditations may bring. But in the real contemplative work you must set all this aside and cover it over with a *cloud of forgetting*. (pp. 54–55)

And then the master tells the neophyte the one positive thing he can do to prepare himself for union with God, and governed by God's grace, to obtain it.

Then let your loving desire, gracious and devout, step bravely and joyfully beyond it [anything not God himself] and reach out to pierce the darkness above. Yes, beat upon that thick cloud of unknowing with the dart of your loving desire and do not cease come what may. (p. 55)

The passage reminds one of Juliana's discussion of praying by "means" in Chapter 6. The conclusions are the same: God is to be loved for himself alone and so prayed to. But where Juliana presents the matter as conclusions drawn from vision

ind insight, applicable to herself as to her fellow Christians,
the author of the *Cloud* offers it as a lesson, a piece of in-
truction from a more to a less experienced pursuer of the
same art.

The essence of the lesson taught by the author of the *Cloud*
is that the neophyte is to forget creation, not to put it out of
mind. The direct attempt to put something out of one's
mind results, as anyone who has tried it can testify, in fixing
it there more firmly, for the most part. One looks at what
one consciously rejects.

Forgetting, on the other hand, is a kind of mental slippage.
A forgotten item escapes mental grasp, evades the attention,
and vanishes.

The best way to forget something successfully is to concen-
trate so hard on something else that everything besides this
object fades and vanishes. Hence, the author's primary advice
to the neophyte does not consist of a program of rigorous exercises in exclusion or mental concentration. Instead, he commands the pupil to keep on trying to love God directly,
striking the cloud with "the dart of your loving desire," and
orders him not to give up. The pupil is, in short, to look at
what he is looking at, not at what he is trying not to look at.

The process requires relaxation as well as concentration, as
the author suggests with his two "techniques" for dealing
with temptation, for both are ways of surrendering the self to
God, and both result in the self-forgetfulness essential to
union with God.

Whether the temptation is to allow otherwise valuable
thoughts, such as the awareness of one's own past sins, to
come between a person and God, or is to allow "temptation
to new ones" to "plague" the mind, "forming an obstacle"
between him and God, the novice is to "crush them" beneath his feet and "bravely step beyond them" (p. 88).
"Try," says the master in Chapter 31, "to bury the thought
of these deeds beneath the thick cloud of forgetting, just as if
neither you nor anyone else had ever done them" (p. 88).

To assist his pupil further, he then offers his two "techniques" for beating temptation, in Chapter 32. The first
requires concentration.

When distracting thoughts annoy you try to pretend that you do not even notice their presence or that they have come between you and your God. Look beyond them— over their shoulder, as it were—as if you were looking for something else, which of course you are. For beyond them, God is hidden in the dark *cloud of unknowing.* (p. 88)

He goes on to explain how this technique tends, in fact, to a further penetration of the cloud of unknowing:

I can vouch for the orthodoxy of this technique because in reality it amounts to a yearning for God, a longing to see and taste him as much as possible in this life. And desire like this is actually love, which always brings peace. (p. 88)

The second "dodge," which requires relaxation, is for use in the case of more difficult and more persistent temptation. The first presentation may sound somewhat quietistic:

When you feel utterly exhausted from fighting your thoughts, say to yourself: "It is futile to contend with them any longer," and then fall down before them like a captive or coward. For in doing this you commend yourself to God in the midst of your enemies and admit the radical impotence of your nature. (pp. 88–89)

Following the author's initial charge, however, we read on and find this explanation:

And surely when this attitude is authentic it is the same as self-knowledge, because you have seen yourself as you really are, a miserable and defiled creature less than nothing without God. This is, indeed, experiential humility. When God beholds you standing alone in this truth he cannot refrain from hastening to you and revenging himself on your enemies. Then like a father rescuing his small child from the jaws of wild swine or savage bears, he will stoop to you and, gathering you in his arms, tenderly brush away your spiritual tears. (p. 89)

Thus we see that the author of the *Cloud,* like Juliana, is orthodox in theology, speaks of a God of love, and urges surrender to him by every person, so that each may be united with him forever in heaven, and by his grace, particularly on earth. Where Juliana relates her personal experience to an audience of fellow Christians, her brothers and sisters, in order to share with them the joy she has found in the fact that God himself has loved and continues to love each of them personally, wishing only to be loved in turn, the author of the *Cloud* is in a real sense *magister* (teacher). He regards his audience as his pupils and seeks to instruct them in the art of communication with his Lord and theirs on a level beyond the common.

Where Juliana speaks from the heart of a present experience, the author of the *Cloud* regards the same experience from the outside, as it were, and invites his pupils to study it with him, with the view of bringing it to their own lives.

These differences are reflected most clearly, perhaps, in the tone established in each book. Juliana speaks quietly and reflectively, telling her story as exactly as she can, filling it in as she goes with further insights gleaned in the meditative prayer of twenty years. One feels the work growing as one reads.

The author of the *Cloud*, on the other hand, is a teacher with a sort of syllabus, complete as it stands, though by no means rigidly, nor even logically, ordered. His role is to instruct his pupils, to encourage their progress, to warn them against dangers, delusions, pitfalls and difficulties, and to do all in his power to bring about their perseverance and success. To this end he is brisk, friendly, blunt, understanding, and ironically aware of human foibles, his own as well as those of his pupils. Wit and good humor are evident, and common sense pervades the whole. The author of the *Cloud* plainly walks with his feet on the ground, as befits one who must lead and guide others.

Not that Juliana lacks these qualities; indeed, as even a cursory reading of her book will indicate, she possessed them to a remarkable degree. But the role of the author of the *Cloud*, as leader, not show-er, and his sense of responsibility for an audience of pupils dependent on him for clarity and guidance, encouragement and practical suggestions as well as light, brings them into a particular prominence in his book, quite different from the form they take in the revelations of the anchoress of Norwich. If it may be put so, the work of the *Cloud* is to prepare the audience to receive experiences

like those of Juliana, as God will, and this task has deter
mined its tone.

Walter Hilton (died c. 1396), like Richard Rolle and th
author of the *Cloud*, and quite unlike Juliana, was a teache
with a program for the spiritual life. But where the author c
the *Cloud* and Rolle are allusive—associatively rather tha
logically organized—and Rolle focuses on the value of th
emotions rather than on the intellect and insists upon th
physical and psychic expressions of divine love as most rea
Hilton is logical (though not scholastic), orderly and some
what detached, and sees true contemplation as a combinatio
of light granted the intellect and "stirrings" granted th
heart.

In his *Scale of Perfection* (trans. by Dom Gerard Sitwel
and pub. by The Newman Press) Hilton describes contem
plation as occurring in three sometimes successive, sometimes
independent, stages or degrees.

The first he defines in Chapter 4 as "the knowledge of
God and spiritual matters, which can be attained by reason"
(p. 6). This stage he calls "only a figure and shadow of true
contemplation, for it carries with it no inward experience of
God and no interior sweetness" (p. 6). Rolle altogether ex
cludes this kind of knowledge from the sphere of contem
plation in his vigorous rejection of "philosophers and sages of
this world" and "theologians bogged down in their inter
minable questionings" (Rolle, Prologue, p. 46) as part of his
audience. The author of the *Cloud*, though not as anti
intellectual as Rolle, also rejects the learned, and unlearned as
well, "who are merely curious." For both, the important
thing in contemplation is not so much what is thought as
what is done and willed.

Juliana, on the other hand, though she is not intentionally
teaching anybody anything, but simply sharing with all her
fellow Christians as fully as she can her experience of union
with God, does not follow this affective emphasis. Through
out the *Revelations* she continues to insist that both knowing
and loving (activities respectively of intellect and will, in me
dieval terms) are part of the experience. "For," she remarks
in Chapter 6, "he wills that we be occupied in knowing and

loving until the time that we shall find fulfillment in heaven."

Hilton sees in his second degree of contemplation the reality Rolle took for the whole. "The second degree of contemplation," he says in Chapter 5, "consists principally in the act of love, and the intellect receives no special light on spiritual matters" (p. 8). Remarking that this kind of experience "is given generally to simple, unlearned people" (Rolle's intended audience), "who devote themselves wholly to God" (the audience demanded by the author of the *Cloud of Unknowing*), he goes on to describe the experience in detail, in language Rolle would have recognized and approved. Says Hilton:

> From this feeling spring sweet tears, burning of desires, silent sorrow, all of which purify the soul from sin and make it melt with the love of Jesus Christ, pliant and obedient to God's will. So much so that a man has no care what becomes of him, if only God's will is fulfilled. All this, and more, will he feel, and it is all the outcome of great grace. (p. 8)

In Chapter 6, Hilton divided this second stage into two degrees, one available to those who lead the so-called "active" life and the other to those "who live in great tranquillity of body and soul, and who by the grace of Jesus Christ and long bodily and spiritual exercises have attained peace of heart and a good conscience, so that their greatest happiness is to remain tranquil and continually praying, keeping their minds on our Lord" (Chapter 7, p. 10)—contemplatives, in short.

The description suggests Juliana, whose work seems to be the result of this way of life, and certainly reflects its tranquillity. It also suggests the audience envisioned by the author of the *Cloud*, who specifically addressed only those aspiring to this state, and attempted to teach them how to lead such a life.

Hilton, however, ostensibly addressing a female recluse, an anchoress (scholars are divided on the issue), sees even this second stage of the second degree of contemplation as incomplete. He defines a third stage, which combines the illumination of the intellect with the stirring of the emotions in an overwhelming experience. This stage, he says in Chapter 8,

> comes about when a man, first of all reformed in the image of Jesus by the practice of virtue, then visited by grace, is detached from all earthly and carnal love, from useless thoughts and imaginations, and is carried out of his bodily senses. By the grace of the Holy Ghost his intellect is illumined to see Truth itself, which is God, and spiritual matters, and his will is inflamed with a soft, sweet, burning love. So powerfully does this come about that by an ecstasy of love the soul for the time being becomes one with God and is conformed to the image of the Trinity. (p. 11)

Thus, the final stage of union, for Hilton, both subsumes and transforms the lower two.

The point of it all, of course, is union with God, and the cultivation of a growing awareness of this oneness. Since any awareness of union with God, whether by faith or by mystical experience, is God's gift, the third and most complete stage of contemplation is particularly in his giving. He gives it "where He will," Hilton notes in Chapter 9, "to learned and to ignorant, to men and to women, to prelates and to solitaries" (p. 14).

"But it is a special gift and not a common one," he continues, "and though a man in active life may have it by a particular favor, the plenitude of it is reserved for the contemplative and the solitary" (p. 14). It is upon this distinction that Hilton builds his work. If the contemplative and the solitary are more likely to receive the third stage of contemplation, it may be partly because they are more ready to receive it. Their readiness consists in their choice of this way of life and their active pursuit of it. The pursuit requires purgation, first, and the exclusion of all that is not God from the consciousness and will. Hilton calls this process "reformation," declaring in Chapter 9, "No man may have this gift [the third stage of contemplation] within him unless he is first reformed in the image of Jesus by the practice of virtue" (p. 12).

To this process of "reformation" Hilton devotes the rest of his work. It is arranged as a *scala*, a stairway or ladder, in which each element depends upon the working together of all the elements that precede it. Hilton sees the virtues of humility, faith and charity as essential to and springing from the practice of prayer and meditation. Perseverance in attempting to acquire these habits, in turn, leads to self-knowledge, particularly the awareness of the roots of each of the seven deadly sins within oneself. The desire for Jesus which prompts all efforts made in these directions also serves as motive and means for the destruction of the seven deadly sins within.

The seven deadly sins are seen first as blocks to contemplation. Finally, when the neophyte contemplative has persevered in his purification and begun to receive God's gift of contemplation, they are destroyed by it. The climber has, as it were, entered into the mystery of sin and redemption at one end of the process, where sin is to be overcome that union may be attained, and come out the other, to find that attainment of union has accomplished the work of purgation that was supposed to prepare for it.

Throughout the work, Hilton maintains his instructive tone. He brings to bear years of experience, as is evident in his treatment of the discovery of the roots of the seven deadly sins. The image of Jesus, which is to be re-formed in the contemplative, is to be used as his touchstone in arriving at the self-knowledge essential to the process. In Chapter 69, for example, speaking of the linked sins of anger and envy, he advises:

Look again at this image [of Jesus] if you will discover how much anger and envy is hidden in your heart, without your being aware of it. Take careful note of yourself when such movements arise in you. The more swelling of anger there is, and the more melancholy bitterness or ill-will you feel the greater is this image. For the more you complain with impatience, either against God, because of trouble or sickness, or bodily discomfort which He sends you, or against your neighbor, the less is the image of Jesus reformed in you. (p. 107)

The two books into which the *Scale of Perfection* is divided may represent two treatments of the same material, with the second "a rehandling of the matter with emphasis on the higher part of contemplation instead of on the attainment of the prerequisite virtues," as Dom Gerard Sitwell, the 1952 translator, maintained ("Contemplation in the 'Scale,'" *Downside Review*, 67, 277). On the other hand, they may form "a structural unity based on a constant progress of the soul, the progress or specifically the reform from the image of sin to the image of God," as Joseph Milosh argues (*"The Scale of Perfection" and the English Mystical Tradition*, 1966). Which of these interpretations is correct is less important than the weight of the whole work in the mystical tradition.

We do not know exactly when Hilton wrote, nor can we pinpoint his influence in any of the other mystics we have considered, but his insistence on the integral workings of intellect and emotions in human prayer, and his awareness of the reciprocal flow of grace and human response in the progress of purgation from sin, and growth in love, earn him a place of fundamental importance to anyone in pursuit of the goal of union with God.

Juliana herself attained in vision, prayer, insight and illumination to the same fundamental awareness, as her work makes evident. But where Juliana shares, Hilton teaches. Each has a distinct and essential function in the development of the English mystical tradition.

The fourth of Juliana's contemporaries, Margery Kempe of Lynne (c. 1373–after 1436), is about as different from the anchoress of Norwich, and indeed from any of the other mystics we have thus far examined, as can be imagined. Save their Christian faith and single-minded love of, and submission to, a loving God, with whom each conversed, Juliana and Margery had very little in common.

Where Juliana lived as a solitary, attached to the church of St. Julian at Norwich, as far as we know until her death, Margery was a wife, mother of fourteen children, traveler throughout England and maker of pilgrimages as far as Jerusalem, Rome and Compostella. The external differences in their lives suggest their internal divergence and prepare one for the dramatic contrasts in their experiences of union with God, and of their accounts.

Margery Kempe was a center of controversy for almost the whole of her adult life. She seems to have been as much cause as victim of the acrimony she stirred up, though, as she assures us, she was not responsible for the conduct that occasioned most of the furor.

Margery, like Juliana, found contemplation of the passion of Christ most moving, but unlike the contemplative Juliana, whose life and demeanor were marked by peace and quiet, Margery responded to the stimulus of church sermons, services and the sacraments, particularly the Eucharist, "with boisterous sobbings," as she tells us. In fact, such "loud cryings" were Margery's common outward response to any sense she had of divine action within her, and they earned her the frank scorn and active hostility of most of her neighbors and associates for most of her life. Bishops summoned her to appear, fellow pilgrims refused to travel with her and abandoned her without mercy in foreign countries, her maid deserted her, and at least one preacher refused to allow her in the church when he preached, all because of her extremely loud, public weeping.

Now, Margery was not a stupid woman. She was well aware of the reaction most people had to her, and aware as well of the vast improvement she might effect in communal relations if she could stop her noisy crying, as she herself reports in her account. But she could not, as she explains frequently, either choose to weep or choose not to weep. Commenting on a particularly violent spell of weeping that came to her one Good Friday, and speaking of herself in the third person, she says, "And the more she tried to keep herself from crying, the louder she cried, for it was not in her power to take it or leave it, but as God would send it" (Butler-Bowdon, *The Book of Margery Kempe*, Chapter 57, p. 128).

Margery saw her tears, and the rejection and humiliation they occasioned her, as a direct gift from God. She reports confirmation of this view throughout her book, quoting the Lord's words to her, as in Chapter 56. Reporting her habit of abundant weeping at the reception of the Eucharist, and the

distress of the local clergy, who administered it to her pri-
vately (whether because of parish complaints, or out of
regard for Margery herself, is not made clear), she says:

> Then Our Blissful Lord said to her mind: "Daughter, I
> will not have My grace hidden, that I give thee, for the
> busier the people are to hinder and prevent it, the more
> will I spread it and make it known to all the world." (p.
> 126)

Margery accepted her gift, and made as good use of it as
she could. She wept, she tells us, for her own sins, for the
sins of the world, and in compassion for the sufferings of
Jesus. The unfriendly responses of almost everyone around
her, and the cruelties they practiced upon her, she accepted
as penances, which she offered for the same intentions, and
as personal purifiers.

She could not explain any of this to those who "wondered"
at her behavior, and there were many. Like other mystics, she
found the experience beyond her power to put into words. As
the priest who wrote the Proem explains:

> She herself could never tell the grace that she felt, it was so
> heavenly, so high above her reason and her bodily wits, and
> her body so feeble in time of the presence of grace that she
> might never express it with her word as she felt it in her
> soul. (p. 236)

It is as if when he stirred her soul, God touched the limits of
his creature, reducing her to tears and inarticulate love.

Thus we see the pattern of mystical union Juliana enjoyed
—the Lord "stirring" her soul to loving response, enlighten-
ing her when and as he willed—repeated in Margery's life
but in terms of Margery's temperament and character.

Margery's account of her experiences is also a reflection of
her character and temperament. Margery wrote an autobiographical account of her relationship with God and her adventures among men. Unexpectedly enough, she is not at all
troubled about chronological order, preferring an associative
method of narration. One incident reminds her of another,
perhaps far distant in time and place, and she does not always trouble to identify either, or to establish sequence. The

fact that she had to dictate the memoir, being unable to read or write, probably had a contributory effect upon this ordering.

In the Proem the priest who finally completed the manuscript of her book says:

> This book is not written in order, each thing after another as it was done, but like as the matter came to the creature in mind when it should be written; for it was so long ere it was written that she had forgotten the time and the order when things befell. And therefore she had nothing written but what she knew right well for very truth. (p. 237)

In the above quotation, "therefore" has the weight of "for this reason." Margery could not give a verbatim chronological account of events that had occurred twenty or more years previous to the recording of them, so she made sure that what was written was accurate and said nothing about what she was unsure of, however plausible it might be.

Although Margery is telling her own life story, with a wealth of personal detail, she is not primarily interested in herself. It is God who matters, and all she says, she says because it has to do with him or shows forth his glory and power.

Margery sees herself only as God's creature. She tells her story in the third person. Her sharp wit, observant eye and gift for vivid description would have produced an admirable memoir had Margery never known God. One result of her knowing him as she did, in the extraordinary way we have been discussing, was a shrinking of ego and a detachment from the scenes she reports. She can thus convey without anger or malice, and with a measure of wit and wry humor, the responses people made to her untoward behavior as she was gripped by and responded to divine power. So effective is her detachment, one tends to forget that the events reported happened to the reporter and to accept them as a genuine third-person account. Amusement, amazement and perhaps good-humored scorn at the follies of Margery give way to psychic shock as one recalls that every "she" in the account should properly be read "I." Margery knows herself, her nothingness and her absolute security in the love of God well enough to be able to afford this stripping, this complete reve-lation of herself, this abandonment of masks.

Here in action, in a vivid, unusual and, according to the judgment of most of her contemporaries, peculiar woman is the reduction to nothingness Juliana speaks of in Chapter 5 as a precondition for union with God.

Most of Margery's account is spent recording the ongoing conversation between her and the Lord. Margery claims no visions. She uses her imagination to re-create scenes from the passion and the life of Christ and his mother, and enters them. She does not pray to the images she has imagined, but converses with the real beings they represent. Ignatius Loyola, in the sixteenth century, would call this practice a "composition of place" and recommend it as a preparation for meditative prayer.

Margery's conversations with the Lord reflect her character and temperament. She questions, complains at times, repents her sins and declares her love. The Lord in his turn declares his love for her, tells her the future, rebukes her, explains his actions and asks her submission. Here is no unfolding illumi-nation from a single sentence, as we find in Juliana's account, but straightforward dialogue.

The central, internal difficulty Margery found with her ex-periences of union with God reflects her external problems. People around her did not know how to judge whether her weepings—the outward sign of her inner experiences—were of God, of the devil, or of her own hypocrisy. Most decided on the second or the third hypothesis. The reason for their difficulty, and their judgment, was, for the most part, that they found Margery's manifestations embarrassing and with-out precedent or official sanction. Despite certification from at least two bishops that Margery was in God's hands, not the devil's, people persisted in asking questions and passing usually negative judgments.

Margery herself was continually troubled about the source of her illumination. The Lord, Mary and other saints spoke to her not audibly but "in her mind"—and Margery was frequently troubled lest "the fiend" might have gotten in and deceived her. Many of her early travels, and most of her converse with friars, priests, confessors and holy people was aimed at easing her mind on precisely that point.

Again and again, Margery tells us, she "showed her life" to this or that holy person, to make sure she was walking in God's way. Assurance gave her comfort, but only for a relatively brief time, and then she had to ask again. The Lord does not seem to have quieted her fears directly but, according to Margery, always sent her to good men who could.

One of the people Margery consulted was Juliana of Norwich. Her account of the conversation appears in Chapter 18 of the first part of her book, and deserves quotation in full, since it is the only glimpse we get of Juliana in action as seen by another person, and gives a sense of her local reputation. Says Margery:

Then she was bidden by Our Lord to go to an anchoress in the same city [Norwich], named Dame Jelyan, and so she did, and showed her the grace that God put into her soul, of compunction, contrition, sweetness and devotion, compassion with holy meditation and high contemplation, and full many holy speeches and dalliance that Our Lord spake to her soul; and many wonderful revelations, which she shewed to the anchoress to find out if there were any deceit in them, for the anchoress was expert in such things, and good counsel could give.

The anchoress, hearing the marvelous goodness of Our Lord, highly thanked God with all her heart for His visitation, counselling this creature to be obedient to the will of Our Lord God and to fulfill with all her might whatever He put into her soul, if it were not against the worship of God, and profit of her fellow-Christians, for if it were, then it were not the moving of a good spirit, but rather of an evil spirit. "The Holy Ghost moveth ne'er a thing against charity, for if He did, He would be contrary to His own self for he is all Charity. Also He moveth a soul to all chasteness, for chaste livers are called the Temple of the Holy Ghost, and the Holy Ghost maketh a soul stable and steadfast in the right faith, and the right belief.

"And a double man in soul is ever unstable and unsteadfast in all his ways. He that is ever doubting is like the flood of the sea which is moved and borne about with the wind, and that man is not likely to receive the gifts of God.

"Any creature that hath these tokens may steadfastly believe that the Holy Ghost dwelleth in his soul. And much more when God visiteth a creature with tears of contrition, devotion and compassion, he may and ought to believe that the Holy Ghost is in his soul. Saint Paul saith that the Holy Ghost asketh for us with mourning and weeping unspeakable, that is to say, He maketh us to ask and pray with mourning and weeping so plenteously that the tears may not be numbered. No evil spirit may give these tokens, for Saint Jerome saith that tears torment more the devil than do the pains of Hell. God and the devil are ever at odds and they shall never dwell together in one place, and the devil hath no power in a man's soul.

"Holy Writ saith that the soul of a rightful man is the seat of God, and so I trust, sister, that ye be. I pray God grant you perseverance. Set all your trust in God and fear not the language of the world, for the more despite, shame and reproof that ye have in the world, the more is your merit in the sight of God. Patience is necessary to you, for in that shall ye keep your soul." (pp. 33–34)

Thus we see Juliana in action. Her calm, common sense and gentle encouragement of the troubled Margery are what we should expect, as are the balanced wisdom, caution and reliance on God, who can be known unfailingly by his actions, as can the fiend Margery so feared.

We do not see in the *Revelations* the straightforward teaching that goes on here, logic buttressed by Scripture, but it is not out of character. The interview seems to have given Margery some comfort, but only for the time. It did not end her anxieties.

Like the rest of her dealings with other people, Margery's attempts to get her book written met difficulties caused by people's conflicting opinions about her and the nature of her experiences. Since Margery could neither read nor write, getting someone to write down her account became a major problem. Her difficulties are recorded in the Proem, which her second amanuensis, a priest, attached to the manuscript.

When she first began receiving her revelations, he tells us, several clerks suggested she have them written, but "she was commanded in her soul that she should not write so soon" (p. 236), and she refused. Twenty years later, when the Lord bade her have them written, the only one she could find to do the job wrote them poorly—though Margery had no way of knowing that at the time—and died. The priest who eventually completed the task found the account ill-written, "neither good English nor Dewch, nor were the letters shaped or formed as other letters were" (p. 236).

He tried to make a new copy, but in addition to the difficulties provided by the text, as he confesses, "there was such evil speaking of this creature and of her weeping that the priest durst not for cowardice speak with her but seldom nor would he write as he had promised . . ." (pp. 236–37). He delayed for four years, then turned Margery and her book over to another man, who, for "a great sum of money," tried to transcribe the poor copy and failed.

The priest, meanwhile, developed a guilty conscience about his treatment of Margery, got the copy back and tried again to read and transcribe it. A mysterious blindness then came upon the priest. As he describes it,

> his eyes failed so that he might not see to make his letters and could not see to mend his pen. Everything else he could see well enough. He set a pair of spectacles on his nose, and then was it well worse than it was before. (p. 237)

He complained to Margery about his disease, and she told him it was caused by the devil, who was envious of the good deed he was trying to do in copying her book. She then "bade him do as well as God would give him grace and not give up" (p. 237).

The result of his obedience was startling, and finally convinced the priest that Margery's experiences were of God,

and that he had done wrong to impede her for the four years
he had delayed in the copying of the book. He says:

> When he came again to his book he could see, he thought,
> as well as ever he did before, by day-light and by candle-
> light both. And for this cause, when he had written a
> quire, he added a leaf thereto, and then wrote he this
> proem, to express more openly than doth the next follow-
> ing [the Preface], which was written earlier than this.
> Anno Domini 1436. (p. 237)

He then completed the copying of the book and added ten
more chapters at Margery's dictation.

In addition to detailing Margery's problems in getting her
book written, the writer of the Proem indicates the purpose
such a recording served. Besides the conversations with the
Lord and his saints, which could easily serve the didactic purpose so dear to the heart of the medieval writer, the book records Margery's adventures among men. These were included
neither for comic relief nor to provide a context for the conversations, but because, in themselves, they showed the workings of God in apparent chaos and the control of Providence
over all creation. Says the priest:

> All the works of our Savior be for our example and instruc-
> tion and what grace that He worketh in any creature is our
> profit, if lack of charity be not our hindrance.

> And therefore . . . this little treatise shall treat some-
> what in part of His wonderful works, how mercifully, how
> benignly, and how charitably He moved and stirred a sinful
> caitiff unto His love. . . . And ever she was turned aback
> [from her good intentions to reform] in time of tempta-
> tion, like unto the reed-spear, which boweth with every
> wind, and never is stable unless no wind bloweth, unto the
> time that our merciful Lord Christ Jesus, having pity and
> compassion on his handiwork and His creature, turned
> health into sickness, prosperity into adversity, worship into
> reproof, and love into hatred.

> Thus, everything turning upside down, this creature who
> for many years had gone astray and ever been unstable, was
> perfectly drawn and stirred to enter the way of high perfec-
> tion. (p. 235)

Margery's life, illustrating some of the ways God can draw a person to himself and to awareness of union with him, and some of the ways a person can respond or fail to respond, thus becomes a visual lesson on the practical level. She herself does not teach and is not interested in teaching, for she does not see herself as an authority, but simply as one of God's creatures. He has commanded the book be written, for his own inscrutable reasons, which she has no way of knowing and does not question. Although Margery is not acting as a teacher, an attentive audience can learn simply by listening to her account of herself.

Lessons drawn from experience, such as those provided by Margery's life, were less common in medieval times than those drawn from "authority": conclusions based upon philosophical reasoning on theological premises found in Scripture or the Fathers and Doctors of the Church.

The closest parallel in the motive for this kind of writing can be found among the hagiographers, who offered the *vitae* of saints as mirrors of Christ and direct models for Christian conduct. The material in Margery's case was so different from that usual with medieval hagiographers, that the manner of application would also have had to be drastically altered for a medieval audience to derive similar profit from reading Margery's book. It is no wonder, then, that only one copy of this unorthodox work survived, and that that one was lost sight of for several hundred years, to be rediscovered only in the twentieth century, by W. Butler-Bowdon.

And that, briefly, answers the third section of the original question: How does Juliana differ from contemporary English mystics? By examining similarities as well as differences, we have hoped to show that it was the same God who revealed himself so diversely to, and within, these five men and women, who had in common only their total commitment to him and his extraordinary working in their lives. A longer study than there is space for here would be able to clarify both the image of this God and the lineaments of each of the human respondents, by allowing their records of their individual experiences of union with God to speak at greater length for themselves.

Further talk *about* the mystical experience would probably not be profitable, as, in the last analysis, it exists not in general but only in particular. The mystical experience is the working of God within the individual, coupled with his personal response, and can best be approached through the study of the record of a particular mystic. In this case, the study of Juliana's *Revelations* will reveal to the attentive reader both Juliana's experience of union with God, and the God who is both revealed and revealer in this experience.

## The Manuscript Tradition

Juliana's account of the sixteen showings of May 8, 1373, exists in two versions, a longer and a shorter. Scholars examining the possible relationships between the two have concluded, almost universally, that the shorter is not a series of extracts from the longer, but a separate, independent account of the same experience, since the shorter includes language and incidents that do not appear in the longer.

The first editor of the shorter version, Rev. Dundas Harford, argues (*The Shewings of Lady Julian*, 1925, p. 8) that it was a kind of "first edition" of the revelations. He saw the longer version as "the outcome of the twenty years' subsequent meditation, thought and experience referred to in the fifty-first and in the last chapters of the later version." Most scholars have come to agree with Harford's analysis.

The oldest surviving manuscript of the *Revelations* records the only copy we have of the shorter version. It appears in an anthology of a dozen fifteenth-century devotional and theological treatises having for their object the reader's spiritual enlightenment and encouragement in perseverance. The theme that seems to unite the selections is their emphasis on the central role of love in the spiritual life—the love of God for the soul, and the soul's loving response to her creator.

Keeping Juliana's *Revelations* company are, among others,

Richard Rolle's *Amending of Life*, his *Incendium amoris*, a treatise on "the perfection of the sons of God," another called "The Mirrour of Symple Souls," and a discussion of the three stages of spiritual progress: the purgative, illuminative and unitive ways.

The manuscript (British Museum, MSS Additional, No. 37790) came into the possession of Rev. Francis Peck (1692–1743) sometime during the eighteenth century (Blomefield, *History of Norfolk*, iv, 8). Of its previous history we know nothing. Of its subsequent history we know only that it came to rest in the library of Lord Amherst and was brought to light again only when the British Museum purchased it at the dispersal of that collection, in March 1910.

In the scribe's preface to the shorter version of the *Revelations*, which appears only in this manuscript, we learn that it was made during Juliana's lifetime. He says:

> Here is a vision, shown by the goodness of God to a devout woman named Juliana, who is a recluse at Norwich, and is still alive in this year of our Lord 1413. In this vision, there are a great many comforting and deeply moving words for all those who desire to be Christ's lovers.

We do not learn from this preface how much time elapsed between the sixteen showings and the written record of them, only that when *this* copy was made Juliana was still alive.

The phrase "that is recluse atte Norwyche" is equally limited in the evidence it offers. We do not learn that Juliana was a recluse at the time of the showings, only that in 1413 she was well enough known as a recluse at Norwich to allow the scribe to use the designation as a ready means of identification.

Of the longer version, we have three manuscripts. The earliest is a sixteenth-century production currently in possession of the Bibliothèque Nationale, Paris (Fonds Anglais, No. 40, Bibliotheca Bigotiana 388). We know nothing of its origin and nothing of its history, though Dom Roger Hudleston, O.S.B. (*Revelations of Divine Love*, 1927, pp. v–vi), judging it to be "the original from which Dom Serenus

Cressy published his printed version" in 1670, conjectures, "it may *perhaps* have belonged to the convent of Benedictine nuns at Paris, to whom Cressy acted as Chaplain during the years 1651–53."

The other two surviving complete manuscripts of the longer version are in the British Museum. The first (British Museum, MSS Sloane, No. 2499) is a seventeenth-century production that does not name Juliana as author. It has chapter headings supplied by the scribe. We do not know the origin of the manuscript, nor its history previous to its arrival in the Sloane collection. The second (British Museum, MSS Sloane, No. 3705) is an eighteenth-century work with some modernization of spelling and language. It may have been copied from Sloane 2499, but it has several unique readings and an added colophon.

Thus, the three manuscripts we have of the longer version of the *Revelations* are respectively two hundred, three hundred and four hundred years distant from the experiences and meditations they record. Though between the showings and the first recording of the longer version a minimum of twenty years has elapsed, on the evidence of its own Chapters 51 and 86, we have no way of knowing the maximum possible time that elapsed, or the history of the chain of manuscripts lying between the first copy and the three we now possess.

It is evident that one or more manuscript copies of the longer version have disappeared. Of the three copies that have survived, the Paris manuscript and Sloane 2499 appear, according to Hudleston, to have derived "from a fourteenth-century original, the spelling and dialect of which they have retained. This lost archetype seems to have been written in a mixed East Anglian and Northern dialect." Which of the two is closer to the lost original is matter for scholarly conjecture.

Each manuscript has its adherents. In 1927, Dom Hudleston found Sloane 2499 as "perhaps nearer to the original text." He declares, "Unless, therefore, the lost fourteenth-century original of the longer version is found, we are not likely to obtain a better text of this than appears in Sloane 2499" (p. xi).

In 1961 Rev. James Walsh, S.J. (*The Revelations of Divine Love of Julian of Norwich*, Abbey Press, pp. v–vi), accepting the conclusions of Sister Anna Maria Reynolds, C.P., agreed that "The Paris MS represents more nearly the MS tradition." Father Walsh urges in support of this conclusion the series of extracts from the *Revelations* found in the fifteenth-century *Florilegium* held at Westminster Cathedral Library. The extracts from the *Revelations* which appear here "consistently favour the readings of the Paris MS against those of the Sloane MSS."

And there the matter stands. Neither argument is irrefutable, and each has great likelihood. Further resolution of the issue seems unlikely, barring the discovery of an earlier text or other conclusive evidence.

## This Translation

In preparing any translation of Juliana's showings, one faces the question of whether to use the shorter or the longer version. Rev. Paul Molinari, S.J. (*Julian of Norwich: the Teaching of a 14th Century English Mystic*, Longmans, Green, p. 5), outlines the alternatives: "whereas the Shorter Version is little more than a simple record of this experience, the Longer Version . . . is a much fuller account of the same experience . . . seen and exposed in the light of further insight and reflection, the result of twenty years of contemplation in which she was granted deeper understanding."

The revelations were, on the evidence of the text of the longer version, only begun in the original showings. They were still in the process of being completed when the longer version was first recorded, at least twenty years after the sixteen showings were granted.

That the revelations were a process rather than a single event is made clear by Juliana in Chapter 86, the last of the longer version. She says, "This book has been begun by

God's gift and his grace, but it has not yet been completed, as I see it," and then records her learning of the meaning of the revelations as a whole, an insight granted her only after twenty years of prayer and meditation. It seems plain that the longer version, containing as it does the fruit of this twenty years of prayer, illumination, deepened understanding and growth in love, is the richer of the two, and therefore I have chosen to use it.

I have used the Paris manuscript and Sloane 2499 in preparing the translation, with Sloane 3705 as a corrective where this was necessary. I have consulted MSS Additional 37790 where the shorter version amplifies or clarifies the longer. For each chapter, I have used the heading supplied by the scribe of Sloane 2499 and repeated in Sloane 3705.

Since my purpose in preparing a new translation of Juliana's *Revelations* is to render them accessible to a twentieth-century non-specialist audience, I have tried to avoid the confusions occasioned by a slavish adherence to the peculiarities of the text, while remaining as close to its words and spirit as possible. To this end, I have used modern phrasing and locutions throughout. I have sacrificed, with regret, some of Juliana's more elliptical, if colorful, expressions in favor of plainer equivalents, as far as these are available. The word "homely" (unassuming, unpretentious, homelike, friendly, familiar), for example, I have eliminated entirely in favor of the equivalent suggested by the context while I have allowed "courtesy," in all its forms, to remain unchanged, as the various weights of that word have persisted in twentieth-century usage.

In all cases, I have striven to make clear what it is Juliana wishes to convey. Where archaic patterns and vocabulary assist the process they have been allowed to remain; where they have hindered it, they have been sacrificed. This, it seems to me, is what Juliana, who received the revelations "for all my fellow Christians," would have preferred.

M. L. del Mastro
CUNY, *Brooklyn College* NSLA, 1976

# THE REVELATIONS

## *Translator's Note*

This scribal introduction appears in the 1413 manuscript only. The 1413 manuscript contains our only copy of the shorter version of the *Revelations*.)

Here is a vision, shown by the goodness of God to a devout woman named Juliana, who is a recluse at Norwich, and is still alive in this year of our Lord 1413. In this vision, there are a great many comforting and deeply moving words for all those who desire to be Christ's lovers.

# Chapter 1

## A Listing of the Showings

This is a revelation of love which Jesus Christ, our endless bliss, made in sixteen showings.

The first showing is of his precious crowning with thorns. In it are contained and specified the blessed Trinity, with the incarnation, and the uniting of man's soul with God. There are also many fair showings and teachings of eternal wisdom and love. In these, all the showings that follow are grounded and joined.

The second showing is of the discoloring of his fair face, a token of his most valuable passion.

The third showing is that our Lord God Almighty, who is All-wisdom and All-love, does or brings about all that is done, just as truly as he has made all things that exist.

The fourth showing is of the scourging of his tender body and the abundant shedding of his precious blood.

The fifth showing is that the fiend is overcome by the precious passion of Christ.

The sixth showing is of the gratitude full of honor of our Lord God, by which he rewards all his blessed servants in heaven.

The seventh showing concerns the frequent shifts in feeling, between well-being and woe. The feeling of well-being is gracious, touching and buoyant, with a sense of real security in unending joy. The feeling of woe is a kind of temptation coming from the heaviness and weariness of our fleshly living. This showing brings with it the spiritual understanding that we are as well preserved in love when we are in woe as when we are in well-being, by the goodness of God.

The eighth showing is of the last pains of Christ, and of his cruel dying.

The ninth showing is of the pleasure in the blessed Trinity because of the accomplishment of the hard passion and painful death of Christ. In this joy and pleasure, he wills we have solace and mirth with him, until we come to its full glory in heaven.

The tenth showing is of our Lord Jesus, who joyfully shows his blessed heart cloven in two for love.

The eleventh is a noble, spiritual showing of his excellent mother.

The twelfth showing is that our Lord God is Being All sovereign.

The thirteenth showing is that our Lord God wills that we have great regard for all the deeds he has done, for the great nobility of his making of all things, for the excellence of the greatest of his works, his making of man, and for the precious amendment he has made for man's sin, turning all our blame into unending honor. By this showing he means to say, "Behold and see! For by the same might, wisdom and goodness that I have done all this, I shall make well all that is not well, and you will see it." And in this he wills that we keep ourselves in the faith and truth of holy Church, not choosing to know his secrets now, except as is proper to us in this life.

The fourteenth showing is that our Lord God is the ground of our prayer. In this situation there are two benefits: the one is rightful prayer, and the other is secure trust. Both of these he wills to be equally great, and thus our prayer pleases him, and he, of his goodness, fulfills it.

The fifteenth showing is that we shall suddenly be taken from all our pain and from all our woe. And of his goodness we shall come up above, where we shall have our Lord Jesus for our reward, that we may be completely filled with joy and bliss and heaven.

The sixteenth showing is that the blissful Trinity, our maker, in Christ Jesus our savior, dwells without end in our soul, graciously ruling and commanding all things, saving and keeping us mightily and wisely for love, so that we shall not be overcome by our enemy.

## Chapter 2

*Of the time of the revelations and how she asked three petitions.*

These revelations were showed to a simple, uneducated creature living in mortal flesh in the year of our Lord 1373, on the eighth day of May.

This creature had desired beforehand three gifts of God by his grace. The first was to enter into the spirit of Christ's passion. The second was bodily sickness in youth, at thirty years of age. The third was to have from God the gift of three wounds.

As far as the first petition was concerned, it seemed to me that I already had considerable feeling for the passion of Christ, but still, I desired to have more, by the grace of God. I wished I could have been with Mary Magdalene and the other lovers of Christ at the time of his passion. Then I might have seen with my own eyes the passion our Lord suffered for me, and I could have suffered with him, as did the others who loved him.

Therefore, I desired a vision in which I might have more knowledge of the bodily pains of our savior, and of the compassion of our Lady and of all his true lovers who were living at that time and saw his pains, for I wanted to be one of them and suffer with him. I never desired any other vision or showing from God until my soul should be parted from my body, for I believed I would be saved by the mercy of God.

I made this first petition so that after the showing I might have a truer understanding of the passion of Christ.

As for the second petition, it came to my mind with contrition, freely, without my seeking it in any way. It was a fully willed desire to have as God's gift a bodily sickness so severe it would bring me to the point of death. I asked that in that sickness I might receive all the rites of holy

Church, and that I, and everyone else who saw me, should re ally believe I was dying. I asked this because I wanted abso lutely no human or earthly comfort in this sickness. I desire to have all the kinds of bodily and spiritual pain I woul have had if I had actually been dying. I wanted all the te rors, the temptations of devils, and every kind of pain excep the actual departure of the soul. I asked all this so that by i I might be purged, by God's mercy, and afterward live mor for the glory of God, because of that sickness. I also hoped i would assist me in my death, for I desired to be soon with my God and maker.

I made these two petitions—for a deeper sharing in th passion, and for the sickness—with a condition (for i seemed to me that this was not the common object o prayer). Therefore I said, "Lord, you know what I want. I it's your will for me to have it, let me have it. If it's not you will, good Lord, don't be displeased, for I only want wha you will."

Concerning my third petition, by the grace of God and th teaching of holy Church I conceived a very great desire to re ceive three wounds in my life—that is to say, the wound o true contrition, the wound of natural compassion, and th wound of fullhearted longing for God. Unlike the first tw petitions, which I had made with a condition, I asked thi third gift very strongly and without any condition.

The first two desires passed from my mind, but the thir dwelled with me continuously.

## Chapter 3

*Of the sickness obtained from God by petition.*

And when I was thirty and one-half years old, God sent me a bodily sickness, in which I lay three days and three nights On the fourth night I received all the rites of holy Church and I believed I would not live until morning.

After that I lay sick two more days and nights. On the
third night, I thought many times that I would die, and so
did those who were with me. Since I was still young, I
thought it a great hardship to die, but not because there was
anything on earth I wanted to live for, nor because I feared
the pain, for I trusted in God's mercy. I would have preferred
to live so that I could have loved God better, for a longer
time, and thus, by the grace of God, have been able to know
and love him better in the bliss of heaven.

For all the time I had lived on earth seemed to me so in-
significant and brief, compared to the reward of endless bliss,
that I thought it nothing. That is why I thought, "Lord, is it
possible that my living no longer is for your honor?" And I
understood by my reason, and because of the pain I was feeling, that I was going to die, so I assented fully, with all my
heart and will, to be at God's disposal.

Thus I endured until daylight, and by then my body, from
the middle downward, was dead, having no feeling at all.
Then I was moved to ask to be set upright, and, with help,
propped up, so that I could have more freedom of heart to be
at God's disposal, and to think about him while my life
would last.

My curate had been sent for to be at my deathbed, but by
the time he came my eyes had become fixed and I could not
speak. He set the cross before my face and said, "I have
brought you the image of your maker and savior. Look on it,
and be comforted by it." It seemed to me I was all right as I
was, for my eyes were fixed upward, gazing in the direction of
the heaven into which I trusted I should come by the mercy
of God. But nevertheless I assented to fix my eyes on the face
of the crucifix, if I could do it, and so I did. It seemed to me
that I might last longer looking straight ahead than directly
upward.

After this my sight began to fail, and it grew as dark
around me in the chamber as if it had been night. I could
only see, I don't know how, the image on the cross, in daylight. Everything besides the cross was ugly to me and frightening, as if it had been fully occupied by devils.

After this, the other part of my body began to die, to the

point where I had scarcely any feeling, and my greatest pa
was shortness of breath. At that point, I was sure I was goi
to die.

And then, suddenly, all my pain was taken from me, and
was as whole and healthy in every part of my body as I ha
ever been before. I marveled at this sudden change, for
seemed to me that this was a secret working of God, and n
the work of nature. And yet this feeling of ease did not co
vince me that I should live, nor, indeed, was it a comple
comfort to me. For I would have preferred to be freed fro
this world, and had had my heart set on it.

Then it came suddenly into my mind that I should desi
the second wound [natural compassion] as a gracious gift
our Lord, so that my body might be filled completely wit
understanding and experience of his blessed passion, as I ha
previously prayed. I desired with compassion that his pa
should be my pain, and afterward, that I should be con
pletely filled with longing for him.

It seemed to me that with his grace I might have th
wounds I had previously desired. But in this prayer I nev
desired any vision, or any kind of showing from God—onl
compassion, as, it seemed to me, a soul following its natur:
bent might have for our Lord Jesus, who for love chose to be
come a mortal man. And therefore, I desired to suffer wit
him, living in my mortal body, as God would give me grace.

## Chapter 4

*Here begins the first revelation, of the precious crowning o*
*Christ, as described in the first chapter, of how God fully fill*
*the heart with greatest joy, of his great meekness, of how th*
*light of the passion of Christ is sufficient strength against a*
*temptations of the fiends, and of the great excellency an*
*meekness of the blessed virgin Mary.*

At this moment suddenly I saw the red blood runnin;
down from under the garland; it was hot and fresh, and jus

plenteous and lifelike as it was at the time the garland of
thorns was pressed on his blessed head, when he, who was
both God and man, suffered for me. I conceived truly and
strongly that it was he himself who showed it to me, without
any intermediary.

And in the same showing, suddenly the Trinity completely
filled my heart with the greatest joy. And so, I understood, it
will be in heaven, without an end, for those who come there.
For the Trinity is God; God is the Trinity. The Trinity is
our maker. The Trinity is our keeper. The Trinity is our everlasting lover. The Trinity is our endless joy and our bliss,
through our Lord Jesus Christ and in our Lord Jesus Christ.
This truth was shown in the first showing and in all the
showings, for where Jesus appears, the blessed Trinity is understood, as I see it.

I said, "Bless the Lord!" in a loud voice, but intending reverence. I was completely astonished, wondering and marveling, that he, who is so worthy of reverence and dread should
be so friendly to a sinful creature living in this wretched
flesh.

This showing I took as a strengthening comfort for the
time of my temptation, for I supposed that, by the permission of God and with his protection, I would be tempted by
devils before I died.

With this vision of his blessed passion, and with the understanding of the godhead I had just been given, I knew
well that I, and indeed, all creatures living, had been given
enough strength to overcome all the devils of hell and all
spiritual temptations.

In this showing, he brought our blessed Lady Mary to my
understanding. I saw her spiritually, in bodily likeness, a simple, meek maiden, young in age, little grown beyond childhood, in stature as she was when she conceived her child.

Also, God showed me in part the wisdom and the integrity
of her soul, and I understood in this the reverence with
which she beheld her God, who is her maker. She marveled
with great reverence that he had chosen to be born of her, a
simple creature of his making. Her wisdom and truth recognized the greatness of her maker and the littleness of herself

who was made; they caused her to say most humbly
Gabriel, "Behold me here, God's handmaiden." In this sigh
I understood truly that she is greater than all that God ha
made. All creation is beneath her in worthiness and i
fulness of grace, for above her is nothing that is made excep
the blessed manhood of Christ, as I see it.

## Chapter 5

*How God is everything that is good, tenderly wrapping u*
*how everything that is made is nothing, compared to A*
*mighty God; and how man has no rest until he sees himse*
*and all things as nothing, for the love of God.*

At the same time that I saw the vision of his bleedin,
head, our Lord gave me spiritual insight into the unpreter
tious manner of his loving. I saw that for us he is everythin
that is good, comforting and helpful; he is our clothing, who
for love, wraps us up, holds us close; he entirely encloses u
for tender love, so that he may never leave us, since he is the
source of all good things for us, as I understood it.

And with this insight he also showed me a little thing, the
size of a hazelnut, lying in the palm of my hand. It was a
round as a ball, as it seemed to me. I looked at it with the
eyes of my understanding and thought, "What can this be?"
My question was answered in general terms in this fashion
"It is everything that is made." I marveled how this could be
for it seemed to me that it might suddenly fall into noth
ingness, it was so small. An answer for this was given to my
understanding: "It lasts, and ever shall last, because God
loves it. And in this fashion all things have their being by the
grace of God."

In this little thing, I saw three properties. The first is that
God made it. The second is that God loves it. The third is
that God keeps it. But I cannot tell the reality of him who is
my maker, lover and keeper, for until I am united to him in
substance, I may never have complete rest or real bliss, that

until I am so fastened to him that there is absolutely no
created thing between my God and me.

It is necessary for us to know the littleness of creatures in
order to reduce them to nothingness in our judgment, so that
we may love and have the uncreated God. The reason we are
not fully at ease in heart and soul is because we seek rest in
these things that are so little and have no rest within them,
and pay no attention to our God, who is Almighty, All-wise,
All-good and the only real rest.

God wills to be known, and it pleases him that we rest in
him, because nothing less than he can satisfy us. This is why
no soul can be at rest until it has judged all created things as
nothing. When one has deliberately valued all things as
nothing in order to possess him who is all, then is he able to
receive spiritual rest.

Our Lord also showed that it is a very great pleasure to
him when a simple soul comes to him nakedly, plainly and
unpretentiously, for he is the natural dwelling of the soul
touched by the Holy Spirit. This is what I understand from
his showing, at any rate.

God, of your goodness, give me yourself, for you are
enough for me. I can ask for nothing less that is completely
to your honor, and if I do ask anything less, I shall always be
in want. Only in you I have all.

These words, by the goodness of God, are of great delight
to the soul, and touch the will of God and his goodness
directly, for his goodness encompasses all his creatures and all
his blessed works, and passes beyond them without end. For
he is endlessness, and he has made us only for himself, restores us by his blessed passion and keeps us in his blessed
love. And all this he does of his goodness.

## Chapter 6

*How we should pray; and of the great tender love that o<br>
Lord has for man's soul—willing us to be occupied in kno<br>
ing and loving him.*

This showing was given to my understanding to teach o<br>
souls wisely to cleave to the goodness of God. And at th<br>
same time our custom of praying was brought to my min<br>
how, for lack of understanding and knowing love, we u<br>
many means [reasons for God to grant our prayers]. An<br>
then I truly saw that it is more to the honor of God an<br>
more real pleasure to him to have us pray, full of faith, t<br>
him in himself, of his goodness, and cleave to him by h<br>
grace, with real understanding, steadfast by love, than if w<br>
used all the means the heart can think of. For if we use a<br>
these means it is still too little, and not full honor to Go<br>
But his goodness encompasses all of them, and in it nothin<br>
at all is lacking.

Concerning this, the following example came to my min<br>
at the same time. We pray to God, asking him to hear us fo<br>
the sake of his holy flesh, his precious blood, his holy passior<br>
his most valuable death and glorious wounds, all his blesse<br>
kindness and the endless life we have. All this is given u<br>
through his goodness.

Again, we pray to him to hear us for the sake of the love o<br>
the sweet mother who bore him; all the help we have from<br>
her is from his goodness.

And we pray asking him to hear us for the sake of the hol<br>
cross he died on; all the help and all the strength we hav<br>
from that cross is from his goodness. In the same way, all th<br>
help we have from particular saints and from the whol<br>
blessed company of heaven, all their most precious love an<br>
their holy, unending friendship for us is from his goodness.

God, of his goodness, has ordained many lovely means t

help us. The chief and principal one among them is the blessed nature he took from the maiden. With this are included all the means that come before and follow after, which belong to the process of our redemption and eternal salvation. For this reason it pleases him that we seek him and worship him using means, while understanding and knowing that he is the goodness of all of them.

For the loftiest prayer is to God of his goodness, and it comes down to the lowest part of our need. It quickens our soul and brings it to life; it makes it grow in grace and in virtue. It is nearest to our nature and readiest to give grace, for it is the same grace that the soul feels and ever shall feel until we know in reality him who has us all enclosed in himself.

A man walks upright and his soul is enclosed in his body as in a beautiful purse. In time of necessity, the purse is opened and closed again, quite properly. And that it is God who does this work is shown where he says he comes down to us to the lowest part of our need, for he has no contempt for what he has made. Further, he does not disdain to serve us in the simplest requirements the nature of our body demands, for love of the soul he has made in his own likeness.

For as the body is clad in the clothes, and the flesh in the skin, and the bones in the flesh, and the heart in the whole, so are we, soul and body, clad and enclosed in the goodness of God. Yes, and more intimately than this, for all these may waste and wear away, but the goodness of God is ever whole and closer to us than any comparison can show. Truly, our heavenly lover desires that our soul cleave to him with all its might, and that we continuously cleave to his goodness. For of all the things the heart may think, that most pleases God, and soonest succeeds.

Our soul is so specially loved by him who is the highest that it goes far beyond the ability of any creature to realize it. That is to say, there is no creature made who can realize how much, how sweetly and how tenderly our maker loves us. And therefore we may, with his grace and his help, stand in spirit, gazing with endless wonder at this lofty, unmeasurable love beyond human scope that Almighty God has for us of his goodness. And therefore we may ask our lover, with reverence, all that we will.

Our natural will is to have God, and the good will of God is to have us, and we may never cease willing or longing for him until we have him in the fulness of joy, and then we shall will no longer. For he wills that we be occupied in knowing and loving until the time that we shall find fulfillment in heaven.

And that is the reason this lesson of love was shown, with all that shall follow, as you shall see. For the strength and ground of everything was shown in the first vision.

Of all things, the beholding of and longing for the maker most makes the soul become less in its own sight; it most fills one with reverent dread, true meekness and fulness of charity toward one's fellow Christians.


## Chapter 7


*Of how our Lady, beholding the greatness of her maker, thought herself least; of the great dropping of blood running from under the garland; of how the greatest joy for man is that God most high and mighty is holiest and most courteous.*


And to teach us this, as I understand it, our Lord God showed me our Lady, Saint Mary, at that same time, that is to say, the lofty wisdom and strength she had when she beheld her maker, so great, so noble, so mighty, so good. The greatness and nobility she saw in God filled her full of reverent dread, and with it she saw herself so little, so low, so simple, so poor in comparison to her Lord God that her reverent dread filled her full of meekness. And thus, on these grounds she was filled full of grace and of all manner of virtues, and passed beyond all other creatures.

And all the time he was showing me in spirit the things I have just said, I continued to see with my eyes the severe bleeding of the head. Great drops of blood poured down from under the garland like pellets, just as if they had come out of the veins. In coming out of the head, the drops were brown-red, for the blood was very thick, but in spreading out, the blood was bright red. When the blood came to the brows, it vanished, but notwithstanding, the bleeding continued, until many things had been seen and understood; nevertheless, the fairness and lifelikeness continued to have the same beauty and loveliness.

The fairness and lifelikeness is like nothing but itself. The plenteousness of the bleeding is like drops of water that fall from the eaves of the house after a great rainstorm; they fall so thick no man can count them with his human powers. As they spread over the forehead, the drops of blood were like herring scales in their roundness.

These three images came to me at that time. The drops were round like pellets in coming out of the head, and like herring scales in spreading out on the forehead; in their unnumberable plenty, they were like raindrops falling from the eaves.

This showing was vivid and lifelike, hideous and dreadful, sweet and lovely. And of all the visions that I saw, this one was the greatest comfort to me—that our God and Lord, who is so worthy of reverence and so awesome, is so unassuming and courteous. This most completely filled me with delight and security of soul.

For the better understanding of this, he gave this clear example. The greatest honor a solemn king or a great lord can do a poor servant is to treat him as an equal, revealing himself to him in a completely honest way and treating him in friendly fashion both in private and in public. Then this poor creature thinks thus, "Ah, how could this noble lord give me more honor and joy than by showing me, who am so little and simple, this marvelous, unassuming friendliness? Truly, it is a greater joy and delight to me than if he gave me great gifts and were himself distant in manner." This human example was shown so intensely in order that man's heart might be ravished and he might almost forget himself for joy at this great unassuming friendliness.

And thus it is between our Lord Jesus and us, for truly, it is the greatest joy possible, as I see it, that he who is highest and mightiest, noblest and worthiest, becomes lowest and meekest, friendliest and most courteous. And really and truly, this marvelous joy shall be shown us all when we see him. And our Lord wills that we believe, choose and trust him, enjoy and delight in him, comforting and solacing ourselves as best we can with his grace and his help until the time we see it in reality. For the greatest fulfillment of joy we shall have, as I see it, is the marvelous courtesy and unassuming friendliness of our Father who is our maker, in our Lord Jesus Christ, who is our brother and our savior. But this marvelous familiarity no man may experience in this present life unless he does so through a special showing of our Lord, or through great fulness of grace given him inwardly by the Holy Spirit. But faith and belief, with charity, deserve their reward, and thus it is attained by grace. For in faith, with hope and charity, our life is grounded.

The showing, made to whomever God wills, plainly teaches the same thing, open and declared, and shows many secret points belonging to our faith, which are good for us to know.

And when the showing, which is given at a single time, has passed away and is hidden, then the faith, by the grace of the Holy Spirit, preserves it to the end of our lives. Thus the showing is not other than the faith, neither less nor more, as can be seen in our Lord's teaching on the same matter, about when each shall come to its end.

## Chapter 8

*A recapitulation of what has been said, and how it was shown to her for all in general.*

And as long as I saw this sight of the severe bleeding of the head, I couldn't stop saying, "Bless the Lord." In this showing I understood six things: The first is the tokens of the blessed passion and the abundant shedding of his precious blood; the second is the maiden who is his excellent mother; the third is the blissful Godhead that ever was, is, and shall be, Almighty, All-wisdom and All-love. The fourth is all things he has made. I know well that heaven and earth and all that is made is great, large, fair and good. The reason it looked so little to me was that I saw it in the presence of him who made it all. For to a soul that sees the maker of all things, everything created seems very small.

The fifth thing I understood from this showing is that he who made all things for love, keeps them in the same love and shall do so forever. The sixth is that God is everything that is good, as I see it, and the goodness anything has is he.

All these things our Lord showed me in the first vision, and gave me the time and space in which to behold them. What I saw with my eyes stopped, but the spiritual insight dwelled in my understanding. I waited at rest, with reverent dread, rejoicing in what I had seen, and desiring, as far as I dared, to see more, if it were his will, or to see the same thing for a longer time.

In all this I was greatly moved with charity toward my fellow Christians. I wished they might see and know what I was seeing, as a comfort to them. For this whole vision was shown to all in general.

Then I said to those who were with me, "Today is my judgment day." I said this because I was sure I was going to die, and the day a person dies he is judged in particular, and fixed as he shall remain forever, as I understand it. My reasons for saying this were that I wanted them to love God better, and I wanted to remind them that life is short, as they could see by example in me.

All this time I was sure I was going to die, and it was somewhat of a marvel and a wonder to me, for it seemed to me this vision was shown for one who should live.

What I say of myself I say in the person of all my fellow Christians, for I was taught by the spiritual showing of our Lord that he intends it so. And therefore I beg you all for God's sake, and advise you for your own profit, stop looking at the wretch to whom this revelation was shown. Intently, wisely and meekly look at God, who because of his courteous love and unending goodness wills to show it to all of us in general, for our comfort. For it is God's will that you receive it with as great joy and delight as if Jesus had showed it to you.

## Chapter 9

*Of the meekness of this woman, who keeps always in the faith of holy Church; and of how one who loves his fellow Christians for God, loves all things.*

Receiving the showing doesn't make me good, unless I love God better as a result. And to the degree that you love God better than I do, it is more profit to you than to me. I'm not saying this to those who are wise, for they already know it well. I'm saying it to you who are simple, for your ease and comfort, for we are all one in love. For in truth, it was not shown me that God loved me any better than he loves the least soul that is in grace; I am certain that there are many who have never had a showing or a vision, nothing but the common teaching of holy Church, who love God better than I.

For if I look just at myself I am really nothing, but if I consider myself in general, I am in hope, because I am united in charity with my fellow Christians, and in this oneness are grounded the lives of all men who shall be saved. For as I see it, God is all that is good, God has made all that is made, and God loves all he has made. He who loves all his fellow Christians in general, for God, loves all that is, for in that part of mankind that shall be saved is included all, that is to say, all that is made and the maker of all. In man is God, and God is in all, and he who loves this way loves all.

I hope by the grace of God that whoever beholds it thus shall be truly taught and greatly comforted if he needs comfort.

I speak of those who shall be saved, for at this time God

showed me no others. But in all things I believe as holy Church believes, preaches and teaches. For the faith of holy Church that I had beforehand understood and, as I hope by the grace of God, deliberately kept in use and custom, stood continuously in my sight. I chose and intended never to receive anything that might be contrary to it. With this intention I beheld all this blessed showing as one in God's meaning.

All his revelation was shown in three ways, that is to say, by what I saw with my eyes, by words formed in my understanding and by spiritual insight. The spiritual insight I neither can nor may show as openly and fully as I would like to, but I trust in our Lord God Almighty that he shall, of his goodness and for your love, make you understand it more spiritually and sweetly than I can or may tell it.

## Chapter 10

*The second revelation: it is of the discoloring of his face and of our redemption; of the discoloring of Veronica's veil; and of how it pleases God that we seek him diligently, abiding in him steadfastly and trusting him greatly.*

And after this I saw with my own eyes on the face of the crucifix that hung before me part of his passion continually depicted: men's contempt, spitting, sullying and buffeting, his many exhausting pains—more than I can tell—and frequent changes of color. Once I saw half the face, beginning at the ear, redden over with dried blood until it was covered up to the middle of the face; then the other half was covered in the same manner, while in the first half the color vanished as it had come.

I saw this with my own eyes, dimly and unclearly, and I desired more bodily light so that I could see it more clearly. I was answered in my reason, "If God will show you more, he will be your light; you need none but him."

For I saw him as he is sought. We are now so blind and so unwise that we never seek God until he, of his goodness, shows himself to us. And when we see anything of him, through his graciousness, we are stirred by the same grace to seek with great desire to see him more blissfully. Thus I saw him and sought him, I had him and I wanted him—and this is, and should be, the way we commonly work in this, as I see it.

Once, my understanding was led down to the seashore. There I saw hills and valleys, green as if they were moss-overgrown, with wrack and gravel. Then I understood thus: If a person were there under the broad water and could have sight of God as God is continuously with a man, he should be safe in soul and body and take no harm. And beyond this, he should have more solace and comfort than all this world may or can tell.

For God wills that we believe that we see him continuously, though it seems to us that we see him only a little, and in this belief he causes us evermore to receive grace. For he will be seen, and he will be sought; he will be waited for, and he will be trusted.

This second showing was so humble and so small and so simple that my spirits were in great distress as I beheld it—mourning, full of dread and longing—for I was, for some time, in doubt whether it was a showing or not. And then, at different times, our Lord gave me more light, by which I understood that it really was a showing.

It was a symbol and an image of the shame of our foul deeds, which our fair, bright, blessed Lord bore for our sins. With its frequent changes of color, it reminded me of the holy veil of Veronica at Rome, on which he imprinted his own holy face when he suffered his hard passion, going by free choice to his death. Many wonder at the brownness, the blackness, the ruefulness and the leanness of this image, questioning how it can be that the image is so discolored and so far from fair, since he imprinted it with his blessed face, which is the fairness of heaven, the flower of earth, and the fruit of the maiden's womb.

I want to explain it as I have understood it by the grace of

God. We know in our faith, and believe by the teaching and preaching of holy Church, that the blessed Trinity made mankind to his image and likeness. In the same manner we know that when man fell so deeply and so wretchedly by sin, there was no other help to restore man but through him who made man. He who made man for love wills, by the same love, to restore him to his former bliss, and give him even more. And just as we were created like the Trinity in our first making, our maker wills that we should be like Jesus Christ our savior in heaven forever, by virtue of our remaking. Then, between these two makings, he wills, for the love and honor of man, to make himself as like man in this mortal life, in our foulness and our wretchedness, as a man might be if he were without guilt. That's what I meant when I said before that the showing was the image and likeness of our foul black deeds' shame in which our fair, bright, blessed Lord God hid his godhead.

But with full certainty I dare to say (and we ought to believe) that there was never so fair a man as he, up to the time his fair color was changed with hard suffering and sorrow, his passion and dying. This is further discussed in the eighth revelation, which also speaks of this likeness. And where it speaks here of the veil of Veronica at Rome, the eighth revelation explains what is meant by the different changes of color and expression—sometimes more comforting and lifelike, sometimes more rueful and marked by death.

This vision was a lesson to my understanding that the continual seeking of the soul for God pleases him greatly. For the soul may do no more than seek, suffer and trust, and this disposition is wrought in the soul that has it by the Holy Spirit.

Finding God in clarity is a gift of his special grace, and comes when he wills. The seeking of him with faith, hope and charity pleases our Lord; the finding of him pleases the soul and completely fills it with joy. Thus was my understanding taught that seeking is as good as seeing, during the time God allows the soul to labor in distress.

It is God's will that we seek him until we behold him, for it is by this means that God, of his special grace, will show himself to us when he wills. God himself shall teach the soul how it shall have him in beholding him, and that is the greatest honor to him and the greatest profit to the soul. This gift is most often received through meekness and virtue with the grace and leading of the Holy Spirit. For a soul that simply fastens itself to God with absolute trust, either in seeking or in seeing, does the greatest honor to God it can do, as I see it.

Two kinds of work can be seen in this vision. The first is seeking. The second is seeing.

The seeking is a common work which every soul can do with God's grace; it ought to be done with discretion and the teaching of holy Church. It is God's will that we have three things in our seeking of him. The first is that we seek him determinedly and diligently without sloth, as well as we can, through his grace, and that we do so gladly and merrily, without unreasonable depression and vain sorrow.

The second is that for love of him we wait for him steadfastly, without grumbling and striving against him, to the end of our lives: for it will only last for a little while.

The third is that we trust very strongly in him, in the full certainty of faith. For it is his will that we know that he shall appear suddenly and blissfully to all his lovers. His working is in secret, and yet he wills to be perceived; his appearing will be very sudden, and he wills to be trusted, for he is very near at hand, friendly and courteous, blessed may he be!

## Chapter 11

*The third revelation: how God does all things (except sin) with a purpose forever unchanging, for he has made all things in the fulness of goodness.*

And after this I saw God in a point—that is to say, I saw him in my understanding. In seeing this, I saw that he is in all things. I watched with attention, seeing and knowing in that sight that he does all that is done. I wondered at that sight with quiet doubt, and thought, "What is sin?" For I saw in truth that God does everything, no matter how little it is.

I also saw for a fact that nothing is done by chance or accident, but all is done by the foreseeing wisdom of God. If it looks like chance or accident in the sight of man, our blindness and lack of foreseeing is the cause. The things that are in the foreseeing wisdom of God are there eternally. These he rightly, gloriously and continually leads to their best ends as they occur. These same things come suddenly upon us, who are not expecting them, and thus, because of our blindness and lack of foreseeing, we say they are chance happenings or accidents. But to our Lord God, they aren't.

Therefore, I must and ought to grant that everything that is done is well done, because our Lord God does it all. (At this time, you see, the working of creatures was not shown—just the working of our Lord God in the creatures, for he is in the mid-point of all things and of all he does.) I was certain that God does not sin. And here I saw in truth that sin is not a deed, for sin was not shown in any of this.

I no longer wanted to marvel at this, so I looked to our Lord to see what he willed to show me next. And thus the rightfulness of God's working was showed to the soul as clearly as it might be at that time.

Rightfulness has two lovely qualities: it is right, and it is full. All the works of our Lord possess these qualities, without needing the work of either mercy or grace, for they are all rightful and their rightfulness does not fail in any respect. (At another time, he showed where he uses the working of mercy and grace, when he had me see sin openly, as I shall tell you.) And this vision was showed to my understanding because our Lord wills to have the soul truly turned inward to behold him and all his works generally, for they are completely good. All his doings are comforting and sweet, and bring great ease to the soul which has turned from beholding the blind judgment of man to contemplating the sweet judgment of our Lord God.

Man sees some deeds as well done, and some deeds as evil,

but our Lord doesn't see things that way. For as everything that has natural being is made by God, so everything that is done is done by virtue of God's doing. It is easy to understand that the best deed is well done; just as well as the best and highest deed is done, so well is the least deed done. And everything is done well by the properties and in the order our Lord has ordained for it from eternity, for there is no doer but he.

I saw with full certainty that God never changes his purpose in the slightest degree, and never shall forever. Because there was nothing unknown to him in his rightful laws from eternity, all things were set in order before anything was made, as it should stand endlessly. No kind of thing shall fail in this regard, for he made all things in the fulness of goodness. Therefore, the blessed Trinity is forever pleased in all his works.

All this he showed most blissfully, intending this to be understood: "See! I am God. See! I am in all things. See! I do all things. See! I never take my hands off my works, and never shall forever. See! I lead all things to the end I ordained for them from eternity, by the same might, wisdom and love by which I made them. How should anything be amiss?"

Thus, mightily, wisely and lovingly was the soul examined in this vision. Then I really saw that I needed and ought to assent with great reverence, rejoicing in God.

## Chapter 12

*The fourth revelation; how it pleases God better rather to wash us clean from sin in his blood than in water, for his blood is most precious.*

And after this, looking at the body bleeding as severely as it had at the scourging, I saw the following. The fair skin was broken all over the sweet body with very deep cuts into the tender flesh, by sharp blows. The hot blood ran out so abundantly that neither skin nor wound could be seen—as if all the body were blood. But when the blood came to where it should have fallen down from the body, it vanished. Notwithstanding, the bleeding continued awhile, until it could be observed with attention. The bleeding was so abundant as I saw it that I thought if it had been actually happening that way in nature and substance at that time, it would have filled the entire bed with blood and spilled over on all sides.

And then it came to my mind that God has made the waters plentiful on earth for our service and bodily ease, because of the tender love he has for us. But it pleases him even more when we accept simply his blessed blood to cleanse ourselves from sin. For there is no liquid made that gives him more pleasure to give us, and it is as precious as it is plentiful, by virtue of the blessed godhead. It is of our own kind, and most blissfully flows over us by virtue of his precious love. As truly as the most valuable blood of our Lord Jesus Christ is most precious, so truly is it most plentiful.

Behold and see the virtue of the precious plenty of his blood, so very valuable. It descended down into hell, and breaking their bonds, delivered all those there who belonged to the court of heaven. The precious plenty of his most highly valued blood overflows the entire earth, and is ready to wash clean from sin all creatures who are, have been and shall be of good will. The precious plenty of his most valuable blood ascends into heaven in the blessed body of our Lord Jesus Christ. It is there in him bleeding, praying for us to the Father; it is and shall be as long as there is need. It flows in all of heaven forever, enjoying the salvation of all mankind who are there, and it shall fill up the number that is lacking [of those who are to be saved].

## Chapter 13

*The fifth revelation is that the temptation of the devil is overcome by the passion of Christ, giving us an increase of joy and the devil everlasting pain.*

And after that, before God showed any words, he allowed me to look at him for a measurable period of time. And all that I had seen and all that I had understood was there, as far as the simplicity of my soul could take in.

Then, without voice or the opening of lips, he formed these words in my soul: "Herewith is the fiend overcome." When he said these words, our Lord was referring to his blessed passion, as he had shown previously.

In this our Lord showed part of the devil's malice and all of his powerlessness, for he showed that his passion is the overcoming of the fiend. God showed that the devil has the same malice now that he had before the Incarnation, and the harder he works, the more continually he sees that all salvation's souls escape from him gloriously, by virtue of Christ's precious passion. And that is his sorrow.

His end is attained very badly, for all that God allows him to do turns to joy for us and to shame, pain and woe for him. He has as much sorrow when God gives him permission to work as when he does not work. The reason for this is that he can never do as much evil as he would like to, because all his power is locked in God's hands.

But, as I see it, there can be no wrath in God. For our good Lord endlessly has regard for his own honor and for the profit of all who shall be saved. With might and right, he withstands the discredited, who, with malice and shrewdness, busy themselves to contrive and work against God's will.

Also, I saw our Lord scorn his malice and reduce his powerlessness to nothing, and he wills that we do the same thing. On account of this sight, I laughed loud and long, which made those who were around me laugh too, and their laughter was a pleasure to me. Then I thought I would like all my fellow Christians to have seen what I saw, for then they should all laugh with me. I didn't see Christ laugh, but I knew well that it was the sight he had shown me that had made me laugh. For I understood that we may laugh, comforting ourselves and rejoicing in God that the devil has been overcome.

When I saw God scorn the devil's malice, it was by the leading of my understanding into our Lord, that is to say by a showing of truth from within, without any change of his outward expression. For as I see it, it is a glorious property of God that he is unchanging.

And after this, I fell into a more sober mood and said, "I see three things: a jest, scorn and earnest. I see a jest in that the fiend is overcome. I see scorn in that God scorns him, and he shall be scorned. And I see earnest in that he is overcome by the blessed passion and death of our Lord Jesus Christ, which was done in absolute earnest and with sorrowful, difficult labor.

And where I said the devil is scorned, I meant that God scorns him, that is to say, God sees him now as he shall see him forever. In this God showed that the fiend is damned, and that's what I meant when I said the devil should be scorned. For I saw he shall be scorned generally at the day of judgment, by all who shall be saved, for whose consolation and salvation he has had great envy. For then he shall see that all the woe and tribulation he has caused them shall be changed to an increase of their joy without end. And all the pain, tribulation and sorrow he has tried to bring them to shall forever go with him to hell.

## Chapter 14

*The sixth revelation is of the gratitude full of honor with which God rewards his servants, and it has three joys.*

After this our Lord said, "I thank you for your service, and for your distressful labor, and especially for your youth."

And in this my understanding was lifted up into heaven, where I saw our Lord like a lord in his own house who has called all his valued servants and friends to a solemn feast. Then I saw the lord take no place in his own house, but royally reign there, and he completely filled it with joy and mirth. He himself endlessly gladdened and solaced his valued friends most modestly and courteously with the marvelous melody of endless love in his own fair, blessed face. This glorious countenance of the godhead completely fills all heaven with joy and bliss.

God showed three degrees of bliss that every soul that has willingly served God in any degree on earth shall have in heaven.

The first is the gratitude full of honor that he shall receive from our Lord God when he is delivered from pain. This thanks is so lofty and so full of honor that it seems to the recipient that it would satisfy him even if there were nothing further. For it seemed to me that all the pain and painful labor that could be suffered by all living men could not deserve this thanks full of honor that one man, who has freely served God, shall have.

The second degree of bliss is that all the blessed creatures who are in heaven shall see that glorious thanking, and God shall make his service known to all who are in heaven. At this time, this example was shown. If a king thanks his subjects, it is a great honor to them; if he makes his thanking known to all the realm, their honor is greatly increased.

The third degree of bliss is that it shall last forever, just as new and pleasing as it is when it is first received.

And I saw this shown, simply and sweetly—that the age of every man shall be known in heaven, that each shall be rewarded for his willing service and for his time, and especially that the years of those who deliberately and freely offer their youth to God are exceedingly rewarded and wonderfully thanked. For I saw that when, for whatever time, a person is truly turned to God, even for a single day's service and for God's eternal will, he shall have all these three degrees of bliss. And the more the loving soul sees this courtesy of God the more anxious it is to serve him all its life.

## Chapter 15

*The seventh revelation is of frequent alternations of feeling: well-being to woe; and of how it is expedient that man sometimes be left without comfort when sin is not the cause.*

And after this he showed me a very lofty spiritual delight in my soul, and in it I was completely filled with everlasting certitude, firmly sustained, without any painful dread. This feeling was so glad and so spiritual that I was entirely at peace, at ease and at rest, so that there was nothing on earth that could have disturbed me.

This lasted only for a while. Then I was transformed and left to myself in depression, weary of my life and irked with myself, so that I kept the patience to go on living only with difficulty. There was no comfort and no ease for me, except faith, hope and charity, and these I had in reality, though I had very little feeling of them.

And immediately after this our Lord again gave me comfort and rest of soul in delight and certitude, so blessed and so mighty that no dread, no sorrow, no bodily or spiritual pain that could be suffered should have caused me distress.

And then the pain returned to my feelings, again followed by the joy and delight—first the one and then the other, at, I suppose, about twenty different times. In the time of joy I could have said with Saint Paul, "Nothing shall separate me from the love of Christ." And in the pain I could have said, "Lord, save me! I perish!"

This vision was showed to me to teach my understanding that it is profitable for some souls to experience these alternations of mood—sometimes to be comforted and sometimes to fail and to be left to themselves. God wills that we know that he keeps us ever equally safe, in woe as in well-being.

For the profit of a man's soul, he is sometimes left to himself, although sin is not ever the cause. For at this time I had committed no sin that should have caused me to be left to myself, it came on me so suddenly; besides, I didn't deserve to have the blessed feeling either, but our Lord gave it to me freely when he chose. Sometimes he allows us to suffer misery, but both well-being and woe express the same love.

For it is God's will that we hold ourselves in his comfort with all our might, for bliss is everlasting, while pain is passing and shall be reduced to nothingness for those who shall be saved. Therefore, it is not God's will that we follow the feelings of pain, in sorrow and mourning on their account, but that we immediately pass beyond them and hold ourselves in the endless delight that is God.

## Chapter 16

*The eighth revelation is of the last, precious pains of Christ's dying; of the discoloring of his face; and of the drying of his flesh.*

After this, Christ showed a part of his passion near his death. I saw his sweet face as if it were dry and bloodless, pale with dying. Next it became more pale and dead-looking with increasing weakness, and then it turned more dead-looking, to blue and then to brown-blue as the flesh continued more and more to die. For his passion was visible to me most completely in his blessed face, particularly in his lips. There I saw these four colors, though they were previously fresh, ruddy, lifelike and pleasing to my sight.

This deep dying caused a change pitiful to watch. The nose clogged and dried as I watched, and the sweet body was brown and black, changed entirely from his own fair, lifelike color to dry dying. For, as I saw it, at the same time our Lord and blessed savior died upon the cross, a dry, sharp, extremely cold wind arose. When all the precious blood that would come from it was bled out of the sweet body, moisture still remained in the sweet flesh of Christ, as was shown.

Bloodlessness and pain, drying from within and the blowing of wind and cold coming from without, met together in the sweet body of Christ. And these four—two without and two within—dried the flesh of Christ by the process of time.

And though this pain was bitter and sharp, yet it lasted for a very long time, as I saw it, and painfully dried up all the vital forces in Christ's flesh. Thus I saw the sweet flesh dry, as it seemed, piece by piece, drying with incredible pain. And as long as any part of Christ's flesh retained its vital force, so long he suffered pain.

This drawn-out pining seemed to me as if Christ had spent seven nights of death, dying, always at the point of passing away, suffering the great last pain. And when I said it seemed to me as if he had spent seven nights of death, I meant that the sweet body was so discolored, so dry, so clogged, so dead-looking and so piteous that it looked as if he had spent seven nights of death, continually dying. And it seemed to me the dying of Christ's flesh was his greatest pain and the last of his passion.

## Chapter 17

*Of the grievous bodily thirst of Christ, caused four ways; of his piteous crowning; and of the greatest pain to a natural lover.*

And in this dying there was brought to my mind the word of Christ "I thirst." For I saw in Christ a double thirst, one bodily, another spiritual, which I shall speak of in the thirty-first chapter. For this word was shown for the bodily thirst.

I understood that the bodily thirst was caused by the absence of moisture, for the blessed flesh and bones were left all alone without blood and moisture. The blessed body dried all alone for a long time with the wringing of the nails and the weight of the body. I understood that because of the tenderness of the sweet hands and feet and the large size, hardness and painfulness of the nails, the wounds would widen and the body sag—both because of its weight and because of the length of time it had hung.

Another cause of the bodily thirst was the piercing and wringing of the head and the binding on of the crown, all baked on with dried blood, with the sweet hair and the dry flesh clinging to the thorns, and the thorns to the drying flesh. And in the beginning, while the flesh was fresh and bleeding, the continuous gripping of the thorns made the wounds wide.

And furthermore I saw that the sweet skin, with the tender flesh, hair and blood, was all raised above and loosened from the bone by the thorns. These cut it in many pieces, like a cloth, and it sagged as if it were on the verge of falling off, it was so heavy and loose while it had natural moisture. This was a great sorrow and dread to me, for it seemed to me I would not, for my life, have seen it fall. I did not see how it was done, but I understood it was by the sharp thorns and the rough and painful, unsparing seating of the garland, done without pity.

This continued for a while, and before it began to change, I looked at it [the loosened, ragged flesh] and wondered how it could be. Then I saw it was because it had begun to dry and its weight had lessened somewhat. It set around the garland, and surrounded the whole head, as if it were a garland upon a garland: the garland of the thorns was dyed with the blood and the other garland. The head was all one color, like clotted blood when it is dry. The skin of the flesh that seemed to belong to the face and the body was finely wrinkled with a tanned color, like a dry board when it is stripped. The face was browner than the body.

I saw four kinds of drying. The first was bloodlessness. The second was the pain following after. The third was the hanging up in the air, as men hang a cloth to dry. The fourth was that his bodily nature asked for something to drink, and there was no kind of comfort ministered to him in all his woe and discomfort. As hard and grievous was his pain, it was much harder and more grievous when the moisture failed and all began to dry and cling this way.

There were two pains that were shown in the blessed head. The first accomplished the drying while it was moist. The second was slow, with the drying and clinging of the flesh, and worked with the blowing of the wind from without that dried him more, and more pained him with cold than my heart can take in. I saw that anything I might say about all his other pains would be too little, for they cannot be expressed.

This showing of Christ's sufferings filled me full of pain. I knew well that he had suffered only once, but that he willed to show his suffering to me, and to fill me with the experience of it, as I had previously desired. During all the time I was experiencing Christ's pain, I felt no pain except his.

Then it occurred to me that I little knew what pain it was I had asked, and like a wretch, repented of my request, thinking that if I had known how bad it would be I'd have been loath to ask for it. For it seemed to me my pain went beyond bodily death. I thought, "Is any pain in hell like this?" And I was answered in my reason, "Hell has another pain, for despair is there. But of all the pains that lead to salvation, the greatest is to see your love suffer." How could any pain be greater to me than to see him, who is all my life, all my bliss and my joy, suffer?

Here I felt truthfully that I loved Christ himself so much more than myself that there was no pain that could be suffered like the sorrow I had to see him in pain.

## Chapter 18

*Of the spiritual martyrdom of our Lady and other lovers of Christ; and how all things suffered with him, good and ill.*

Here I saw a part of the compassion of our Lady Saint Mary for Christ. She was so much one with him in love that the greatness of her loving was the cause of the intensity of her pain. For in this I saw the substance of the natural love his creatures have for him extended by grace. This natural love was most fully showed in his sweet mother, and it passed the usual limits, for to the degree that she loved him more than all others, her pain exceeded theirs. Always, the higher, the mightier, the sweeter the love is, the more sorrow it is to the lover to see the body he loves in pain.

And all his disciples and all his true lovers suffered pain greater than their own bodily dying. For I am sure, judging by my own feeling, that the least of them loved God so much more than himself that it goes beyond anything I can say.

Here I saw in my understanding a great joining together between Christ and us, for when he was in pain, we were in pain, and all creatures that could suffer pain suffered with him—that is to say, all creatures God has made for our service.

The firmament and the earth failed for sorrow, according to their nature, at the time of Christ's dying, for it belonged naturally to them as a property to know him for their lord and the one in whom all their strengths were grounded. When he failed, then it was suitable and necessary to them by their nature to fail with him, as far as they could, for sorrow at his pain.

And those who were his friends suffered pain for love, and all in general suffered as well—that is to say, those who did not know him suffered because all kinds of comfort failed except for that which God's hidden might kept. By "those who knew him not" I mean the two kinds of people who can be seen in two persons. The one was Pilate; the other was St. Dionysius of France, who was a pagan at that time. For when he saw the strange and terrible sorrows and dreads that happened at that time, he said, "Either the world is now at an end, or else he who is the maker of nature suffers." That is why he wrote on an altar, "This is the altar of an unknown god."

God, who of his goodness made the planets and the elements work naturally both for the blessed man and for the cursed, at this time withdrew from both. It was for this reason that they who knew him not were in sorrow at that time. Thus did our Lord Jesus suffer and become nothing for us, and in the same manner we suffer and are made nothing with him and shall until we come into his bliss, as I shall tell you later.

## Chapter 19

*Of the comforting beholding of the crucifix; how the desire of the flesh, without consent of the soul, is no sin; and that the flesh must be in pain, suffering until both soul and body are joined to Christ.*

At this time I wanted to look away from the cross, and I dared not do so, for well I knew that while I gazed upon the cross I was secure and safe. Therefore I would not agree to put my soul in peril, for outside of the cross there was no security against the temptations of fiends.

Then, as if it had been a friend, my reason made me a suggestion, saying, "Look up to heaven, to his father." I saw clearly, with the faith I felt, that there was nothing between the cross and heaven that could have disturbed me. I had either to look up, or to answer.

I answered inwardly with all the strength of my soul, and said, "No! I may not, for you are my heaven." I said this, for I would not look away from the cross. I would rather have been in that pain until Judgment Day, than have come to heaven by any means other than him, for I knew well that he who had bound me so painfully would himself unbind me when he willed to do so.

Thus was I taught to choose for my heaven Jesus, whom I saw only in pain at that time. No other heaven pleased me but Jesus, who shall be my bliss when I come there. It has been a comfort to me ever since that, by his grace, I chose Jesus for my heaven in all this time of passion and sorrow. It has also been a lesson to me that I should always, in well-being and woe, choose only Jesus for my heaven, in the same way.

And though, like a wretch, I had repented of my request (as I said before, if I had realized what intense pain it would be, I'd have been loath to ask it), here I saw in truth that that was the grumbling and judgment of the flesh, without the soul's assent. To this God assigns no blame.

Regret and deliberate choice were two contraries which I felt simultaneously at that time. They are the two parts of a whole, the one outward and the other inward.

The outward part is our mortal flesh, which is now in pain and misery and shall continue so in this life. Most of what I felt at this time was from this part, and it was in this part that I regretted my request.

The inward part is a noble, blissful life, which is entirely settled in peace and love and is felt more secretly. It was in this part that, powerfully, wisely and deliberately, I chose Jesus for my heaven and in this part that I saw in truth that the inward part is master and sovereign to the outward. The inward part neither commands nor takes heed of the will of the outward. Its whole intent and will is endlessly fixed upon being made one with our Lord Jesus.

That the outward part should draw the inward part to assent was not shown to me; only that the inward part draws the outward part by grace, and that both shall be made one in bliss without end, by the virtue of Christ, was shown.

## Chapter 20

*Of Christ's passion beyond words; and of three things always to be remembered about the passion.*

And thus I saw our Lord Jesus lingering in pain for a long time, for the oneness with the godhead gave strength to the manhood to suffer for love more than any man could suffer. I mean not only more pain than any man could suffer but also that he suffered more pain than all saved men who ever existed, from the very beginning to the last day, could say or even fully imagine, considering the worthiness of the noblest, most glorious King, and his shameful, cruel, painful death.

For he who is noblest and worthiest was most completely reduced to nothingness, most foully condemned and utterly despised. For the highest point that can be reached in the passion is to think and to know who he is that suffered. Beyond this there are two other, lesser points to remember. One is what he suffered, and the other for whom he suffered.

And in this he brought to my mind, in part, the greatness and nobility of the glorious godhead, and with it the preciousness and tenderness of the most blessed body, which are together one.

He also brought to mind the loathness our nature has to suffer pain. For just as he was most tender and pure, so was he most strong and mighty to suffer. He suffered for the sin of every man who shall be saved, and he saw the sorrow, desolation and anguish of every man and grieved for kindness and love. For just as much as our Lady sorrowed for his pains, so much did he suffer sorrow for her sorrow, and more, inasmuch as his sweet manhood was more perfect in nature.

As long as he was able to suffer, he suffered for us and sorrowed for us. Now he has risen from the dead, and can no longer suffer. Yet he has suffered with us, as I shall explain later.

And I, beholding all this by his grace, saw that his love for our soul is so strong that he deliberately chose it with great desire, and suffered patiently for it with great joy, paying well for it. For the soul that sees it thus, when it is touched by grace, shall in truth see that the pains of Christ's passion exceed all pains, that is to say the pains that shall be turned into everlasting exceeding joys by virtue of Christ's passion.

## Chapter 21

*Of three ways of beholding the passion of Christ; and how we are now dying on the cross with Christ but his countenance frees us from all pain.*

It is God's will, as I understand it, that we have three ways of looking at the passion of Christ. The first is the harsh pain he suffered, which we should behold with contrition and compassion. That our Lord showed me at this time and gave me strength and grace to see it.

With all my might I focused on his dying, and expected to see the body completely dead, but I did not see him so. And just at the moment that it seemed to me that life could last no longer, and the showing of the end must, of necessity, be near, suddenly, looking at the same cross, I saw him transform his blessed face. The transformation of his blessed face transformed mine, and I was as glad and merry as it was possible to be.

Then our Lord brought joyfully to my mind the question "What do your pain and anguish matter now?" And I was completely happy. I understood that what our Lord means is that we are now on his cross with him in our pains, and dying with him in our sufferings. If we deliberately stay on the same cross, with his help and his grace, up to the final point, suddenly he shall transform his countenance for us and we shall be with him in heaven. Between the one and the other no time shall elapse. Then all shall be brought to joy. That is what he meant by his question "What do your pain and anguish matter now?" We shall be full of bliss.

And here I saw in truth that if he showed us his blissful countenance now, there is no pain on earth or in any other place that could trouble us. All things would be joy and bliss to us. But because he shows us his face as it was in his passion, as he bore his cross in this life, we are disturbed and in sorrowful labor with him, as our frail nature necessitates.

The reason he suffers is because he chooses, of his goodness, to make us the loftier with him in his bliss. For this little pain that we suffer here, we shall have a lofty, endless knowing in God, which we could never have had without it. And the harsher our pains have been with him on his cross, the greater shall our glory be with him in his kingdom.

## Chapter 22

*The ninth revelation is of the delight of three heavens; of the infinite love of Christ; and of his desiring to suffer every day for us if he could do so, though it is not necessary.*

Then our good Lord Jesus Christ asked me, "Are you really pleased that I suffered for you?"

I said, "Yes, good Lord, thank you so much! Yes, good Lord, blessed may you be!"

Then our good, kind Lord Jesus said, "If you are satisfied, I am satisfied. It is a joy, a bliss, an endless delight to me that I ever suffered the passion for you, and if I could suffer more, I would."

In feeling this, my understanding was lifted up into heaven and there I saw three heavens. I was greatly astounded at this sight, and though I saw three heavens, all in the blessed manhood of Christ, none of them was greater, none was less, none was higher, none was lower, but all were equally alike in bliss.

For the first heaven, Christ showed me his Father—in no bodily likeness, but in his properties and in his working. That is to say, I saw in Christ what the Father is. The working of the Father is that he gives reward to his Son, Jesus Christ. This gift and this reward is so blissful to Jesus that his Father could have given him no reward that could have pleased him better. The first heaven, which is the pleasing of the Father, was shown to me as a heaven. It was completely blissful because he is completely pleased with all the deeds Jesus has done for our salvation.

Therefore, we are his not only because he has bought us, but also by the courteous gift of his Father. We are his bliss, we are his reward; we are his glory, we are his crown. It was a singular marvel and a thing most delightful to behold, that we are his crown. All of this (which I have just said) is so great a joy to Jesus that for it he counts all his painful labor, his difficult passion, his cruel and shameful death, as nothing.

In the words "If I could suffer more, I would" I saw in truth that he would have died as often as he could have, and love would never have let him rest until he had done it. I looked with great diligence to learn how often he would die if he could, and in truth, the number exceeded the power of my understanding and my wits to such an extent that my reason might not and could not comprehend it or take it in.

And even when he had died, or would have died, this many times, he still would count it as nothing for love, for all seems to him very small compared to his love.

Though the sweet manhood of Christ could suffer only once, the goodness in him can never cease offering itself: he is ready to do the same thing every day, if such a thing were possible. If he said he would, for my love, make new heavens and a new earth, it would be a very small thing compared to this, for he could do that every day if he wanted to, without any painful labor, but to die so often for my love that the number goes beyond created reason is the greatest offer our Lord God could make to man's soul, as I see it.

By all this he meant the following to be understood: "How should it, then, be that, for your love, I should not do all I could? The deed does not distress me, since for your love I should die so often with no regard for my intense pain."

For the second heaven, I saw here, looking at the blessed passion, that the love that made him suffer exceeds all his pains by as much as heaven is above earth. For the pain was a noble glorious deed done at a single time by the working of love, and love was without a beginning, is, and shall be without an ending. For this love he said most sweetly these words: "If I could suffer more, I would." He did not say, "If it were necessary to suffer more," because even though it were not necessary, if he could suffer more, he would. This deed and this work concerning our salvation was ordained as well as God could ordain it. It was done as gloriously as Christ could do it. And here I saw complete bliss in Christ, for his bliss would not have been complete if it could have been done better.

## Chapter 23

*How Christ wills that we greatly rejoice with him in our redemption and desire grace from him that we may do so.*

And in these three words, "It is a joy, a bliss, an endless delight to me," three heavens were showed, as follows:

For the joy I understood the pleasure of the Father; for the bliss, the glorification of the Son, and for the endless delight, the Holy Spirit. The Father is pleased, the Son is glorified, the Holy Spirit is delighted.

That is what I saw, looking at his blessed passion, for the third heaven—that is to say, the joy and bliss that make him delight in it. For our courteous Lord showed me his passion in five ways. The first is the bleeding of the head; the second is the discoloring of his face; the third is the extensive bleeding of the body in the likeness of his scourging, and the fourth is the drying of the dying. These four are the pains of the passion, as I have said before.

The fifth is that which was shown for the joy and bliss of the passion, for it is God's will that we take true delight with him in our salvation. In it he wills that we be greatly comforted and strengthened. That is why he wills that our souls be cheerfully occupied with his grace, for we are his bliss. In us he delights without end, and in the same way we shall delight in him, with his grace.

All he has done for us, and does, and ever shall do was never a cost or charge to him, nor could it be, except only that he died in our manhood; the cost and charge of our redemption in deed, beginning at the sweet Incarnation, lasted until the blessed Resurrection on Easter morning, and extended only that far. In this deed he rejoiced endlessly, as I have said before.

Jesus wills that we pay attention to the bliss that is in the blessed Trinity on account of our salvation and that we desire to have as much spiritual delight with his grace as I have already said; that is to say that our delight in our salvation may be as like the joy Christ has in our salvation as it can be while we are here.

The whole Trinity has worked in the passion of Christ, ministering an abundance of virtues and a fulness of grace to us through him, but only the maiden's son did the suffering in which the whole blessed Trinity endlessly delights.

And this was showed in Christ's words "Are you really pleased . . . ?" and "If you are satisfied, then I am satisfied." It is as if he were saying, "It is joy and delight enough for me, and I ask nothing else of you for my bitter labor but that I might really please you."

And in this he brought to my mind the quality of a cheerful giver. A cheerful giver pays little attention to the thing he gives. All his desire and all his intent is to please and comfort the one to whom he gives it. And if the receiver takes the gift nobly, gladly and thankfully, then the courteous giver counts all his cost and all his difficult labor as nothing, for his joy and delight that he has pleased and comforted the one he loves. This was showed completely and at length.

Also, consider wisely the greatness of this word "ever," for in it was shown a noble insight into the love he has for our salvation and the manifold joys that, because of it, flow from the passion of Christ. One joy is that he delights that he has done it in deed and will suffer no more. Another is that he has brought us up into heaven and made us his crown and endless bliss. The third is that, by it, he has bought us away from the endless pains of hell.

## Chapter 24

*The tenth revelation is that our Lord Jesus Christ, rejoicing, shows his blessed heart cut in two for love.*

Then, with a happy face, our Lord looked at his wounded side and gazed into it, rejoicing. With his sweet gazing he drew forth the understanding of his creature through that same wound into his side within. And there he showed a fair, delectable place, large enough for all of mankind who shall be saved to rest there in peace and love. With this, he brought to my mind his most valuable blood and the precious water which he let pour out completely, for love.

With this sweet vision, he showed his blissful heart cut even in two, and with the sweet rejoicing he showed my understanding the blessed godhead, in part (as far as he willed at that time), stirring the poor soul to understand it as it may be put into words—that is, to comprehend the endless love that was without beginning, is, and ever shall be.

With this, our good Lord said most blissfully, "See how I loved you!" It was as if he had said, "My darling, behold and see your Lord, your God, who is your maker and your endless joy! See what delight and endless bliss I have in your salvation. For my love, enjoy it now with me."

In addition, for my greater understanding, this blessed word was said: "See how I loved you! Behold and see that I loved you so much before I died for you that I chose to die for you, and now I have died for you, and freely and deliberately have suffered all I can. Now all my bitter pain and all my difficult labor are turned to endless joy and bliss for me and for you. How should it be, now, that you should ask me for anything that pleases me, without my granting it to you with the greatest pleasure? For my delight is your holiness, and your endless joy and bliss with me."

This is the understanding, as simply as I can say it, of this blessed word, "See how I loved you!" Our good Lord showed this to make us glad and merry.

## Chapter 25

*The eleventh revelation is a noble, spiritual showing of his mother.*

And with this same expression of mirth and joy, our good Lord looked down and to his right, and brought to my mind the place where our Lady stood at the time of his passion. He said, "Do you want to see her?"

And in this sweet word it was as if he had said, "I knew well you wanted to see my blessed mother, for after myself she is the greatest joy I could show you. She is my greatest delight and glory, and the one my blessed creatures most desire to see."

And because of the noble, marvelous, singular love he has for this sweet maiden, his blessed mother, our Lady Saint Mary, he showed her in bliss and greatly rejoicing, as these sweet words had promised. It was as if he had said, "Do you want to see how I love her, so that you can rejoice with me in the love that I have in her, and she in me?"

And for our greater understanding our Lord God also spoke this sweet word to all of mankind that will be saved, but addressed them as a single person. It was as if he said, "Will you see in her how you are loved? For your love I made her this important, this noble, and this worthy. This pleases me, and I will that it please you in the same way."

After himself, she is the most blissful sight. But in this regard, I am not taught to long to see her in her bodily presence while I am here, but to see the virtues of her blessed soul: her truth, her wisdom, her charity. By seeing these I can begin to know myself and to be reverently in awe of my God.

And when our good Lord had showed this and said this word, "Do you want to see her?" I answered, saying, "Yes, good Lord, thank you very much! Yes, good Lord, if it be your will." I prayed this prayer frequently, and I supposed I would see her bodily presence, but I did not see her this way. Jesus, in this word, showed me a spiritual picture of her. First he showed her just as I had seen her before—little and simple—and then he showed her as important, noble, glorious, and pleasing to him above all creatures. He wills that it be known that all those who delight in him should delight in her, and in the delight he takes in her and she in him.

And for our greater understanding, he showed this example. If a man loves a creature singularly, above all creatures, he will make all creatures love and delight in that creature he loves so much. And the word Jesus said, "Do you want to see her?" seemed to me, with the spiritual showing of her he gave me, to be the most delightful word he could have given me about her.

Our Lord showed me no one in particular except our Lady Saint Mary, and he showed her to me three times. The first was as she conceived, the second was as she was in her sorrows under the cross, and the third was as she is now, in delight, glory and joy.

## Chapter 26

*The twelfth revelation is that the Lord our God is Being All-sovereign.*

And after this our Lord showed himself more glorious in my sight than I had ever seen him before. In this I was taught that our soul shall never have rest until it comes to him, knowing that he is the fulness of joy, familiarly and courteously blissful, and life itself.

Our Lord Jesus frequently said, "I am it! I am the one! I am that which is the highest! I am what you love! I am what delights you! I am the one you serve! I am what you long for! I am what you desire! I am what you intend! I am all! I am what holy Church preaches and teaches you! I am the one who has shown myself to you here."

The number of the words exceeded my wit, all my understanding and all my powers, and as I see it, this is the highest
point, for in these words is comprehended— I cannot tell;
but the joy I saw in the showing of them goes beyond anything heart may will and soul may desire. That is why the
words are not repeated here. But let every man, according to
the grace God gives him in understanding and loving, receive
them as our Lord intends them.

## Chapter 27

*The thirteenth revelation is that our Lord God wills that we
have great regard for all the deeds he has done in the great
nobility of his making of all things, and of how sin is not
known except by the pain.*

After this, the Lord brought to my mind the longing I had
had for him before, and I saw that nothing stood in my way
but sin. I saw that this is generally true of all of us. It seemed
to me if sin had not existed, we would all have been pure and
like our Lord, as he made us. Thus, in my folly, before this
time, I often wondered why, by the great foreseeing wisdom
of God, the beginning of sin had not been prevented, for
then, I thought, all would have been well.

This stirring definitely ought to have been given up; nevertheless, I mourned and sorrowed on its account without
reason or discretion. But Jesus, who in this vision informed
me of all I needed to know, answered in these words, saying,
"Sin is necessary, but all shall be well, and all shall be well,
and all manner of things shall be well."

In this naked word "sin" our Lord brought to my mind all
that is not good in general, the shameful contempt and utter
reduction to nothingness he bore for us in this life, his dying,
and all the pains and passions, spiritual and bodily, of all his
creatures. For we are all, in part, made nothing, and following our master Jesus, we shall be made nothing until we are
fully purged—that is to say, until we are fully stripped of

our mortal flesh and of all our inward affections that are not truly good.

In beholding all this, together with all the pains that ever were or ever shall be, I understood the passion of Christ as the greatest pain, passing beyond all the rest. All this was shown in a touch, and immediately was transformed into comfort, for our good Lord did not choose to have the soul made afraid by this ugly sight.

But I did not see sin, for I believe it has no kind of substance and no part of being and that it cannot be known except by the pain it causes. And thus pain is something for a time, as I see it, for it purges us and makes us know ourselves and ask for mercy. The passion of our Lord is a comfort to us against all this, and so is his blessed will.

Because of the tender love our good Lord has for all those who shall be saved, he gives comfort readily and sweetly, assuring us, "It is true that sin is the cause of all this pain, but all shall be well, and all shall be well, and all manner of things shall be well."

These words were said most tenderly, showing no kind of blame assigned to me or to anyone who shall be saved. Consequently, it would be a most unnatural act for me to blame or wonder at God on account of my sin, seeing that he does not blame me for sin.

And in these same words, I saw a marvelous, lofty secret hidden in God, which he shall make known openly to us in heaven. In knowing it we shall see in truth the reason why he allowed sin to come, and in this sight we shall endlessly rejoice in our Lord God.

## Chapter 28

*How the children of salvation shall be shaken in sorrows, but Christ rejoices with compassion; and a remedy against tribulation.*

Thus I saw how Christ has compassion on us because of sin. And just as before I was completely filled with pain and compassion in the passion of Christ, so now I was filled, in part, with compassion for all my fellow Christians—for that well, well-beloved people that shall be saved—for he loves most fully the people that shall be saved. What I mean is that God's servants, holy Church, shall be shaken in sorrows, anguish and tribulation in this world as men shake a cloth in the wind.

Our Lord answered that in this way: "I shall make a great thing of all this in heaven, a thing of endless glories and ever-lasting joys."

Indeed, I saw that our Lord rejoices at the tribulations of his servants with pity and compassion to the extent that, in order to bring each person he loves to his bliss, he lays on him some thing that is no lack in his sight but by which the person is lowered and despised in this world—scorned, mocked and cast out. This he does in order to prevent the harm that his servants would suffer from the pomp and vain-glory of this wretched life, to make ready their way to come to heaven, and to raise them in his bliss lasting without an end. For he says, "I shall shatter you in your vain affections and your vicious pride, and then I shall gather you together and make you mild and meek, pure and holy, by making you one with me."

And then I saw that each act of natural compassion a man performs for his fellow Christians in charity is Christ in him and that every kind of reduction to nothingness Christ suf-fered in his passion is repeated here in this compassion.

In this our Lord intended two kinds of understandings: The one was the bliss that we are brought to, in which he wills to be enjoyed. The second is for comfort in our pain, for he wills that we understand that all of it shall be turned into glory and profit by virtue of his passion. He also wills that we understand that we do not suffer alone, but with him, and that we see him as our ground. He wills that we see that his pains and his reduction to nothingness so far surpass all that we can suffer that it can't really be imagined.

The careful contemplation of this will save us from grumbling and despair as we experience our pain, especially if we see that, in truth, our sin deserves it, yet his love excuses us. He does away with all our blame by his noble courtesy and regards us with compassion and pity, like innocent children, who can't be hated.

## Chapter 29

*Adam's sin was the greatest, but the satisfaction for it is more pleasing to God than ever the sin was harmful.*

But I continued to look at this in general, in mourning and darkness, saying mentally to our Lord with very great respect, "Ah, good Lord, how can all be well, with the great harm that has come to your creatures by sin?" And here I desired, as much as I dared, to have some more open declaration in which I could find ease in this regard.

To this request, our blessed Lord answered most meekly and with a very lovely expression. He showed that Adam's sin was the greatest harm that was ever done, or ever shall be done to the world's end. He also showed that this is known openly on earth throughout holy Church. Furthermore, he taught me that I should behold the glorious satisfaction. For this making of satisfaction is, beyond comparison, more pleasing to God and more valuable for man's salvation than ever Adam's sin was harmful.

By this teaching our blessed Lord means us to understand and pay attention to this: "For since I have made well the greatest harm, then it is my will that you know thereby that I shall make well all that is less."

## Chapter 30

*How we should rejoice and trust in our savior, Jesus, not presuming to pry into his secret purposes.*

He gave me understanding of two parts [of truth]. The first part is our savior and our salvation. This blessed part is open, clear, fair, light and abundant, for all men who are, and shall be, of good will are included in this part. To this part we are bound by God, and to it we are drawn, counseled and taught, inwardly by the Holy Spirit and outwardly by holy Church, by the same grace.

In this first part our Lord wills that we be occupied rejoicing in him, for he rejoices in us. The more fully we take from this source with reverence and meekness the more thanks we earn from him and the more success we gain for ourselves. Thus we can say, rejoicing, that our part is our Lord.

The second part of truth is hidden and barred from us—that is to say, everything that is unrelated to our salvation. These are our Lord's secret purposes. It belongs to the royal lordship of God that he have his secret purposes in peace; to his servants belong obedience and reverence, not full knowledge of his purposes.

Our Lord has pity and compassion on us, because there are some of us who so busy ourselves in his secret purposes; I am sure if we knew how very greatly we would please him and ease ourselves by abandoning this curiosity, we would do so. The saints who are in heaven will to know nothing but what our Lord wills to show them. Their charity and desire are also ruled according to the will of our Lord. We ought, like them, to will in this way; then we would will and desire nothing but the will of our Lord, as they do, for we are all one, as God sees things. Here I was taught that we should trust and rejoice only in our savior, blessed Jesus, for all things.

## Chapter 31

*Of the longing and the spiritual thirst of Christ, which lasts and shall last until Judgment Day; and by reason of his body he is not yet fully glorified or entirely unable to suffer.*

And thus our good Lord answered all the questions and doubts I could invent, saying most comfortingly, "I may make all things well, I can make all things well, I will to make all things well, and I shall make all things well. And you yourself shall see that all manner of things shall be well."

That he says, "I may," I understand for the Father; that he says, "I can," I understand for the son. Where he says, "I will to," I understand the Holy Spirit, and where he says, "I shall," I understand the unity of the blessed Trinity, three persons and one truth. Where he says, "You yourself shall see," I understand the joining of all mankind who shall be saved in the blissful Trinity.

In these five words God wills we be enclosed in rest and in peace, and thus shall the spiritual thirst of Christ have an end. For the spiritual thirst of Christ is the love-longing that lasts and ever shall until we see that sight on Judgment Day. For of us who shall be saved and shall be Christ's joy and his bliss, some are still here and some are yet to come—and so shall it be right up to that day. Therefore, this is his thirst: a love-longing to have us all together, whole in him, for his bliss, as I see it, for we are not as fully whole in him as we shall be then.

We know in our faith, and it was also showed in all of this, that Christ Jesus is both God and man. In the godhead, he is himself the highest bliss, was so from before the beginning, and shall be so without end. This endless bliss can never be made higher or lower in itself. This was abundantly seen in every showing, and specifically in the twelfth, where he says, "I am that which is highest."

In Christ's manhood, it is known through our faith, and

also shown here, that he, by virtue of the godhead, suffered pains and passions and death for love, to bring us to his bliss. These are the works of Christ's manhood, by which he rejoices. He showed that in the ninth revelation, where he says, "It is a joy, a bliss, an endless delight to me that I ever suffered the passion for you." And this is the bliss of Christ's works.

That's what he means where he says, in the same showing, that we are his bliss, we are his reward, we are his glory, we are his crown. For insofar as Christ is our head he is glorified and unable to suffer, but as far as his body, into which all his members are knit, is concerned, he is not yet fully glorified or entirely unable to suffer. For the same desire, longing and thirst that he had upon the cross and which, as I see it, were in him from eternity, he has yet, and ever shall have, until the last soul to be saved has come up into his bliss.

As truly as there is in God a property of compassion and pity, so truly is there in him a property of thirst and longing. By virtue of this longing in Christ, we have to long for him in response. Without this response, no soul comes to heaven. The property of longing thirst comes from the endless goodness of God, just as the property of pity comes from his endless goodness. And though he has longing and pity, they are two different properties, as I see it. In this stands the point of the spiritual thirst that will last in him as long as we are in need, drawing us up to his bliss. All this was seen in the showing of compassion, for that shall cease on Judgment Day. Thus he has pity and compassion on us, and he has longing to have us, but his wisdom and his love do not allow the end to come until the best time.

## Chapter 32

*How all things shall be well, and how Scripture shall be fulfilled; and that we must steadfastly hold ourselves in the faith of holy Church, as is Christ's will.*

At one time our good Lord said, "All shall be well," and at another time he said, "You yourself shall see that all manner of things shall be well." In these two sayings the soul took several different understandings.

One was that he wills that we grasp that he pays attention not only to noble and great things but also to little and small, lowly and simple things. He takes heed of both the one and the other, which is what he means when he says, "All manner of things shall be well." He wills that we understand that not even the smallest thing will be forgotten.

Another understanding of these two sayings is this: As we see it, there are many deeds evilly done. So great is the harm they cause, that it seems to us impossible that they should ever come to good. We look upon these deeds sorrowing and mourning so that, on their account, we cannot be at rest in the blissful contemplation of God as we should be. The cause is this: the reasoning we can use now is so blind, so low and so simple that we cannot know the lofty, marvelous wisdom, the power and the goodness, of the blessed Trinity. That is what he means where he says, "You yourself shall see that all manner of things shall be well." It is as if he said, "Pay attention now, faithfully and trustfully, and at the last end you shall see it in truth, in the fulness of joy."

And thus from these same five words I have mentioned before ("I may make all things well," etc.), I took very great comfort concerning all the works of our Lord God that are yet to come.

There is a deed that the blessed Trinity shall do on the last day, according to what I saw. When and how the deed shall be accomplished is and shall remain unknown to all creatures beneath Christ until the day it is done. What our Lord wills that we know, through his goodness and love, is that the deed will be done. His power and wisdom, by the same love, will to conceal and hide from us what the deed will be and how it shall be done.

The reason he wills that we know that the deed will be done is because he wants us to be more at ease in soul and more peaceful in love and to stop looking at all the tempests that could keep us from true rejoicing in him.

This great deed is the one ordained by God from eternity, treasured and hidden in his blessed breast, and only known to himself. By this deed, he shall make all things well. Just as the blessed Trinity made all things from nothing, so the same blessed Trinity shall make well all that is not well.

At this sight I wondered greatly. I looked at our faith, marveling thus: "Our faith is grounded in God's word, and it is part of our faith that we believe that God's word shall be saved in all things. But one point of our faith is that many creatures shall be damned, like the angels who fell from heaven because of their pride and are now devils. Men, too, who die outside the faith of holy Church (that is to say, heathens), and men who are baptized Christians yet live unchristian lives and so die outside of charity, shall all likewise be damned to hell forever, as holy Church teaches me to believe. Considering all this, it seemed to me impossible that all manner of things should be well, as our Lord had showed me at this time.

Concerning all this, I had no other answer in any showing from our Lord God but this: "What is impossible to you is not impossible to me. I shall save my word in all things, and I shall make all things well."

Thus was I taught by the grace of God that I should steadfastly hold myself in the faith as I had before understood it and that I should seriously believe that all manner of things would be well, as our Lord at that same time had showed me. For by the great deed that our Lord shall do he shall save his word in all things and he shall make well all that is not well—though how it shall be done no creature below Christ knows or shall know until it is done. This is what I understood from what our Lord communicated to me at this time.

## Chapter 33

*All damned souls are despised in the sight of God, like the
devil; these revelations do not detract from the faith of holy
Church but strengthen it; and the more we busy ourselves to
know God's secrets the less we know.*

And yet in this showing I wished, as much as I dared, that
I could have had a complete view of hell and purgatory. In
wishing this, it was not my intention to test anything that
faith teaches, for I believed steadfastly that hell and purgatory exist for the same ends that holy Church teaches they
do. My intention was to see so that I could learn all about
the things that belong to my faith, and because of them
live more for God's glory and my profit.

But, for all my desire, I could see nothing of this except
what I told you before: the showing where I saw that the
devil is reproved by God and endlessly damned. In that sight
I understood that all creatures who share the devil's condition in this life, and die in it, whether they are Christians or
not, are no more made mention of by God and all his holy
ones than is the devil, despite the fact that they belong to
mankind.

Although this was a revelation of goodness and made little
mention of evil, I was still not drawn by it from any point of
faith that holy Church teaches me to believe. I saw the passion of Christ in several different showings—the first, the second, the fifth and the eighth—as I have said before. I had in
part a sense of the sorrow of our Lady and of his true friends
who saw him in pain, but I did not see properly specified the
Jews, who did him to death, despite the fact that I knew in
my faith that they were accursed and damned without end,
except for the ones who were converted by grace.

I was strengthened and taught in general to keep myself in
the faith at every point, and in all that I had understood be-

fore. I hoped that, with the mercy and grace of God, I was doing so, and in my intentions I desired and prayed that I might continue to, until the end of my life.

It is God's will that we have great regard for all the deeds he has done, for he wills that by them we shall know, trust and believe all he shall do, but it is forever necessary for us to stop ourselves from speculating on what the great deed shall be. We should desire to be like our brothers who are saints in heaven; they will nothing but what God wills. Then we would rejoice only in God and would be well satisfied both with what he hides and with what he shows. For I saw in truth that our Lord means us to understand that the more we busy ourselves to know his secrets, in that or anything else, the further away we shall be from knowing them.

## Chapter 34

*God shows the secrets necessary for his lovers; and how those who diligently receive the preaching of holy Church please God greatly.*

Our Lord God showed two kinds of secrets. One is this great secret with all the hidden points belonging to it. He wills that these secrets remain hidden from us in this way until the time he chooses to show them to us clearly.

The second kind are the secrets he wills to make known and open to us, for he wills that we grasp that it is his will that we know them. They are secrets to us not only because he wills that they be hidden from us but because of our blindness and ignorance. On these he has great pity, and therefore he wills to make them more open to us himself so that we may know him, love him and cling to him. For, all that it is expedient for us to grasp and know, our Lord will most courteously show us—and that showing is this revelation with all the preaching and teaching of holy Church.

God showed the very great pleasure he has in all men and

women who enthusiastically, humbly, wisely and deliberately accept the preaching and teaching of holy Church. For it is his holy Church. He is the ground, he is the substance, he is the teaching, he is the teacher, he is the end, he is the reward for which every soul following its nature does difficult labor. This is known, and shall be known to every soul to which the Holy Spirit declares it. I hope, truly, that he will assist all those who seek this, for they seek God.

All this that I have said up to now, and more that I shall say after this, is a comfort against sin. For in the third showing, when I saw that God does all that is done, I saw no sin. And then I saw that all is well. But it was when God showed me sin that he said, "All shall be well."

## Chapter 35

*How God does all that is good and suffers honorably all that is evil, by his mercy; and that this will cease only when sin is no longer allowed.*

And when God Almighty had shown me some of his goodness so plentifully and completely, I desired to learn whether a certain creature I loved continued in the good living I hoped had been begun by the grace of God. And it seemed that I got in my own way with this desire to know about a particular person, for I received no teaching about it at this time. But then I was answered in my reason, as it were by a friendly adviser, "Take what you are shown as general, and look at the courtesy of the Lord God as he shows it to you. For it is a greater honor to God for you to see him in everything than in any one, special thing."

I assented, and thus I learned that it is a greater honor to God for us to know all things in general than to delight in any one thing in particular. And if I want to act wisely according to this teaching, not only should I not be glad for any one thing specifically, I should not be greatly disturbed for any kind of thing, for all shall be well. The fulness of joy is to behold God in everything, for by the same blessed power, wisdom and love that he made everything, our good Lord leads it to the same end continuously, will himself bring it there, and when it is time, we shall see it.

The ground of this teaching was seen in the first showing, and more openly in the third, where it says, "I saw God in a point. . . . All that our Lord does is done rightfully, and all that he suffers is full of honor." And in these two are encompassed good and evil. For all that is good our Lord does, and what is evil our Lord suffers.

I'm not saying that evil is full of honor, but that our Lord God's endurance of evil is full of honor. By it his goodness shall be known without end in his marvelous humility and mildness, by the working of mercy and grace.

Rightfulness is that quality which is so good that nothing can be better than it is, for God himself is true rightfulness and all his works are done rightfully by his noble might, his high wisdom, his lofty goodness, as they have been ordained from eternity. And as he has ordained them for the best, just so he works continuously, leading them to the same end. He is always completely pleased with himself and with all his works.

Looking at this blessed harmony is very sweet to the soul that sees it by grace. All the souls that shall be saved in heaven without end are made rightful in the sight of God and by his own goodness. In this rightfulness we are endlessly and marvelously preserved, above all creatures.

Mercy is a work that comes from the goodness of God. In its working, it shall last as long as sin is allowed to pursue the rightful soul. When sin no longer has permission to pursue, the working of mercy shall cease and all shall be brought to rightfulness and be established in it without end.

By his permission we fall, in his blissful love with his might and his wisdom we are preserved, and by mercy and grace we are raised to many more joys.

Thus in rightfulness and mercy he wills to be known and loved now and forever, and the soul that, in grace, wisely sees this is well pleased with both and endlessly rejoices in them.

## Chapter 36

*Of another excellent deed that our Lord shall do, which, by grace, may be known in part here; how we shall delight in this same deed; and how God still does miracles.*

Our Lord God showed that a deed shall be done and that he himself shall do it. And the deed he shall do himself will be glorious, marvelous and generous. That he shall do it himself is the loftiest joy the soul understood. I can do nothing except sin, but my sin will not prevent the working of his goodness.

And I saw that contemplating this truth is an uplifting, heavenly joy in an awe-filled soul that evermore, following its proper nature by grace, desires God's will.

This deed shall be begun here, and it shall be full of honor to God and abundantly profitable to his lovers on earth and forever. As we come to heaven we shall see it in marvelous joy, and it shall last thus, in its working, until the last day. The glory and the bliss of it shall last in heaven before God and all his holy ones without end.

Thus was this deed seen and understood as our Lord intended. The reason he showed it is to make us delight in him and all his works.

When I saw his showing continue, I understood that it was shown as a great thing that would happen in the future. God showed that he himself would do this deed which would have the properties I mentioned before. He showed this most blissfully, intending that I should receive it wisely, faithfully and trustfully. But what this deed would be was kept secret from me.

In this I saw that he does not will that we dread to know the things he shows. He shows them because he wills that we know them, and by knowing them, that we love him, delight in him and endlessly rejoice in him. Because of the great love he has for us, he shows us everything that is proper and profitable for us to know at the time. Because of his great goodness, even the things he wills to keep secret now he shows us in a hidden way, and he wills that we believe and understand of this showing that we shall see its reality in his endless bliss. Thus we ought to rejoice in him both for all he shows and for all he keeps hidden. If we do this deliberately and meekly, we shall find great ease in the doing, and we shall have his endless thanks for it.

Here is the understanding of this word: the deed shall be done for me, that is for all men in general who shall be saved; it will be glorious, marvelous and generous, and God himself shall do it; it will be the soul's loftiest joy to see the deed that God himself shall do; and men will do absolutely nothing but sin. What our Lord God intends by that is this. It is as if he were saying, "Look and see! You have matter for humility here, and here you have matter for love. You have matter here by which you can know yourself and judge yourself as nothing, and you have matter here for delighting in me. For my love, rejoice in me, for of all the things you could do, this would please me most."

As long as we are in this life, every time we, by our folly, turn ourselves to the contemplation of the damned, our Lord God touches us tenderly and blissfully calls us, saying in our soul, "Let all your love, my precious child, be directed toward me. I am enough for you. Delight in your savior and your salvation." I am sure that the soul that experiences it by grace will see and feel that this is our Lord's working in us.

Though it is true that this deed is to be properly understood as referring to man in general, it does not exclude particular individuals, for what our good Lord wills to do by means of his poor creatures is now unknown to me.

But this deed and that great deed we spoke of before are not the same, but two different deeds. This deed shall be done sooner than the other—when we come to heaven. This deed may be known here, in part, by those to whom our Lord gives this knowledge, but the great deed I spoke of before shall be known neither in heaven nor on earth until it is done.

In addition, he gave me a special understanding of and

teaching about the working of miracles, as follows: "It is known that I have done miracles here before, many and terrible, lofty and marvelous, glorious and great. Just as I have done, I do now continually, and so shall I do in time to come."

It is known that before miracles come sorrow, anguish and tribulation. This is so that we will know our own feebleness and the bad situation we have fallen into by sin; it humbles us and makes us dread God and cry for help and grace. Great miracles come after that, from the noble power, wisdom and goodness of God. They are given in charity, to show us his strength and the joys of heaven (as far as that can be done in this transitory life), in order to strengthen our faith and to increase our hope. For this reason, it pleases him to be known and adored in miracles. Then he indicated that he does not will that we be overly depressed by the sorrows and storms that come our way, because that has always been the condition before miracles come.

## Chapter 37

*God preserves his chosen ones in complete security; although they sin, there is a godly will in them that never assents to sin.*

God brought to my mind that I should sin, but because of the delight I had in looking at him, I did not readily pay attention to that showing. Most mercifully our Lord waited for me and gave me the grace to pay attention.

I took this showing to refer to me alone, but by all the gracious comfort that followed, as you can see, I was taught that it referred to all my fellow Christians in general, with nothing intended just for me. Even though our Lord showed me I should sin, "all" is to be understood for "me alone."

All this made me somewhat afraid, and our Lord answered my dread this way: "I keep you most securely." This word was said with more love and sureness of spiritual preservation than I can or may tell. For just as it was showed that I should sin, so was the comfort shown: security and preservation for all my fellow Christians.

What can make me love my fellow Christians more than to see in God that he loves all who shall be saved as if they were all one soul? For in every soul that shall be saved, there is a godly will that has never assented to sin and never shall. Just as there is a beastly will in the lower part of a man that cannot will any good, so there is a godly will in the higher part. This will is so good that it can never will evil but only and always good. That is why we are what he loves and endlessly do what delights him.

Our Lord showed in the wholeness of love in which we stand in his sight that, indeed, he loves us as well now, while we are here, as he shall when we are there, before his blessed face. It is the failure of love on our part that causes all our distressful labor.

## Chapter 38

*The sins of the chosen shall be transformed to joy and glory; examples of David, Peter and John of Beverley.*

God also showed that sin will be no shame but an honor to man, for just as for every sin there is an answering pain in reality, so for every sin a bliss is given to the same soul. Just as different sins are punished by different pains according to their seriousness, so shall they be rewarded by different joys in heaven according to the pain and sorrow they have caused the soul on earth. For the soul that shall come to heaven is so precious to God, and the place itself is so glorious, that the goodness of God never allows the soul which will come there to sin without giving it a reward for suffering that sin. The sin suffered is made known without end, and the soul is blissfully restored by exceeding glories.

In this sight my understanding was lifted up into heaven, and there God suggested to my mind David and others without number in the Old Law. In the New Law he brought to my mind first how Mary Magdalene, Peter, Paul, Thomas of India, Jude, Saint John of Beverley and others, also without number, are known in the Church on earth with their sins, and how these sins are no shame to them but have all been transformed to their glory. By this honor, our courteous Lord shows for them here, in part, something similar to what is done for them in fulness there, for there the token of sin is transformed into glory.

And for the sake of familiarity, our Lord showed Saint John of Beverley in comfort, most clearly, reminding me that he is a neighbor near to hand, one whom we know. And God called him Saint John of Beverley plainly, just as we do, and did so with a most glad, sweet expression, showing that he is a very high, blissful saint in heaven in God's sight.

With this showing God made mention that Saint John of Beverley, in his youth and tender years, was a most valuable servant to God, extremely good, loving and reverencing him. Nevertheless, God allowed him to fall, mercifully preserving him from perishing or losing time. Afterward God raised him to grace many times greater, and by the contrition and humility he practiced in his living, God has given him joys in heaven many times surpassing what he would have had, had he not fallen. And God shows on earth that this is the truth with abundant miracles, performed continually around the body of Saint John of Beverley. All this was shown and done to make us glad and merry in love.

## Chapter 39

*Of the sharpness of sin and the goodness of contrition; how our compassionate Lord wills that we do not despair because we fall frequently.*

Sin is the sharpest scourge that any chosen soul can be struck with. This scourge beats a man or woman completely to a pulp, makes him so entirely noxious in his own sight that after a while he judges of himself that he is worthy only to sink into hell. He feels this way until contrition takes hold of him, by the touch of the Holy Spirit, and transforms the bitterness into hope of God's mercy.

Then his wounds begin to heal, and his soul, turned to the life of holy Church, quickens. The Holy Spirit leads him to confession of his own free will, to confess his sins nakedly and honestly, with great sorrow and great shame, because he has befouled the fair image of God. Then, for each sin, he undertakes the penance given him by his confessor, who is grounded in holy Church by the teaching of the Holy Spirit.

This is an act of meekness that greatly pleases God. So is accepting the bodily sickness God sends, the sorrow and shame that come from without, the reproof and contempt of this world, and all the kinds of grievance and temptations that are cast upon body and soul. Our Lord perserves us most carefully when it seems to us that we are nearly forsaken and cast away for our sins, and because we have deserved it. But because of the meekness we get through these trials, we are wholly raised in God's sight by his grace. We are moved with such great contrition, compassion and true longing for God that we are suddenly delivered from sin and pain, are taken up to bliss, and are made fellows with the noble saints.

By contrition we are made clean; by compassion we are made ready, and by true longing for God we are made worthy. These are the three means, as I understand it, by which all souls—that is to say, all souls that have been sinners on earth and shall be saved—come to heaven, for by these medicines it would profit every sinful soul to be healed.

Though the sinner be healed, his wounds are seen before God—not as wounds but as honors. And likewise, as we are punished here with sorrow and penance, we shall be rewarded in heaven by the courteous love of our Lord God Almighty, who wills that no one who comes there shall suffer any loss at all for his bitter labor. For he sees sin as sorrow and pain to his lovers, to whom, for love, he assigns no blame.

The reward that we shall receive will not be little; it will be high, glorious and full of honor. In the same way, shame shall also be transformed into honor and more joy. Our courteous Lord does not will that his servants despair, either for frequent or for serious failures, for our failures do not prevent him from loving us.

Peace and love are ever in us—being and working—but we are not always in peace and love. He wills, however, that we pay attention to the fact that he is the ground of our whole life in love, and furthermore that he is our everlasting preserver. He defends us powerfully against our enemies, who are most deadly and fierce in their attacks upon us, and our need is all the greater in that we give them the advantage by our failures.

## Chapter 40

*We need to long in love with Jesus, renouncing sin for love; the vileness of sin exceeds all pains; God loves us most tenderly while we are in sin; and we need to do the same thing for our neighbor.*

It is an act of sovereign friendship on the part of our courteous Lord that he tenderly preserves us while we are in sin, and that, furthermore, he touches us most secretly, showing us our sin by the sweet light of mercy and grace. But when we have seen how foul we are, we imagine that God must be angry with us for our sin. Then we are stirred by the Holy Spirit, by means of contrition, to pray and desire to amend our lives, and with all our powers, to lessen God's wrath until such time as we can find rest of soul and relief in confession. Then we hope that God has forgiven us our sins, and that it is true.

Then our courteous Lord shows himself to the soul most merrily and with a glad expression. With a friendly welcome, as if the soul had been in pain and imprisoned, he says sweetly, "My darling, I am glad you have come to me. In all this misery I have ever been with you. Now you see my loving, and we are made one in bliss."

Thus are sins forgiven by mercy and grace, and thus our soul is received with honor, in joy, just as it shall be when it comes to heaven—and this as many times as it comes to be forgiven, by the gracious working of the Holy Spirit and the virtue of Christ's passion.

By this I understood in truth that every kind of thing is made ready for us by the great goodness of God, to the extent that when we ourselves are in peace and love we are, in reality, saved. But because we may not possess this in its fulness while we are here, it happens that we must ever live in sweet prayer and love-longing with our Lord Jesus. For he longs always to bring us to the fulness of joy, as was described previously, where he showed his spiritual thirst.

But now, if any man or woman, because of all this spiritual comfort that I have described, should be stirred by folly to say or think, "If this is true, then it would be a good thing to sin so one could have a greater reward," or to judge sin less evil, let him beware of this stirring. For, in truth, if it comes it is untrue, and emanates from the enemy of the same true love that teaches us all this blessed comfort. For the same true love that touches us all by his blessed comfort teaches us that we should hate sin for the sake of love alone. I am sure, from my own feelings, that the more often any soul following its proper nature sees this in the courteous love of our Lord God, the more loath it is to sin and the more ashamed it is. For if all the pains in hell, in purgatory, and on earth—death and all the rest—were laid before us next to sin, we should rather choose all that pain than sin. Sin is so vile, and so greatly to be hated that it can't be compared to any pain that is not itself sin. No harder hell than sin was showed to me, for a soul following its proper nature has no hell but sin, because all is good except sin, and nothing except sin is evil.

When, by the working of mercy and grace, we fix our will in love and humility, we are made entirely fair and clean. And God is as anxious to save man as he is powerful and wise to accomplish it.

Christ himself is the ground of all the laws of Christian men, and he taught us to return good for evil. Here we can see that he himself is this charity and does to us as he teaches us to do to others, for he wills that we be like him in the wholeness of endless love for our fellow Christians. No more than his love for us is broken because of our sin does he will that our love toward ourselves and our fellow Christians be broken. Rather, he wills that we nakedly hate the sin and endlessly love the soul as God loves it. Then we will hate sin as God hates it and love the soul as God loves it, for this word the Lord said is an endless comfort: "I keep you most securely."

## Chapter 41

*The fourteenth revelation is what was said before: it is impossible that we should pray for mercy and lack it; how God wills that we continue to pray even though we are dry and barren, because that prayer is acceptable and pleasing to him.*

After this our Lord gave me a showing about prayer, in which I saw the two conditions our Lord intends for it. The first is rightfulness. The second is sure trust.

But still many times our trust is not full, because we are not sure that God hears us as we think he does, because of our unworthiness and because we feel absolutely nothing, for we are frequently as barren and dry after our prayers as we were before them. And this folly in our feelings is the cause of our weakness. I have felt this way myself.

Our Lord brought all this suddenly to my mind, and showed these words, saying, "I am the ground of your beseeching. First, it is my will that you have what you ask, and then, I make you will it. Since I make you ask it, and you do ask it, how should it, then, be that you should not have what you ask?"

Thus, as its words make clear, in the first reason, with the three that follow, our good Lord showed a powerful comfort. And in the first reason, where he said, ". . . and you do ask it," he showed the very great pleasure and the endless reward that he wills to give us because of our beseeching. In the sixth phrase, where he says, "how should it then be . . . ?" the question is intended as an impossibility. For it is most impossible that we should ask for mercy and grace and not receive them. Everything our good Lord makes us ask him for, he himself has ordained for us from eternity.

Here we can see that our asking is not the cause of the good things God does for us and the grace he gives us. This he showed in truth when he said all these sweet words: "I am the ground. . . ."

Our good Lord wills that this be known by his lovers on earth, and the more clearly we know it, the more we should ask, if we take it wisely, for so our Lord intends. This "beseeching" is a true, gracious, lasting disposition of the soul which is united and fastened into the will of our Lord by the sweet, secret work of the Holy Spirit.

Our Lord himself is the first receiver of our prayer, as I see it, and takes it most thankfully. Rejoicing greatly in it, he sends it up above and sets it in among his treasure, where it shall never perish. It is there, before God with all his holy ones, continually being received and continually assisting our needs. And when we shall enter into our bliss, it shall be given to us as a degree of joy, with his endless thanks so full of honor.

Our Lord is most glad and delighted with our prayer. He looks for it, and he wills to have it, for with his grace he makes us as like himself in condition as we are in nature. This is his blessed will, for he says, "Pray inwardly, though you think it gives you no satisfaction. For the prayer is profitable though you feel nothing, though you see nothing, yes, though you think you can do nothing. In dryness and in barrenness, in sickness and in feebleness—then is your prayer most pleasing to me, though you think it gives you but little satisfaction. And so it is with all your believing prayers, in my sight."

Because of the reward and the endless thanks he will give us for it, he covets our continual prayer in his sight. God accepts the good will and the bitter labor of his servant, however we may feel. Therefore, it pleases him that we work reasonably, with discretion, both in our prayers and in our good living by his help and his grace, concentrating our powers on him until we have, in fulness of joy, him whom we seek; that is, Jesus. This he shows in the fifteenth revelation, in this word: "You will have me for your reward."

Thanking also belongs to prayer. Thanking is a new, inward knowing, with great reverence and loving awe. It is a turning of our self with all our might to the working that our good Lord stirs us to, rejoicing and thanking him inwardly. Sometimes, because of its abundance, it breaks out audibly and says, "Good Lord, many thanks! Blessed may you be!" Sometimes, when the heart feels nothing because it is dry or else because of the temptation of our enemy, it is driven by reason and by grace to cry to our Lord, audibly going over his blessed passion and his great goodness. Then the virtue of our Lord's word turns into the soul, quickens the heart, by his grace starts it working properly, and makes it pray most blissfully. To rejoice truly in our Lord is a most blissful, lovely thanking in his sight.

## Chapter 42

*Of three things that belong to prayer; how we should pray; and of the goodness of God, which always supplies for our imperfection and feebleness when we do what we are supposed to do.*

Our Lord God wills that we have true understanding, especially of the three things that belong to our prayer.

The first is from whom and how our prayer springs up. He shows "from whom" when he says, "I am the ground"; "how" is goodness, for he says, "It is my will, first."

The second thing that belongs to our prayer is in what manner and how we should make our prayer. We should pray in such a way that our will is turned toward the will of our Lord, rejoicing. That's what he intends when he says, "I make you will it."

The third thing that belongs to our prayer is that we know that the fruit and end of our prayer is to be made one with our Lord and to live for him in all things. It was with this intention and for this end that the whole of this lovely lesson was shown. He will help us, and we will make our prayer just as he himself says, blessed may he be!

It is our Lord's will that our prayers and our trust should be equally far-reaching. For if our trust is not as far-reaching as our prayer, we do not give complete honor to our Lord in our prayer, and we waste time and cause ourselves pain. I believe the cause of this fault is that we do not know, in truth, that our Lord is the ground from which our prayer springs up. Further, we do not know that the prayer is given us by the grace of his love, for if we realized that, it would make us trust that we would receive, as a gift from our Lord, all that we desire. For I am certain that no man asks mercy and grace with a true intention unless mercy and grace have first been given to him.

But sometimes it occurs to us that we have prayed for a long time and still, as we think, have not received what we have asked. We should not be depressed on this account, for I am sure, from what our Lord said, that we are waiting either for a better time, or for more grace, or for a better gift. He wills that we have a real knowledge that in himself he is Being. In this knowledge he wills that our understanding be grounded with all our powers, all our attention, and all our purpose. In this grounding he wills that we have our place and our dwelling.

By the gracious light of himself, he wills that we have an understanding of the following things: the first is the nobility and excellence of our creation; the second is the preciousness and the extremely great value of our redemption; the third is that he has made all things beneath us to serve us, and that he preserves them for love of us.

What he means is this. It is as if he said, "Behold and see that I have done all this before you prayed. Now you exist

nd pray to me." He means that it is our place to know that
hese great deeds have been done as holy Church teaches and
hat, gratefully seeing them, we ought to pray for the accomplishment of the deed that is now being done, namely that
ne rule us and guide us for his glory in this life and bring us
to his bliss.

It is to accomplish this deed that he has done everything,
and he intends us to see that he is doing it and to pray for it
to be done. To do only one is not enough, for if we pray and
do not see that he does it, it makes us depressed and doubt-
ful, and that is not an honor to him. But if we see that he
does it and do not pray, we do not pay our debt, and that
can't be; that is to say, in his sight, that does not exist. But
to see that he does it and to pray that it be done—that is
the way he is honored and the way we profit.

Everything that our Lord has decided to do, he wills that
we pray for—either in particular or in general. The joy and
bliss this is to him, and the thanks and honor we shall have
for doing so, surpass the understanding of creatures, as I see
it. For prayer is a just understanding of the fulness of joy
that is to come, with intense longing and certain trust. The
savoring of our bliss, to which we are by our proper nature ordained, makes us long; true understanding and love, with the
sweet mentality of our savior, graciously makes us trust. In
these two workings, our Lord sees us continuously, for this is
our debt, and his goodness may assign us no less. Thus it is
our part to do our duty diligently, and when we have done it,
then we should still think that it is nothing—which is the
truth.

But we are to do what we can, and truly ask mercy and
grace, and all that we lack we shall find in him. This is what
he means where he says, "I am the ground of your beseeching." And thus, in this blissful word, with this showing, I saw
the complete overcoming of all our weakness and all our
doubt-filled dreads.

## Chapter 43

*What prayer does, ordained to God's will; how the goodness*
*of God has great delight in the deeds he does by us (as if he*
*were beholden to us), doing all things most sweetly.*

Prayer makes the soul one with God. For though the soul,
restored by grace, is always like God in nature and substance,
it is often unlike him in condition, because of sin on man's
part. Then prayer is a witness that the soul wills as God wills.
It comforts the conscience and fits a man for grace.

And thus God teaches us to pray, and to trust intensely
that we shall receive what we ask for, for he looks at us with
love and wills to make us the partner of his good deed. For
this reason he stirs us to make the prayer that it delights him
to grant. In return for the prayer and good will that he wills
us to have by his gift, he will reward us and give us endless
payment. This was showed in the word "And you do ask for
it."

In this word God showed as much pleasure and delight as
if he were beholden to us for every good deed we do; yet it is
he who does it, because we ask him intensely to do everything that delights him. It is as if he said, "What could you
do to please me more than to ask me, intensely, wisely and
deliberately, to do the thing I will to do?" And thus the soul
is brought into agreement with God by prayer.

But when our courteous Lord, of his special grace, shows
himself to our soul, we have what we desire. And for that
time, we do not see what more we could pray for, because all
our attention and all our powers are wholly fixed in looking
at him. This is a lofty prayer, beyond human conception, as I
see it, for the whole cause of our prayer is joined to the sight
and contemplation of him to whom we pray. Marvelously rejoicing with reverent dread, we have such great sweetness and

elight in him for that time that we can pray absolutely
othing except what he stirs us to pray. And well I know that
ie more the soul sees of God the more it desires him, by his
race.

But when we do not see him in this way, then we feel in
ur failure need and cause to pray, in order to ready ourselves
or Jesus. For when the soul is tempted, troubled and left to
self in unrest, then it is time for it to pray, to make itself
pple and obedient to God. But there is no kind of prayer
1at can make God supple to the soul, for he is always the
ame in love.

Thus I saw that when we see a need for which to pray,
ur good Lord follows us, assisting our desire. And when
e, through his special grace, look at him plainly, seeing no
ther need, then we follow him and he draws us into him
y love. For I saw and felt that his marvelous and abundant
oodness completely fills all our powers.

And then I saw that his continual working in every kind
f thing is done so well, so wisely and so mightily that it
urpasses all our imaginings and all that we can suppose and
hink. Then we can do no more than look at him rejoicing,
vith a noble, powerful desire to be entirely made one with
im—to be centered in his dwelling, rejoicing in his loving
nd delighting in his goodness. And then, with his sweet
race, we shall, in our own meek, continual prayer, come in
o him now, in this life, by many secret touchings of sweet,
piritual sights and feelings measured out to us in the degree
hat our simplicity can bear.

This is, and shall be, wrought by the grace of the Holy
pirit, until we die in longing for love. Then shall we all
ome in to our Lord, knowing ourselves clearly and possess-
ng God most fully. We shall endlessly be completely pos-
essed by God, seeing him in truth, most fully feeling him,
piritually hearing him, delectably smelling him, sweetly
wallowing him. Then shall we see him face to face, famil-
rly and most fully. The creature that is made shall see and
ndlessly gaze at God, who is its maker. No man can see God
his way and continue to live afterward—that is to say, in

this mortal life. But when God of his special grace wills
show himself here, he strengthens the creature beyond i
own self, and measures the showing according to his ow
will, as it is profitable for that time.

## Chapter 44

*Of the properties of the Trinity; how man's soul, a creatur
has the same properties, doing what it was made for: seein
contemplating, and marveling at its God; and that, by
doing, it seems as nothing to itself.*

God frequently showed in all the revelations that man fo
ever works his will and his honor, continually, without a
stinting. What this work is was shown in the first revelatio
and that was a marvelous foundation, for it was shown in th
working of the most blessed soul of our blissful Lady Sai
Mary, as truth and wisdom. And how I hope by the grace
the Holy Spirit that I can say what I saw.

Truth sees God, and wisdom contemplates God. Fro
these two comes the third, which is a holy, marvelous deligh
in God, who is love. Where truth and wisdom are, in truth
there is love, coming in reality from both of them, and all a
of God's making. For he is endless sovereign truth, endle
sovereign wisdom and endless sovereign love, all of the
uncreated.

And man's soul is a creature of God that has the sam
properties in created form. It does forever what it was mad
for: it sees God, it contemplates God, and it loves God. B
cause of this, God rejoices in the creature and the creatu
rejoices in God, marveling endlessly. In this marveling, it se
its God, its Lord, its maker—so noble, so great, and so goo
in comparison to one who is created, that it is with difficult
that the creature seems like anything to itself. But th
brightness and clearness of truth and wisdom make it see an
recognize that it is made for the love in which God endless
preserves it.

## Chapter 45

*f the firm and deep judgment of God, and the variant judg-
*ent of man.*

God judges us on our natural substance, which is forever
*ept one in him, whole and safe without end. And this judg-
*ent is made out of his rightfulness. Man makes judgments
*a our changeable sensuality, which seems now one thing,
*ow another, according as it draws from one part or the
*ther, and on what shows outwardly. And this judgment is
*uddled. Sometimes it is good and easy, and sometimes it is
*ard and grievous. But inasmuch as it is good and easy, it be-
*ongs to rightfulness. And inasmuch as it is hard and griev-
*us, our good Lord Jesus reforms it by mercy and grace
*rough the virtue of his blissful passion, to bring it into
*ghtfulness. And though these two judgments are thus
*rought into agreement and made one, still both shall be
*nown in heaven without end.

The first judgment, which is from God's rightfulness, is of
*is noble, endless love. This is the fair sweet judgment that
*as shown in all the fair revelations in which I saw him as-
*gn to us no kind of blame. And though this was sweet and
*electable, I could not be fully set at ease in beholding only
*, because of the judgment of holy Church, which I had un-
*erstood before and which was always in my sight. It was by
*is judgment that it seemed to me that I ought and had to
*now myself as a sinner. By the same judgment, I understood
*at sinners are sometimes worthy of blame and wrath. These
*vo things I could not see in God, and my desire to do so
*as greater than I can or may tell. For the higher judgment,
*od himself showed at the same time, and therefore I ought
*nd had to accept it. But the lower judgment had been
*ught me previously by holy Church, and therefore I could
*n no way abandon the lower judgment.

Then it was my desire that I might see in God in what way

the judgment holy Church teaches in this matter is true i
his sight, and how I ought to understand it in truth, so tha
both might be preserved in a way that would give honor t
God and be righteous for me.

And to all this I had no other answer than a marvelous e
ample of a lord and a servant, as I shall tell you later, whic
was shown most powerfully. And yet I remain fixed in desir
and will, until the end of my life, to know by grace how t
reconcile these two judgments as I ought. For all heavenl
things, and all earthly things that belong to heaven, are er
compassed in these two judgments. And the more unde
standing and knowledge we have of these two judgments b
the gracious leading of the Holy Spirit, the more we shall se
and know our failings. And always, the more that we se
them, the more naturally by grace we shall long to be con
pletely filled with endless joy and bliss. For we are made fe
endless joy and bliss, and our natural substance is now blis
ful in God, has been so since it was made, and shall be s
without end.

## Chapter 46

*We cannot know ourselves in this life except by faith an
grace; but we must know ourselves as sinners; and how Gc
is never angry, being most near the soul, preserving it.*

But the passing life that we have here in our sensuali
does not know what our self is, except in faith. And when v
know and see clearly what our self is in truth, then we sha
in truth see and know our Lord God clearly, in fulness of jo
For this reason, the nearer we are to bliss, the more we ougl
and have to long, and that both by nature and by grace. W
can have knowledge of ourselves in this life by the continui
help and virtue of our noble, proper nature. In this know
edge, we may increase and grow by the furtherance and a
sistance of mercy and grace, but we may never know ou

selves fully, to the ultimate point. In that point this passing
life and every kind of pain and woe shall have an end. Therefore it properly belongs to us, both by nature and grace,
both to long and desire with all our powers to know ourselves
in the fulness of endless joy. In this complete knowledge we
shall in truth know our God clearly in the fulness of endless
joy.

And yet, during all this time from the beginning to the
end, I had two kinds of showing. The first was of endless,
continuing love, with a security in preservation and blissful
salvation. For that's what all the showings revealed. The second was of the common teaching of holy Church, of which I
had previously been informed; I had been grounded in these
teachings, and deliberately kept them in use and in my understanding. The seeing of all this did not come from me, for
I was not stirred or led in the smallest point from the common teaching of holy Church by the showing, but was taught
in it that I should love and delight in it and that, by doing
so, I could, with the help of our Lord and his grace, increase
in and rise to more heavenly knowledge and more noble love.
And thus, in seeing all of this it seemed to me that I ought
and had to see and recognize that we are sinners, that we do
many evils that we ought to stop doing, and leave undone
many good deeds that we ought to do. For this we deserve
pain, blame and wrath.

And notwithstanding all this, I saw in truth that our Lord
was never angry, and never will be. For he is God: he is
goodness, life, truth, love and peace. His power, his wisdom,
his charity and his unity do not allow him to be angry. For I
saw truly that to be angry is contrary to the property of his
power, the property of his wisdom and the property of his
goodness. God is the goodness that cannot be angry, for he is
nothing but goodness. Our soul is made one with him, who is
unchangeable goodness, and between God and our soul there
is neither anger nor forgiveness, in his sight. For our soul is
most completely made one with God by his own goodness,
so that between God and the soul absolutely nothing can
exist.

The soul was led to this understanding by love and drawn

to it by power in every showing: that this is what our go
Lord showed; that this is how it is truly done by his gre
goodness; and that he wills that we desire to comprehend
that is to say as far as his creatures can comprehend it. F
God willed that everything that the simple soul understo
should be shown to it and known by it. The things that
wills, mightily and wisely, to keep secret, he himself hides f
love. I saw in the same showing that many secret things a
hidden which shall not be made known until the time th
God of his goodness has made us worthy to see them. I a
quite satisfied with this state of affairs, awaiting our Lord
will in this lofty marvel. And now I yield myself to m
mother, holy Church, as a simple child ought.

## Chapter 47

*We must reverently marvel and humbly suffer, ever rejoi
ing in God; and how our blindness, in that we do not s
God, is the cause of sin.*

Our soul must pay its debt in two respects. One is that v
marvel reverently. The second is that we suffer meekly, ev
rejoicing in God. For he wills that we realize that in a sho
time we shall see clearly in himself all that we desire.

And notwithstanding all of this, I stared and wonder
greatly what the mercy and forgiveness of God might be.

For by the teaching I had previously had, I understoo
that the mercy of God was supposed to be the cessation
his wrath after we had sinned. For it seemed to me that to
soul whose intention and desire is to love, the wrath of Go
would be harsher than any other pain. That's why I took
that the cessation of his wrath must be one of the princip
parts of his mercy. But for nothing that I could see an
desire in all the showings could I see this point.

But I shall say something of what I understood and sa
about the works of mercy, as God wills to give me grace.

I understood this. Man is changeable in this life, and by frailty and being overcome, by simplicity and lack of cunning, he falls into sin. In himself he is powerless and unwise, and his will is overborne. In this time he is in tempests and in sorrow and woe. The cause is blindness, for he does not see God. If he saw God continuously, he would have no mischief-making feelings and no kind of stirring or yearning that would urge him to sin.

I saw and felt this at this same time, and it seemed to me that the feeling was noble and abundant and gracious compared to our usual feelings in this life. But I also thought it was small and low compared to the great desire the soul has to see God.

I felt within myself five kinds of working of the spirit, which are these: rejoicing, mourning, desire, dread, and sure, true hope. I felt "rejoicing" because God gave me the understanding and realization that it was he himself whom I saw. I felt "mourning" for my failures. I felt "desire" in that I wished I could see him ever more and more, understanding and realizing that we shall never have complete rest until we see him clearly and in truth in heaven. I felt "dread" because it seemed to me all during that time that the sight would fail and I would be left by myself. I felt "sure, true hope" in the endless love by which I saw I would be kept by his mercy and brought to his bliss. Rejoicing in his sight with this sure, true hope of his merciful preservation gave me feeling and comfort so that the mourning and dread were not very painful.

Yet in all this I saw in the showings of God that this kind of sight of him cannot be a continuing one in this life, both for his own glory and for an increase of our endless joy. That is why the sight of him often fails us. Immediately, we fall into our selves, and we find absolutely no feeling of anything except the contrariness that is in our selves and that which comes from the root of man's first sin, with all that follows of our own contrivance. In this we labor bitterly and are tempted with feelings of sins and pains in the many different ways, spiritual and bodily, that are known to us in this life.

## Chapter 48

*Of mercy and grace and their properties; and how we shall
rejoice that we ever suffered woe patiently.*

But our good Lord the Holy Spirit, who is endless life
dwelling in our soul, keeps us most securely, works a peace
in the soul, brings it to ease by grace, brings it into agreement
with God, and makes it obedient. And this is the mercy, and
the way that our Lord continually leads us in, as long as we
are here in this life, which is changeable.

For I saw no wrath, except on man's part, and that he for
gives in us. For wrath is nothing else but a perversity, and a
contrariness to peace and love. It comes either from the
failing of power, or the failing of wisdom, or the failing of
goodness. These failures are not in God, but are failings on
our part, for by sin and wretchedness we have in ourselves a
wretched and continuing contrariness to peace and love.

He showed this many times in his lovely expression of com
passion and pity. For the ground of mercy is love, and the
working of mercy is our preservation in love. This was
showed in such a way that I could only conceive the property
of mercy as if it were only to be found in love, that is to say
as I saw it.

Mercy is a sweet, gracious working of love, mingled with
abundant pity. For mercy works by preserving us, and mercy
works by turning all things to good for us. Mercy allows us,
for love, to fail up to a certain point, and insofar as we fail, so
far we fall, and insofar as we fall, so far we die, for we must
and ought to die insofar as we fail in the sight and feeling of
God, who is our life.

Our failing is full of dread, our falling is full of shame,
and our dying is full of sorrow. But still, in all this, the sweet
eye of pity and love never departs from us, and the working
of mercy does not cease.

For I saw the property of mercy and the property of grace, which have two ways of working in a single love. Mercy is a property full of pity, which belongs to the motherhood in tender love. Grace is a glorious property, which belongs to the royal lordship in the same love. Mercy brings about preserving, suffering, bringing to life and helping, and all these come from the tenderness of love. Grace brings about raising and rewarding, endlessly surpassing what our loving and our bitter labor deserve, as it spreads abroad and shows the noble, abundant largess of God's royal lordship in his marvelous courtesy. This comes from the abundance of love.

Grace transforms our failings full of dread into abundant, endless comfort; grace transforms our failings full of shame into a noble, glorious rising; grace transforms our dying full of sorrow into holy, blissful life. For I saw with complete certainty that just as our contrariness here on earth brings us pain, shame and sorrow, so grace brings us surpassing comfort, glory and bliss in heaven, to the extent that when we come up and receive the sweet reward which grace has wrought for us, then we shall thank and bless our Lord, endlessly rejoicing that we ever suffered woe. And that shall be a property of blessed love that we shall know in God, which we might never have known without first experiencing woe.

And when I saw all this, I ought and had to grant that the mercy of God and his forgiveness exist to slacken and shrink our wrath.

## Chapter 49

*Our life is grounded in love, without which we perish; but still God is never angry, but in our wrath and sin he mercifully preserves us and makes a treaty of peace with us, rewarding our tribulations.*

It was a great wonder to the soul, continuously shown in everything and watched with great diligence, that our Lord God in himself cannot forgive, because he cannot be angry—

it is impossible. For it was shown that our life is entirely
grounded and rooted in love and without love we cannot live
And therefore to the soul, which because of his special grace
sees this much of the lofty, marvelous goodness of God and
sees that we are endlessly made one with him in love, that
God should be angry is the most impossible thing that could
be, for wrath and friendship are two contraries. He who
shrinks and destroys our wrath and makes us meek and mild
we ought and have to believe is ever, in the same love, meek
and mild, which is contrary to wrath. For I saw most certainly that where our Lord appears, peace is accepted and
wrath has no place.

I saw no kind of wrath in God, neither for the short term
nor for the long, for truly, as I saw it, if God could be angry
even a touch, we should never have life, nor place, nor being.
As true as it is that we have our being from the endless
power of God, from his endless wisdom and from his endless
goodness, it is just as true that we have our preservation from
the endless power of God, from his endless wisdom and from
his endless goodness.

Though we feel in ourselves wrath, wretched debates and
strifes, we are mercifully in all ways fully enclosed in the
mildness of God, in his meekness, in his benignity and in his
obedience. I saw most certainly that all our endless friendship, our place, our life and our being is in God, for the same
endless goodness that preserves us when we sin so that we do
not perish, continually makes treaties of peace in us against
our wrath and our contrary falling, and makes us see our
need to seek God strenuously, with true dread, that we may
have forgiveness with a grace-filled desire for our salvation.

We may not be blissfully saved until we are truly in peace
and love, for that is our salvation. And though we, by the
wrath and contrariness in us, are now in such tribulation,
unease and woe as falls to our blindness and frailty, yet we
are securely safe by God's merciful preservation so that we do
not perish. But we are not blissfully safe in our possession of
endless joy until we are entirely in peace and love, that is to
say, completely pleased with God, with all his works and
with all his judgments, and loving and peaceable with our

selves, with our fellow Christians and with everything God loves as love delights in it. God's goodness accomplishes this in us.

Thus I saw that God is our true peace and he is our reliable preserver when we are ourselves unpeaceful. He continually works to bring us into endless peace. And thus, when we, by the working of mercy and grace, are made meek and mild, we are completely safe. The soul is made suddenly one with God when it is truly at peace in itself, for in him no wrath is found.

And thus I saw how we are entirely in peace and in love. We find no contrariness and no kind of permission for the contrariness that is now in us to act. Our Lord God, of his goodness, makes this most profitable for us, for that contrariness is the cause of our tribulations and all our woe, and our Lord Jesus takes them and sends them up to heaven. There they are made sweeter and more delectable than the heart can imagine or the tongue can tell. When we come to that place, we shall find them ready, all turned into fairness itself and endless honors. Thus, God is our steadfast ground, and he shall be our complete bliss and make us unchangeable, as he is, when we are there.

## Chapter 50

*How the chosen soul was never dead in the sight of God; of a doubt upon the same; and three things emboldened her to ask of God the understanding of it.*

And in this life mercy and forgiveness are our way, and they lead us evermore to grace. And going by the tempests and sorrows we, for our part, fall into, we are often dead, as man judges things on earth. But in the sight of God the soul that shall be saved was never dead and never shall be.

But still I wondered here and marveled with all the diligence of my soul, thinking thus, "Good Lord, I see you, who

are truth itself, and I know in truth that we sin grievously all
the time and are worthy of much blame. I may neither
depart from the knowing of this truth nor see your showing
us no kind of blame. How can this be?"

For I knew by the common teaching of holy Church and
by my own feeling, that the blame for our sins hangs continuously upon us from the first man up to the time that we
come up to heaven. In this was my marveling, that I saw our
Lord God showing us no more blame than if we were as pure
and holy as angels are in heaven.

Between these two contraries my reason was greatly bela-
bored by my blindness. I could have no rest, for fear his
blessed presence should pass from my sight and I should be
left ignorant of how he looks at us in our sin. For either I
ought and had to see in God that sin was entirely done away
with, or else I had and ought to see in God how he sees it, by
which I could truly know how I ought properly to see sin and
the way in which we are blamed.

My longing endured as I continued to gaze at him, and yet
I could have no patience, because of my great anxiety, fear
and perplexity. I was thinking, "If I take it that we are no
sinners and are not blameworthy, it seems that I would err
and fail to know this truth. And if it is true that we are sinners and blameworthy, good Lord, how can it, then, be that
I cannot see this truth? In it are my God and my maker, in
whom I desire to see all truth.

"Three points make me bold enough to ask this. The first
is because it is so small a thing, for if it were a lofty thing, I
should be afraid to ask. The second is that it is so common,
for if it were special and secret, I should also be afraid. The
third is that it is necessary for me to understand it, it seems
to me, in order that, if I should continue to live here, I may
discern good and evil. Then, by reason and grace, I may better separate them from one another, and love goodness and
hate evil, as holy Church teaches."

I cried inwardly with all my might, seeking for help from
God, saying, "Ah, Lord Jesus, King of bliss, how shall I be
eased? Who will teach me and tell me what I need to comprehend if I cannot see it in you at this time?"

## Chapter 51

*The answer to the previous doubt by a marvelous example of a lord and a servant; God will be waited for, because it was nearly twenty years later before she understood this example completely; and how it is to be understood that Christ sits at the right hand of the father.*

And then our courteous Lord answered by showing most sweetly a wonderful example of a lord who had a servant, and gave insight to my understanding about both. The sight was showed double in the lord and double in the servant. The first part was showed spiritually with a bodily image. The second part was showed more spiritually, without a bodily image.

In the first part I saw as follows. There were two bodily images of persons, that is to say a lord and a servant, and with these images God gave me spiritual understanding. The lord sits solemnly, in rest and in peace. The servant stands before his lord reverently, ready to do his lord's will.

The lord looks most lovingly, sweetly and meekly upon his servant. He sends him into a certain place to do his will. The servant not only goes; for love, he jumps up suddenly and runs in great haste to do his lord's will. And immediately he falls into a ravine and suffers very great injury. Then he groans and moans, he wallows and writhes, but he cannot rise or help himself in any kind of way.

And in all this the greatest danger was the failing of his comfort, for he could not turn his face to look up to his loving lord, who was very near him and in whom is complete comfort. But like a man who is very feeble and unwise, he paid attention, for the moment, to his feeling and stayed in misery.

In this woe he suffered seven great pains. The first was the sore bruising he took in his fall, which was great and feelable pain to him. The second was the heaviness of the body. The third was the feebleness that followed these two. The fourth was that he was blinded in his reason and stunned in his mind, to the extent that he had almost forgotten his own love. The fifth was that he could not rise. The sixth pain was the most surprising to me, and that was that he lay alone. I looked all around and stared far and near, high and low, and I saw no help for him. The seventh pain was that the place in which he lay was long, hard and grievous.

I marveled how this servant could suffer all this woe there so meekly. And I gazed with attention to learn if I could perceive any fault in him, or if the lord should assign him any kind of blame. And in truth, none was seen, for the only cause of his falling was his good will and his great desire, and he was zealous, and as willing, and as good inwardly as when he had stood before his lord ready to do his will.

His loving lord looks at him continually in just this way, and has a twofold expression. The first part was outward. It was most meek and mild, with great compassion and pity. The second part was inward. It was more spiritual. This was showed by my spirit's being led into the lord; in the showing I saw him rejoice greatly, because of the glorious and noble raising he wills and shall bring to his servant by his abundant grace. (All this refers to the second part of the showing.)

Now my understanding was led back to the first part of the showing, while keeping both in mind. Then this courteous lord indicated what he meant us to understand: "Look! Look at my beloved servant! See what harm and unease he has suffered in my service, for my love. Yes, and on account of his good will is it not reasonable that I should reward him for his fright and his dread, his hurt and his maiming, and all his woe? Not only this, but does it not fall to me to give him a gift that will be better for him and more to his honor than his own wholeness would have been? Or else it seems to me I have done him no favor."

With this an inward spiritual showing of what the Lord meant descended into my soul. In it I saw that it ought and had to be so, given his great goodness and his own glory, that his most valuable servant, whom he loved so much, should be in truth nobly and blissfully rewarded without end, beyond what he would have received if he had not fallen—so much so that his falling and all the woe that he suffered from it should be turned into lofty, surpassing glory and endless bliss.

And at this point the showing of the example vanished and our good Lord led forth my understanding in vision and in showing of the revelation to the end. But notwithstanding all this leading forth, my wondering at the example never left me, for it seemed to me that it had been given to me as an answer to my desire. And still I could not grasp the complete understanding of it for my ease at that time.

For in the servant, who stood for Adam, as I shall explain, I saw many different properties that could in no way be applied to Adam alone. And thus at that time I was solidly fixed in unknowing, for the full understanding of this marvelous example was not given me at that time.

In this mighty example three properties of the revelation are still greatly hidden. Notwithstanding this, I saw and understood that every showing is full of secret things.

For this reason I now ought and have to tell three properties of the example about which I have been somewhat eased. The first is what I understood of the beginning of the teaching at the time I received it. The second is the inward teaching that I have since understood about it. The third is the entire revelation from the beginning to the end, that is to say of this book. This our Lord God, of his goodness, frequently brings freely to the sight of my understanding. These three are so united, as I understand it, that I cannot and may not separate them.

And from these three as one, I have received teaching such that I ought to believe and trust in our Lord God, that by the same goodness and for the same end that he showed it, he shall declare it to us when it is his will. For, twenty years less three months after the time of the showing, I received inward teaching that I shall tell you: "It is your place to pay attention to all the properties and conditions that were showed in the example, though you may think them misty and indifferent in your sight."

I assented deliberately, with great desire, feeling inwardly with attention all the points and properties that were showed at the same time, as far as my wit and understanding would serve.

Beginning with my seeing the lord and the servant, I noticed the way in which the lord sat and the place he sat on, the color of his clothing and the way it was shaped, his outward expression and his inward nobility and goodness. I noticed the way the servant stood, the kind, color and shape of his clothing, his outward behavior and his inward goodness, and his willingness.

The lord, who sat solemnly in rest and in peace, I understood to be God. The servant who stood before the lord I understood to represent Adam. That is to say, one man and his falling were shown at that time to make us understand by this how God views all of mankind and its falling. For in the sight of God all of mankind is one man, and one man is all of mankind.

This man was hurt in his power and made very feeble, and he was stunned in his understanding, for he was turned away from the seeing of his lord, but his will was kept whole in God's sight. For I saw our Lord commend and approve his will, though he himself was prevented and blinded from knowing this will.

This is a great sorrow and a grievous unease to him, for he neither clearly sees his loving lord, who is completely meek and mild toward him, nor does he see truly what he himself is in the sight of his loving lord. And well I knew that when these two things are wisely and truly seen we shall have great rest and peace, here in part, and the fulness of bliss in heaven, by his abundant grace.

This was a beginning of the teaching that I saw at the time. By it I could come to know in what manner he sees us in our sin. And then I saw that only pain blames and punishes; our courteous Lord comforts and assists. He always wears a cheerful expression for the soul, loving and longing to bring us to bliss.

The place that our Lord sat upon was simply on the earth —barren and a desert. He sat alone in the wilderness. His clothing was ample and full and most beautiful, as becomes a lord. The color of his clothing was as blue as azure, most sober and fair.

His expression was merciful. The color of his face was fair —brownish white—with most beautiful features. His eyes were black, most fair and lovely, appearing full of lovely pity, and having within them a look, lofty, long and broad, all filled with the endless heavens. The lovely look with which he gazed continually upon his servant, specifically in his falling, it seemed to me, would melt our hearts for love and break them in two for joy. This fair gaze appeared to be a beautiful mixture that was marvelous to behold. One part of it was compassion and pity; the other part was joy and bliss. The joy and bliss surpassed the compassion and pity as far as heaven is above earth. The pity was earthly, the bliss heavenly.

The compassion and pity of the Father was for the fall of Adam, who is his most loved creature. The joy and bliss were for his most precious Son, who is equal to the Father. The merciful sight of his loving expression completely filled the whole earth and descended with Adam down into hell. With its continuing pity Adam was kept from endless death. And this mercy and pity dwells with mankind until we come up into heaven.

But man is blinded in this life, and therefore we cannot see our Father, God, as he is. When he of his goodness wills to show himself to man, he shows himself familiarly, as man. Notwithstanding that, I saw that in truth we ought to know and believe that the Father is not man.

But his sitting on the earth, barren and a desert, stands for the fact that he has made man's soul to be his own city and his dwelling place, which, of all his works, pleases him most. And when man fell into sorrow and pain, he was not lovely enough to serve in that office. Therefore our kind Father would have no other place prepared for himself, but seated himself upon the earth waiting for mankind, which is mingled with earth, until by his grace his most precious Son had again brought this city into noble fairness by his hard, bitter labor.

The blueness of the clothing is a symbol of his stead-

fastness. The brownness of his fair face with the lovely blackness of the eyes was most suitable to show his holy seriousness. The fullness of his clothing, which was flaming fair
around him, stands for the fact that he has enclosed in himself the entire heavens and all of endless joy and bliss.

And this was showed to me in a touch, where I saw that
my understanding was led into the Lord. In this touch I saw
him greatly rejoice on account of the glorious restoration that
he wills and to which he shall bring his servant by his abundant grace.

And still I wondered, looking at the lord and the servant I
mentioned before. I saw the lord sit solemnly and the servant
stand reverently before his lord. In this servant there is a double understanding—one from without, the second from
within.

Outwardly he was clad as simply as a laborer who was
ready for hard labor. He stood very near the lord, not directly
in front of him but partly to one side, the left side. His clothing was a single white tunic, old and completely soiled, dyed
with the sweat of his body. It fit him tightly, was short—a
hand's breadth below the knee—and seemed threadbare, as if
it would soon be worn out and ready to be torn into rags.

I wondered greatly at this, thinking, "Now, this is unbe-
coming clothing for a servant who is so greatly loved to stand
in before so glorious a lord."

Inwardly, there was shown within him a foundation of
love which he had for the lord, that was equal to the love the
lord had for him. The wisdom of the servant saw inwardly
that there was one thing to do that would be an honor to the
lord. And the servant, for love, having no regard for himself,
or for anything that could happen to him, when his lord sent
him, hastily jumped up and ran to do the thing that was his
lord's will and for his honor.

It seemed from the servant's outer clothing that he had
been a laborer continuously and had worked very hard for a
long time. But by the inward sight I had, both of the lord
and of the servant, it seemed that he was made anew—that is
to say, newly beginning to labor hard, as a servant who had
never been sent out before.

There was a treasure in the earth which the lord loved. I marveled and thought what it might be. And I was answered in my understanding, "It is a meal which is delightful and pleasing to the lord." For I saw the lord sit as a man, and I saw neither meat nor drink with which to serve him. This was one marvel. A second marvel was that this solemn lord had no servant but this one, and he sent him out.

I looked at this, thinking, "What kind of labor can it be that this servant does?" And then I understood that he was doing the greatest labor and the hardest work; that is, he was a gardener, digging and making ditches, sweating and turning the earth over, seeking the depths and watering the plants at the right time.

He would continue his hard labor in this way, making sweet floods run and a noble abundance of fruit to spring forth. This he would bring before the lord and serve him with it, to the lord's delight. He would never return again until he had prepared this meal, making it completely ready, in the way he knew would please the lord. And then he would take this meal with the drink and carry it most respectfully before the lord. And all this time the lord would sit right in the same place, awaiting the servant whom he had sent out.

And yet I wondered where the servant came from, for I saw in the lord that he had within himself endless life and all kinds of goodness, except for the treasure that was in the earth, and that was grounded within the lord in the marvelous depth of endless love. But all this was not entirely a glory for him until this servant had thus nobly prepared it and brought it before him, in his own person. And without the lord, there was absolutely nothing but wilderness.

I didn't entirely understand what this example meant. That is why I wondered where the servant came from.

In the servant is comprehended the second person of the blessed Trinity, and Adam—that is to say all men. Therefore, when I say "the Son" I mean the godhead which is equal to the Father, and when I say "the servant" I mean Christ's manhood, which is the rightful Adam.

By the nearness of the servant, the Son is to be understood, and by his standing at the lord's left side Adam is to be understood. The lord is God the Father; the servant is this same Jesus Christ; the Holy Spirit is the equal love that is in both of them.

When Adam fell, God's Son fell, because of the rightful union that was made in heaven. God's Son could not be separated from Adam, for by "Adam" I understand all men. Adam fell from life to death into the abyss of this wretched world, and after that into hell. God's Son fell with Adam into the abyss of the womb of the maiden who was the fairest daughter of Adam, in order to excuse Adam from blame in heaven and on earth, and powerfully he fetched Adam out of hell.

By the wisdom and the goodness that are in the servant is to be understood God's Son. By his poor clothing as a laborer standing near the lord's left side is to be understood the manhood of Adam with all the evil consequences and feebleness that follow. For in all this our good Lord showed his own Son and Adam as a single man. The virtue and the goodness that we have is from Jesus Christ; the feebleness and blindness that we have is from Adam. Both of them were shown in the servant.

Thus has our good Lord taken upon himself all our blame. And therefore our Father can and will assign no more blame to us than to his own most precious Son, Jesus Christ. He was the servant before his coming to earth by standing ready before the Father in his purpose, until the time the Father would send him to do the glorious deed by which mankind was brought again to heaven. That is to say, notwithstanding the fact that he is God, equal with the Father as concerns the godhead, he would be as man in his foreseeing purpose, to save man by fulfilling the will of his Father. Thus he stood before his Father as a servant, deliberately taking upon himself all that was charged against us.

And then he jumped up, completely ready at the Father's will. Immediately, he fell very low, into the maiden's womb, having no regard for himself, nor for his hard pains.

The white tunic is his flesh. Its singleness symbolizes the fact that there was absolutely nothing between the godhead and the manhood. The tightness of the tunic is poverty. The age of the tunic comes from Adam's wearing of it. The soiling is from the sweat of Adam's bitter labor. The shortness shows that the servant labors.

And thus I saw the Son, as he intended it, standing and saying, "Look, my dear Father! I stand before you in Adam's tunic, all ready to jump and run. I would be on earth for your glory when it is your will to send me. How long shall I desire it?"

The Son knew most truly when it was the Father's will and how long he would desire, that is to say, in his godhead, for he is the wisdom of the Father. Therefore this meaning was shown to be understood of the manhood of Christ. All of mankind that shall be saved by the sweet Incarnation and the blissful passion of Christ is the manhood of Christ, for he is the head and we are his members. To these members the time when passing woe and sorrow shall have an end and everlasting joy and bliss shall be fulfilled is unknown. All the company of heaven longs and desires to see that day and time.

For all who are under heaven who shall come to it, their way is by longing and desiring. This desiring and longing were showed in the servant standing before the lord, or else by the Son standing before the Father in Adam's tunic. The longing and desire of all of mankind that shall be saved appeared in Jesus. For Jesus is all that shall be saved. And all that are saved are Jesus, as is all of the charity of God, with the obedience, meekness, patience and the virtues that belong to us.

Also in this marvelous example I have teaching within, like the beginning of an ABC, by which I may have some understanding of our Lord's meaning. For the secrets of the revelation are hidden in it, notwithstanding that all the showings are full of secret things.

The sitting of the Father symbolizes his godhead, that is to say in showing rest and peace, for in the godhead there can be no hard labor. That he shows himself as a lord symbolizes our manhood. The standing of the servant symbolizes bitter labor. His standing on lord's left side symbolizes that he was not fully worthy to stand directly before the lord. His jumping up was symbolic of the godhead, and the running symbolized the manhood, because the godhead jumped up from the Father into the maiden's womb, falling into his taking of our nature. In this falling he received a great wound. The wound that he took was our flesh. In it he immediately felt mortal pains.

The fact that he stood, full of dread, before the lord, and not directly in front of him, means that his clothing was not decent enough for him to stand directly in front of the lord, that this could not, and should not, be his office while he was a laborer, and also that he might not sit with the lord in rest and peace until he had won his peace rightfully with his hard, bitter labor. The fact that he stood at the left side means that the Father deliberately left his own Son in his manhood to suffer all man's pain without sparing him.

By the fact that his tunic was at the point of being torn to rags is to be understood the rods, the blows and scourges, the thorns and the nails, the drawing and dragging of his tender flesh, the tearing of it, as I saw in some part the flesh torn from the skull, its falling in pieces until the bleeding stopped, when it began to dry and cleave to the bone again.

And by the wallowing and writhing, groaning and mourning, is to be understood that he could never rise All-powerful from the time he had fallen into the maiden's womb until his body was slain and dead and he yielded his soul into the Father's hand with all mankind for whom he was sent. At this point he first began to show his power, for then he went into hell. When he was there, he raised up out of the deepest depths the great root that was rightfully knitted to him in high heaven.

The body lay in the grave until Easter morning. And from that time he never again lay down dead, for then the wallowing and writhing, the groaning and moaning were rightfully ended. Our foul, mortal flesh, which God's Son took upon himself—Adam's old tunic, tight, bare and short—was then, by our savior, made fair, new, white and bright, of endless cleanness, ample and full, fair and richer than was the clothing I saw on the Father. For the Father's clothing is bliss, and Christ's clothing is now a fair and becoming mixture that is so marvelous that I cannot describe it, for it is all of glory itself.

Now the lord does not sit on earth in the wilderness, but he sits on his rich and noble chair, which he made in heaven to be most to his liking. Now the Son does not stand before the Father as the servant stands before the lord, dreadfully clothed and partly naked, but he stands before the Father directly in front of him, richly clothed in blissful amplitude, with a crown of precious richness on his head. For it was showed that we are his crown, and this crown is the Father's joy, the Son's glory, the Holy Spirit's delight, and endless marvelous bliss to all who are in heaven.

Now the Son does not stand before the Father on the left side like a laborer, but he sits at the Father's right hand in endless rest and peace. But this does not mean that the Son sits at the Father's right hand beside him, as one man sits next to another in this life, for there is no such sitting in the Trinity, as I saw it. He sits at his Father's right hand with "right hand" meaning in the highest nobility of the Father's joy.

Now is the spouse, God's Son, in peace with his beloved wife, who is the fair maiden of endless joy. Now the Son, true God and true man, sits in his city in the rest and peace his Father has prepared for him in his endless purpose. And so sits the Father in the Son, and the Holy Spirit in the Father and the Son.

## Chapter 52

*God rejoices that he is our father, brother and spouse; how the chosen have here a mixture of well-being and woe, but God is with us in three ways; how we may eschew sin but never perfectly, as in heaven.*

And thus I saw that God rejoices that he is our Father; God rejoices that he is our mother; God rejoices that he is our true Spouse and that our soul is his beloved wife. Christ rejoices that he is our brother, and Jesus rejoices that he is our savior. These are the five noble joys, as I understood things, in which he wills that we rejoice, praising him, thanking him, loving him and endlessly blessing him.

All of us who shall be saved have within us during our lifetime a marvelous mixture of both well-being and woe. We have within ourselves our risen Lord Jesus Christ, and we have within us the wretchedness and evil consequences of Adam's falling. Dying in Christ, we are everlastingly preserved, and by the touching of his grace, we are raised to a real trust in salvation.

By Adam's falling we are so broken in our feelings in different ways (by sin and by various pains in which we are made dark and so blind), that only with difficulty can we take any comfort. But in our intentions we wait for God and faithfully trust we shall have mercy and grace—and this is his own working in us. By his goodness it opens the eye of our understanding, in which we have sight, sometimes more, sometimes less, as God gives us the ability to accept it. Now we are raised to the one and now we are allowed to fall into the other. And thus the mixture in us is so puzzling that it is with difficulty that we know of ourselves or of our fellow Christians how we stand, with the strangeness of these different feelings.

But that same holy assent by which we submit to God when we feel him in truth, choosing to be with him with all our heart, with all our soul and with all our power, makes us then hate and despise our evil stirrings and all that might be an occasion of sin, spiritual or bodily.

And yet, nevertheless, when this sweetness is hidden we fall again into blindness and so into woe and into various kinds of tribulations. But then this is our comfort, that we know in our faith that, by the virtue of Christ, who is our preserver, we never assent to these feelings, but we grudge assent to them and endure in pain and woe, praying, until that time when he shows himself to us again.

And thus we live in this mixture of feelings all the days of

our life, but he wills that we trust that he is everlastingly
with us, and that in three ways: He is with us in heaven as
true man, and in his own person he draws us up. This was
showed in his spiritual thirst. He is with us on earth, leading us. This was showed in the third revelation, where I saw
God in a point. And he is with us in our soul, endlessly
dwelling there, ruling and guiding us. That was showed in
the sixteenth revelation, as I shall tell you.

Thus, in the servant was showed the blindness and evil
consequences of Adam's falling and the wisdom and the
goodness of God's son. In the lord was showed God's compassion and pity at Adam's woe and the high nobility and
endless glory that mankind has come to by virtue of the passion and the death of his most precious son. Therefore God
rejoices greatly in Adam's falling, on account of the noble
raising and the fulness of bliss that mankind has come to,
surpassing what we would have had if he had not fallen. And
to see this surpassing nobility, my understanding was led thus
into God at the same time that I saw the servant fall.

And thus we have matter for mourning, for our sin is the
cause of Christ's pains, and we have everlasting matter for
joy, for endless love made him suffer. Therefore the creature
that sees and feels the working of love by grace hates nothing
but sin, for of all things, as I see it, love and hate are the
stubbornest and most unmeasurable contraries.

Notwithstanding all this, I saw and understood as our Lord
intended, that we cannot, in this life, keep ourselves from
sin, in complete purity, the way we will be in heaven. But we
may well, by grace, keep ourselves from the sins that would
lead us to endless pain, as holy Church teaches us, and
reasonably avoid venial sins, to the extent of our power. If at
any time by our blindness and wretchedness we should fall,
we can readily rise, knowing the sweet touching of grace,
amend our lives with determination according to the gravity
of the sin and the teaching of holy Church, and go forth
with God in love. We shall neither, on the one hand, fall too
low in spirit, inclining to despair, nor on the other hand be
overreckless, as if we didn't care, but merely recognize our

feebleness, understanding that we may not stand alone for the twinkling of an eye except with grace preserving us, and clinging reverently to God, trusting only in him. This is how God sees things, though men see things otherwise. It is man's place meekly to accuse himself; it belongs to the goodness proper to our Lord God courteously to excuse him.

There are two things that were shown in the double expression with which the lord beheld the falling of his beloved servant. The first expression appeared outwardly and was most meek and mild, with great compassion and pity. The second expression was an inward one, of endless love. Our good Lord wills that we accuse ourselves in just this way, deliberately and truly seeing and knowing our failures and all the harms that come from them, and seeing and recognizing that we can never make up for them. Together with this, he wills that we deliberately and truly see and know the everlasting love he has for us, and his abundant mercy. To see and know both together in this way by grace is the meek self-accusation that our good Lord asks of us. He himself brings it about where it occurs.

This is the lower part of man's life, and it was showed in the outward expression. In this showing I saw two parts. The one is the pitiable falling of man. The second is the glorious satisfaction that our Lord has made for man.

The other expression was showed inwardly, and that was more noble, and all one. For this life and the virtue that we have in the lower part is from the higher part and comes down to us by grace from the natural love of the self. Between the higher and lower parts nothing can exist, for it is all the same love, which has now a double working in us in blessed love. For in the lower part are pains and passions, compassions and pities, mercies and forgiveness, and such other things as are profitable for us. But in the higher part are none of these; all is a single, noble love and marvelous joy. In this marvelous joy all pains are wholly destroyed and nobly repaid.

In this our good Lord showed not only God's excusing of us but also the nobility, full of honor, to which he shall bring us, turning all our blame into endless glory.

## Chapter 53

*The kindness of God assigns no blame to his chosen ones, for in them is a goodly will that never consents to sin; for it becomes the compassion of God to be so knitted to them that a substance in them is kept which can never be separated from him.*

And I saw that he wills that we understand that he judges the fall of no creature that will be saved any more harshly than he judged the fall of Adam, who, as we know, was endlessly loved and securely preserved in all his time of need and is now blissfully restored in lofty, surpassing joys. For our Lord God is so good, so gentle and so courteous that he can never assign blame to those by whom he shall forever be blessed and praised.

In what I have just said, my desire was answered, in part, and my great difficulty was somewhat eased by a lovely, gracious showing from our Lord God. In this showing I saw and understood most surely that in each soul that shall be saved, there is a goodly will that has never assented to sin and never shall do so. This will is so good that it can never will evil, but forever continually wills good and performs it in the sight of God. Therefore our Lord wills that we know this both in the faith and in our belief, and that we realize, specifically and in truth, that we have all of this blessed will, whole and safe, in our Lord Jesus Christ. This is so because each nature with which heaven shall be made completely full must and ought, on account of God's rightfulness, be so knitted to and made one with him that in each nature there is preserved a substance that never can nor will be parted from him. This is accomplished through his own good will in his endless foreseeing purpose, which I have spoken of before.

Notwithstanding this rightful knitting and this endless joining together, still the redemption and buying back of mankind is necessary and profitable in every way as it has been accomplished, for the same purpose and to the same end that holy Church teaches us in our faith.

I saw that God never started loving mankind. For the condition man shall have in endless bliss, completely filling up the joy of God as far as his works are concerned, shall be exactly the same as that he has had in the foresight of God—known and loved from without beginning in God's rightful intent. By the endless intent and assent of the complete accord of the whole Trinity, Jesus, its mid-person, willed to be the ground and the head of this fair nature. Out of him we all come; in him we are all enclosed; into him we shall all go, finding in him our complete heaven in everlasting joy by the foreseeing purpose of the whole blessed Trinity from eternity.

Before he made us he loved us, and when we were made we loved him. This love is made of the natural substantial goodness of the Holy Spirit. It is powerful by reason of the might of the Father, and wise in mind of the wisdom of the Son. And thus is man's soul made by God and at the same point knitted to God.

Thus I understood that man's soul is made from nothing. That is to say, it is made, but not out of anything that has been made in this fashion: when God went to make man's body, he took the slime of the earth, which is mingled matter, gathered from all bodily things, and he made man's body from it. But for the making of man's soul, God took absolutely nothing. He simply made it. And thus is human nature rightfully made one with its maker, who is substantial, uncreated nature—that is, God. And that is the reason why there can and will be absolutely nothing between God and man's soul.

In this endless love, man's soul is kept whole, as the entire matter of this revelation means and shows. In this same endless love we are led and preserved by God and we shall never be lost. For he wills that we know that our soul is alive, and its life, by his goodness and his grace, shall last in heaven without end, loving him, thanking him and praising him. And just exactly as we shall live without end in heaven, so we have been treasured in God—hidden, known and loved from eternity.

Therefore he wills that we realize that the noblest thing that he ever made is mankind, and that the fullest substance and the highest virtue he ever made is the blessed soul of Christ. Furthermore, he wills that we realize that his most valuable soul was preciously knitted to him in its making. The knot is so subtle and so powerful that it is made one with God. In this joining it is made endlessly holy. Furthermore, he wills that we realize that all the souls which shall be saved in heaven without end are knitted in this knot, are made one in this joining, and are made holy in this holiness.

## Chapter 54

*We ought to rejoice that God dwells in our soul and our soul in God, so that between God and our soul there is nothing, but, as it were, all is God; and how faith is the ground of all virtue in our soul by the Holy Spirit.*

And because of the great, endless love that God has for all mankind, he makes no distinction in love between the blessed soul of Christ and the least of the souls that will be saved. It is very easy to believe and trust that the dwelling of the blessed soul of Christ is completely on high, in the glorious godhead. And in truth, as I understood what our Lord meant, where the blessed soul of Christ is, there is the substance of all the souls that will be saved by Christ. We ought to rejoice greatly that God dwells in our soul, and much more greatly that our soul dwells in God. Our soul is made to be God's dwelling place, and the dwelling place of our soul is God, who is uncreated. It is a lofty understanding inwardly to see and to know that God, who is our maker, dwells in our soul, and it is a still loftier and greater understanding inwardly to see and to know that our soul, which is created, dwells in God's substance. From this substance we are what we are, by God.

I saw no difference between God and our substance, but saw it as if it were all God. And yet my understanding accepted the fact that our substance is in God; that is to say that God is God and our substance is a creature in God. For the almighty truth of the Trinity is our Father, for he made us and preserves us in himself; the deep wisdom of the Trinity is our mother, in whom we are enclosed; the lofty goodness of the Trinity is our Lord, and in him we are enclosed and he in us.

We are enclosed in the Father, we are enclosed in the Son, and we are enclosed in the Holy Spirit. The Father is enclosed in us—All-power, All-wisdom, and All-goodness: one God, one Lord.

Our faith is a virtue that comes from our natural substance into our sensual soul by the action of the Holy Spirit, through whom all our virtues come to us. Without the virtue of faith, no man can receive virtues, because faith is nothing other than a proper understanding of our being, with true belief and certain trust, that we are in God and he is in us, though we do not see it. This virtue, with all the others that God has ordained for us included with it, works great things in us. For Christ's merciful working is within us, and we are graciously being brought into agreement with him through the gifts and the virtues of the Holy Spirit. This working makes us Christ's children and Christian in our loving and living.

## Chapter 55

*Christ is our way, leading and presenting us to the Father; as soon as the soul is infused into the body, mercy and grace work; and how the Second Person took our sensuality to deliver us from double death.*

And thus Christ is our way, securely leading us in his laws, and Christ in his body powerfully bears us up into heaven. For I saw that Christ, having within himself all of us who shall be saved by him, gloriously presents his Father in heaven with us. This present his Father receives most thankfully, and courteously gives it to his Son, Jesus Christ. And this gift and working is joy to the Father, bliss to the Son and delight to the Holy Spirit.

Of all the things that are proper for us to do, it is the greatest delight to our Lord that we rejoice in this joy which is in the blessed Trinity on account of our salvation. This was seen in the ninth showing, which speaks at greater length of this matter. And notwithstanding all our feelings of woe or well-being, God wills that we understand and believe that we exist more truly in heaven than on earth.

Our faith comes from the natural love of our soul, from the clear light of our reason, and from the steadfast mind that we have from God in our first creation. At the very time our soul is breathed into our body, when we are made sensual, immediately mercy and grace begin to work, curing and preserving us by pity and love. In this working, the Holy Spirit forms in our faith the hope that we shall again come up above to our substance, into the virtue of Christ, increased and fulfilled through the Holy Spirit.

Thus I understood that man's sensuality is grounded in nature, in mercy and in grace. This grounding enables us to receive gifts that lead us to endless life. For I saw most surely that our substance is in God. I also saw that God is in our sensuality, for in the same respect that our soul is made sensual, the city of God is ordained for it from eternity. Into this city he comes, and he shall never move away from it, for God is never out of the soul, in which he shall dwell blissfully without end. This will be explained in the sixteenth showing, which says that Jesus shall never move from the place he takes in our soul.

All the gifts that God can give to a creature, he has given to his Son, Jesus, for us. These gifts he, dwelling in us, has enclosed within himself, until the time that we are grown up and mature—our soul with our body and our body with our soul. Either of them can accept help from the other until we are brought to our full stature as nature works. And then, in the ground of nature with the working of mercy, the Holy Spirit graciously breathes into us gifts leading to endless life.

And thus was my understanding led by God to see in him and to recognize, to understand and to know that our soul, known and loved from without beginning, is a created trinity, similar to the uncreated blessed Trinity, and joined to the maker in its making as was said previously. This sight was most sweet and marvelous to behold, peaceful and restful, sure and delectable.

And because of the glorious union that was thus made by God between the soul and the body, it had and ought to be that mankind should be rescued from double death. This restoration could never be accomplished until the Second Person of the Trinity, to whom the highest part had been joined in the first creation, had taken on the lower part of mankind. These two parts, the higher and lower, were in Christ, who is only one Soul. The higher part was ever one in peace with God, in full joy and bliss. The lower part, which is sensuality, suffered for the salvation of mankind. These two parts were seen and felt in the eighth showing, in which my body was filled full of the feeling and the spirit of Christ's passion and his dying.

Furthermore, with this there was a subtle feeling and a secret inward sight of the higher part, and that was shown at the same time, when I might not, in spite of the friendly proposition of my reason, look up into heaven. And that was on account of that overwhelming seeing of the inward life. This inward life is that lofty substance, that precious soul which is endlessly rejoicing in the godhead.

## Chapter 56

*It is easier to know God than to know our own soul, for God is nearer to us than that; therefore, if we will have knowledge of our soul, we must seek in God; and he wills that we desire to have knowledge of nature, mercy and grace.*

And thus I saw most certainly that we come more readily and more easily to the knowing of God than to the knowing of our own soul. For our soul is so deeply grounded in God and so endlessly treasured that we cannot come to the knowing of it until we first have come to the knowing of God, who is the maker to whom it is joined.

But notwithstanding this, I saw that we have, from the fulness of our nature, the power to desire wisely and truly to know our own soul, by which we are taught to seek it where it is, and that it is in God. And thus, by the gracious leading of the Holy Spirit we shall know both God and our soul in one; whether we are stirred to know God or our soul, the stirring is both good and true.

God is nearer to us than our own soul, for he is the ground in whom our soul is rooted, and he is the medium that keeps the substance and the sensuality together for God so that they will never be separated. For our soul sits in God in true rest, and our soul stands in God in sure strength, and our soul is naturally rooted in God in endless love. And therefore, if we will to have the knowing of our soul, communing with it and conversing with it, we ought to seek it within our Lord God, in whom it is enclosed.

Of this enclosing I saw and understood more in the sixteenth showing, as I shall tell you. As far as our substance is concerned, it can rightly be called our soul. And as far as our sensuality is concerned, it, too, can rightly be called our soul —and that is because they are made one in God.

The glorious city in which our Lord Jesus sits is our sensuality, in which he is enclosed, and our natural substance is enclosed in Jesus, with the blessed soul of Christ sitting at rest in the godhead. And I saw most certainly that we ought and should live in longing and in penance until the time that we are led so deeply into God that we really and truly know our own soul. And I saw certainly that our good Lord himself leads us into this lofty deepness in the same love by which he made us and bought us, by mercy and grace, by virtue of his blessed passion.

And notwithstanding all this, we can never come to the full knowing of God until we first know clearly our own soul. For until the time that it is in its full powers, we cannot be entirely holy—and that will be when our sensuality, by virtue of Christ's passion, has been brought up into the substance, with all the profits from our tribulations that our Lord will cause us to receive by mercy and grace.

I had, in part, a touching, and it is grounded in nature. That is to say, our reason is grounded in God, who is substantial nature. From this substantial nature spring mercy and grace. They spread within us, accomplishing all things in fulfilling our joy. These are the groundings in which we have our being, our increase and our fulfillment. For in nature we have our life and our being, and in mercy and grace we have our increase and our fulfillment. These are three properties in a single goodness, and where one works, all work, in the things for which we now long.

God wills that we understand these things, ever desiring with all our heart and all our strength to have more and more knowledge of them until the time we shall be completely filled. For to know them fully and to see them clearly is nothing other than the endless joy and bliss that we shall have in heaven. This God wills, that we begin here in the knowing of his love. For by our reason alone we cannot profit, unless we have with it, in truth, equal spirit and love. Nor can we be saved only in the natural grounding we have in God, unless we have, from the same grounding, skill, mercy and grace. For from these three working all together, we receive all the good things that are ours, of which the first are the good things of nature. For in our first making, God gave us good things—as many, as full, and as great as we could receive in our spirit alone—but his foreseeing purpose in his endless wisdom willed that we have double the capacity.

## Chapter 57

*In our substance we are full, in our sensuality we fail; this God will restore by mercy and grace; how our nature, which is the highest part, is knitted to God in the making; Christ*

*Jesus is knitted to our nature in the lower part, in taking our flesh; of faith spring other virtues; and Mary is our mother.*

And as far as our substance is concerned, he made us so noble and so rich that we may evermore accomplish his will and his honor. Where I say "we" it means "men who will be saved." For in truth I saw that we are what he loves and we do what delights him continuously, without any holding back. And from this great richness and from this lofty nobility, virtues in their measure come into our soul at the time it is knitted to our body. In this knitting we are made sensual.

And thus in our substance we are full, and in our sensuality we fail. This failure God wills to restore and fulfill, by the working of mercy and grace plenteously flowing into us from his own natural goodness. Thus this natural goodness brings it about that mercy and grace work in us and the natural goodness that we have from him enables us to receive the working of mercy and grace.

I saw that our nature is whole in God. In it he causes diversities flowing out of him to work his will; he keeps nature whole, and he restores and fulfills mercy and grace. Of these none shall perish, for the higher part of our nature is knitted to God in the making and God is knitted to the lower part of our nature in taking flesh. And thus in Christ our two natures are joined. For the Trinity is included in Christ, in whom our higher part is grounded and rooted, and the Second Person of the Trinity has taken on our lower part, which nature was first prepared for him.

I saw most certainly that all the works that God has done or ever shall do were completely known to him and previously seen from all eternity. For love he made mankind, and for the same love he willed to become man himself.

The next good that we receive is our faith, in which our profiting begins. It comes from the noble richness of our natural substance into our sensual soul, and it is grounded in us and we in it, through the natural goodness of God, by the working of mercy and grace. From it come all the good things by which we are led and saved.

For the commandments of God come from it. In these we

ought to have two kinds of understanding. The first is that we ought to understand and know the things he commands in order to love them and keep them. The second is that we ought to know the things he forbids, in order to hate them and reject them. For in these two all our working is encompassed.

The seven sacraments also come from our faith. They follow one another in order, as God has ordained them for us.

And all kinds of virtues come from faith, for the same virtue that we have received from our substance, given to us in nature by the goodness of God, by the working of mercy is given to us in grace and renewed through the Holy Spirit. These virtues and gifts are treasured for us in Jesus Christ. For at the same time that God knitted himself to our body in the maiden's womb, he took on our sensual soul. In this taking, having enclosed us entirely within himself, he joined it to our substance. In this joining he was perfect man, for Christ, having knitted each man who will be saved into himself, is perfect man.

Thus, our Lady is our mother, in whom we are entirely enclosed and of whom we are born in Christ. For she who is the mother of our savior is the mother of all who are saved in our savior. And our savior is our true mother; in him we are endlessly born, and we shall never come out of him.

Plenteously, fully and sweetly was this shown. It is spoken of in the first showing, where it is said, "We are all enclosed in him and he is enclosed in us." And it is spoken of in the sixteenth showing, where he says he sits in our soul. For it is his delight to reign blissfully in our understanding, to sit restfully in our soul, and to dwell in our soul endlessly, drawing us completely into him. In this work he wills that we be his helpers, giving him all our attention, learning his teachings, keeping his laws, desiring that all be done which he does, and trusting in him in truth. For in truth I saw that our substance is in God.

## Chapter 58

*God was never displeased with his chosen wife; of three properties in the Trinity: fatherhood, motherhood and lordship; how our substance is in every person but our sensuality is in Christ alone.*

God, the blessed Trinity, who is everlasting Being, just as he is endless from without beginning, so it was in his endless purpose to make man. This fair nature was first prepared for his own Son, the Second Person of the Trinity, and when he willed it with the full agreement of the whole Trinity, he made us all at once.

In our making he first knitted us and joined us to himself. By this joining we are kept as clean and as noble as we were created to be. By virtue of that same precious joining, we love our maker and become like him, praise him and thank him, and endlessly rejoice in him. And this is the work that is wrought continuously in every soul that shall be saved. This is the "goodly will" I mentioned before.

And thus in our creation God Almighty is our natural father, and God All-wisdom is our natural mother, with the love and goodness of the Holy Spirit. These are all one God, one Lord. In the knitting and the joining he is our real, true spouse and we are his loved wife and his fair maiden. With this wife he was never displeased. For he says, "I love you and you love me, and our love shall never be parted in two."

I saw the working of the whole blessed Trinity. In seeing this I saw and understood these three properties: the property of the fatherhood, the property of the motherhood and the property of lordship in one God.

In our Father Almighty we have our preservation and our bliss, as far as our natural substance, which we have by our creation from without beginning, is concerned. In the Second Person we have our preservation in wit and wisdom, as far as our sensuality, our restoring and our saving are concerned. For he is our mother, brother and savior. And in our good Lord the Holy Spirit we have our rewarding and our harvest for our living and our bitter labor, endlessly surpassing all that we desire in his marvelous courtesy from his lofty, plenteous grace.

All our life is in three modes. In the first is our being. In the second we have our increasing. And in the third we have our fulfilling.

The first is nature. The second is mercy. The third is grace.

For the first, I saw and understood that the noble power of the Trinity is our father, the deep wisdom of the Trinity is our mother, and the great love of the Trinity is our Lord. All these we have in nature and in our substantial making.

Furthermore, I saw that the Second, most precious, Person, who is our substantial mother has now become our sensual mother, for we are double by God's making, that is to say, substantial and sensual. Our substance is the higher part which we have in our father, God Almighty.

The Second Person of the Trinity is our mother in nature, in our substantial making. In him we are grounded and rooted, and he is our mother by mercy in our sensuality, by taking flesh.

Thus our mother, Christ, in whom our parts are kept unseparated, works in us in various ways. For in our mother, Christ, we profit and increase, and in mercy he reforms and restores us, and by virtue of his passion, death and resurrection joins us to our substance. This is how our mother, Christ, works in mercy in all his beloved children who are submissive and obedient to him.

And grace works with mercy, specifically in two properties, as it was showed. This working belongs to the third person, the Holy Spirit. He works rewarding and giving. Rewarding is a great gift, that the Lord, honorably fulfilling his pledge, makes to those who have labored hard. Giving is a work of courtesy, which he does freely, by grace, fulfilling and surpassing all that is desired by creatures.

Thus in our Father, God Almighty, we have our being. In our mother, Christ, we have our reforming and our restoration by mercy. In him, our parts are made one, and all is made perfect man. And by the harvest and the giving of grace, we are completely filled by the Holy Spirit.

Our substance is in our Father, God Almighty. Our substance is in our mother, God All-wisdom. And our substance is in our Lord God the Holy Spirit, All-goodness. For our substance is whole in each person of the Trinity, which is one God. Our sensuality is only in the Second Person, Christ Jesus, in whom are the Father and the Holy Spirit. In him and by him we are powerfully taken out of hell, and out of the wretchedness on earth, and are gloriously brought up into heaven and blissfully joined to our substance, increased in richness and nobility by all the virtue of Christ and by the grace and working of the Holy Spirit.

## Chapter 59

*Wickedness is turned to bliss by mercy and grace in the chosen; for the property of God is to do good against evil through Jesus, our mother in natural grace; the noblest soul in virtue is the meekest; and from the ground of meekness we receive other virtues.*

All this bliss we have by mercy and grace. We might never have had and known this kind of bliss unless the property of goodness, which is God, had been opposed. By this opposition we have this bliss, for wickedness has been permitted to rise in opposition to goodness, and the goodness of mercy and grace worked against that wickedness and turned everything to goodness and glory for all those who shall be saved. For goodness is that property in God that does good against evil. Thus Jesus Christ, who does good against evil, is our true mother. We have our being from him, in whom the ground of motherhood begins with all the sweet preservation of love that follows endlessly.

As truly as God is our Father, so truly is God our mother.

That he showed in everything, but especially in these sweet words, where he says, "I am it!"—that is to say, "I am the might and the goodness of the fatherhood. I am it—the wisdom and nature of motherhood. I am it—the light and grace that is all blessed love. I am it—the Trinity. I am it—the Unity. I am it—the noble sovereign goodness of every kind of thing. I am it—that which makes you long and love. I am it—the endless fulfillment of all true desires.

For where the soul is highest, noblest and most full of honor, there it is lowest, meekest and mildest. From this substantial ground we have all the virtue in our sensuality by the gift of nature and by the help and assistance of mercy and grace, without which we cannot profit.

Our high Father, Almighty God, who is Being, knows us and loved us from before any time. From this knowing, in his most marvelous deep charity, he willed that the Second Person should become our mother, our brother and our savior, by the foreseeing endless counsel of all the blessed Trinity. From this it follows that, as truly as God is our Father, so truly is God our mother. Our Father wills, our mother works, and our good Lord the Holy Spirit confirms.

And therefore it is our place to love our God, in whom we have our being, thanking him reverently and praising him for our creation, mightily praying to our mother for mercy and pity and to our Lord the Holy Spirit for help and grace. For in these three is all our life: nature, mercy and grace. From these we have mildness, patience and pity, and the hatred of sin and wickedness, for hatred of sin and wickedness belongs properly to virtue.

Thus is Jesus our true mother in nature from our first making. He is our true first mother in grace by the taking of our created nature. All the fair working and all the sweet natural offices of the most precious motherhood are appropriated to the Second Person, for in him we have this goodly will, whole and safe without end, both in nature and in grace from his own proper goodness.

I understand three ways to look at motherhood in God. The first is that he is the ground of our natural making. The

cond is his taking of our nature, where the motherhood of
ace begins. The third is his motherhood in working. In
ese there is a spreading forth, long and broad, high and
ep, by the same grace without end. And all is one love, his
vn.

## Chapter 60

*ow we are bought again, and spread forth by mercy and
ace, by our sweet, natural and ever-loving mother, Jesus; of
e properties of motherhood; but Jesus is our true mother,
t feeding us with milk but with himself, opening his side
us and challenging all our love.*

But now it is necessary for me to say a little more about
is "spreading forth," as I understood it in our Lord's mean-
g—how we are brought again, by the motherhood of mercy
d grace, into our natural place, for which we were created
the motherhood of natural love. This natural love never
aves us.

Our natural mother, our gracious mother, because he
lled to become our mother entirely in everything, took the
ound for his work most humbly and most mildly in the
aiden's womb. That he showed in the first showing, where
brought that meek maiden before the eye of my under-
anding in the simple stature she had when she conceived.
hat is to say, our high God, the sovereign wisdom of all, ar-
yed himself in this low place and made himself entirely
ady in our poor flesh in order to do the service and the
fice of motherhood himself in all things.

A mother's service is nearest, readiest and surest. It is
arest because it is most natural. It is readiest because it is
ost loving. And it is surest because it is most true. This
fice no one but him alone might or could ever have per-
rmed to the full.

We realize that all our mothers bear us for pain and for

dying, and what is that? But our true mother, Jesus—A
love—alone bears us for joy and for endless living, blesse
may he be! Thus he sustains us within himself in love ar
hard labor, until the fulness of time. Then he willed to suff
the sharpest thorns and the most grievous pains there ev
were or ever will be, and to die at the last.

When he had done this and so borne us to bliss, all th
still could not satisfy his marvelous love. That he showed
these noble, surpassing words of love: "If I could suffer mor
I would suffer more." He could not die any more, but I
would not stop working.

Therefore it was necessary for him to feed us, for the mo
precious love of motherhood had made him a debtor to us.
mother can give her child her milk to suck, but our precio
mother, Jesus, can feed us with himself. He does so mo
courteously and most tenderly, with the Blessed Sacramer
which is the precious food of true life. With all the swe
sacraments he sustains us most mercifully and gracious]
That is what he meant in these blessed words, where he sai
"I am that which holy Church preaches and teaches you
that is to say, "All the health and the life of the sacramen
all the virtue and the grace of my word, all the goodness th
is ordained for you in holy Church, that I am."

The mother can hold her child tenderly to her breast, b
our tender mother, Jesus, can lead us in friendly fashion in
his blessed breast by means of his sweet open side and the
show us something of the godhead and the joys of heav
with a spiritual assurance of endless bliss. This he showed
the ninth revelation, giving the same understanding in t]
sweet word where he said, "See how I loved you!" Look in
his blessed side, rejoicing.

This fair, lovely word "mother" is so sweet and so natu
in itself that it cannot truly be said of anyone but him, or
anyone but him, who is the true mother of life and of ever
thing.

To motherhood as properties belong natural love, wisdc
and knowledge—and this is God. For though it is true th
our bodily bringing forth is very little, low and simple co

pared to our spiritual bringing forth, yet it is he who does the mothering in the creatures by whom it is done.

The natural loving mother, who recognizes and knows the need of her child, takes care of it most tenderly, as the nature and condition of motherhood will do. And continually, as the child grows in age and size, she changes what she does but not her love. When the child has grown older, she allows it to be punished, breaking down vices to enable the child to receive virtues and grace.

This work, with all that is fair and good, our Lord does in those by whom it is done. Thus he is our mother in nature, by the working of grace in the lower part for love of the higher. And he wills that we know it, for he wills to have all our love fastened to him.

In this I saw that all the debts that we owe, by God's command, to fatherhood and motherhood by reason of God's fatherhood and motherhood, are repaid in the true loving of God. This blessed love Christ works in us. And this was showed in everything, especially in the noble, plenteous words, where he says, "I am what you love."

## Chapter 61

*Jesus uses more tenderness in our spiritual bringing forth; though he allows us to fail in the knowing of our wretchedness, he hastily raises us, not breaking his love because of our trespass, for he cannot allow his child to perish; he wills that we have the property of a child, fleeing to him always in our necessity.*

And in our spiritual bringing forth he uses tenderness beyond comparison in keeping us—more than he used in our bodily bringing forth by as much as our soul's worth is greater in his sight than our body's.

He kindles our understanding, he prepares our ways, he eases our conscience, he comforts our soul, he lightens our

heart and gives us, in part, a knowing and loving in hi
blessed, blissful godhead, with the gracious mentality of hi
sweet manhood and his blessed passion, and with a courteou
marveling at his noble surpassing goodness. He makes us lov
all that he loves for his love, and be well satisfied with hin
and with all his works.

And when we fall, he raises us hastily, by his lovely callin
and his gracious touching. When we are strengthened by hi
sweet working, then we deliberately choose him, by his grace
and choose to be his servants and his lovers permanently
without end.

And yet after this he allows some of us to fall harder an
more seriously than we have ever done before, as we imagine
And then we suppose that we are not entirely wise, and tha
all we have begun is nothing. But it is not so. For it is neces
sary for us to fall, and it is necessary for us to see it.

If we did not fall, we would not know how feeble an
wretched we are of ourselves, nor should we know so fully th
marvelous love of our maker. For we shall truly see in heave
without end that we have sinned grievously in this life.

And notwithstanding this, we shall see in truth that w
never lost any of his love, nor were we ever of less worth i
his sight. And by the test of this failure we shall have a nobl
and marvelous knowing of love in God without end, for tha
love is hardy and wonderful. It cannot and will not be broke
on account of trespass.

That was one profitable understanding. Another is the hu
mility and meekness we shall receive from the sight of ou
falling. By it we shall be raised high in heaven. To this rais
ing we might never have come without that meekness, an
therefore we must see our failure. And if we don't see i
though we fall it will not be profitable for us. Commonly
first we fall and then we see our failure, and both are from
the mercy of God.

A mother may allow her child to fall sometimes, and b
made uncomfortable in various ways for his own profit, bu
because of her love she can never allow any kind of peril t
come to her child. And though our earthly mother can allo
her child to perish, our heavenly mother, Jesus, can neve

low us who are his children to perish. For he is Almighty, All-wisdom, All-love, and there is none like him, blessed may e be!

But frequently when our failure and our wretchedness are nown to us, we are so terribly frightened and so greatly shamed of ourselves that it is with difficulty that we know here to put ourselves.

But then our courteous mother does not will that we flee way; for him nothing could be more loathsome. But he wills hen that we act the way a child does. When a child is in discomfort and afraid, he runs hastily to his mother, and if he an do nothing more, he cries out to his mother for help vith all his might. Jesus wills that we act this way, saying like meek child, "My natural mother, my gracious mother, my most precious mother, have mercy on me. I have made myself dirty and unlike you, and I may not and cannot make it better, except with your secret help and your grace."

If we don't feel ourselves eased at that point, immediately we should be sure that he is acting the way a wise mother does. For if he sees that it is for our profit to mourn and to weep, he allows it, with compassion and pity, for love, to last until the time that is best.

And he wills then that we act the way a child acts, who evermore naturally trusts the love of the mother in well-being nd woe. And he wills that we take ourselves with great strength to the faith of holy Church and find there our most precious mother in comfort and true understanding, with the whole communion of blessed ones. For a person by himself an frequently be broken, as it seems to himself, but the whole body of holy Church was never broken and never shall be, without end. Therefore it is a sure thing, a good thing, nd a gracious thing to will meekly and powerfully to be fastened and joined to our mother, holy Church—that is Christ esus.

For the flood of mercy that is his most valuable blood and precious water is plentiful enough to make us fair and clean. The blessed wounds of our savior are open and rejoice to heal us. The sweet, gracious hands of our mother are ready and diligent around us, for he in all this work performs the true

office of a natural nurse who has nothing else to do but to
tend to the salvation of her child. It is his office to save us;
is his glory to do it, and it is his will that we know it. For
wills that we love him sweetly and trust in him meekly a
powerfully. And this he showed in these gracious words:
keep you most securely."

## Chapter 62

*The love of God never allows his chosen ones to lose tim*
*for all their trouble is turned into endless joy; how we are*
*bound to God by nature and by grace; every nature is*
*man; we do not need to look outside for various natures, b*
*only in holy Church.*

At that time, he showed our frailty and our fallings, o
breakings and our nothingness, our malice and what we a
charged with, our exiles and all our misery, to the extent th
these things could befall us in this life, as it seemed to m
With this he showed his blessed power, his blessed wisdon
his blessed love. In these he preserves us during this time
tenderly and sweetly for his glory and as surely for our salv
tion as he does when we have most solace and comfort. An
to achieve these things he raises us high in heaven spirituall
and transforms everything for his glory and for our endle
joy. Because of his precious love, he never allows us to los
time. All this is from the natural goodness of God, by th
working of grace.

God is natural in his being; that is to say, the goodne
that is natural to God. He is the ground, he is the substanc
he is the same thing that nature is. And he is the real fathe
and the real mother of natures. All the natures that he ha
caused to flow out of himself to do his will shall be restore
and brought into him again by the salvation of man throug
the working of grace. For all the natures that he has set i
different creatures in part are all entirely in man in fulnes
and in virtue, in fairness and in goodness, in royalty and i

obility, and in all kind of solemnity, of preciousness and of
lory.

Here we can see that we are entirely bound to God by na-
ure, and we are entirely bound to God by grace. Here we
an see that it is not necessary for us to seek far off in order
o know the different natures. We need only look to holy
Church, into our mother's breast—that is to say, into our
wn soul, where our Lord dwells. We shall find everything
here—now in faith and in understanding, and afterward
learly, in reality, in himself, in bliss.

But let no man or woman take this as applying to himself
lone, for it is not this way. This is true in general, for it is
ur precious mother, Christ, for whom this fair nature was
repared for the glory and nobility of man's creation and for
he joy and bliss of man's salvation, just as he saw, realized
nd knew it from eternity.

## Chapter 63

*Sin is more painful than hell; it is vile and hurts nature; but
grace saves nature and destroys sin; the children of Jesus are
not all born yet; they do not pass from the status of childhood, but live in feebleness until they come to heaven, where
joys are ever beginning anew, without end.*

Here we can see that in truth we are enabled by nature to
hate sin and that, in truth, we are enabled by grace to hate
sin. For nature is entirely good and fair in itself, and grace
was sent out to save nature and to preserve it, to destroy sin
and again to bring fair nature into the blessed point from
which it came—that is, God—with greater nobility and glory
by virtue of the working of grace. It shall be seen before God
by all his holy ones in endless joy that nature has been tested
in the fire of tribulation and no lack or defect was found in
it.

Thus are nature and grace in accord. For grace is God, as
uncreated nature is God. He is two in his manner of working

but one in love, and neither of them works without the other, nor can anything separate them. When we, by the mercy of God and with his help, bring ourselves into agreement with nature and grace we shall see in truth that sin is worse, viler and more painful than hell, without any comparison, because it is contrary to our fair nature. For as truly as sin is unclean, so truly is it unnatural.

All this is a horrible thing to see for the loving soul who would be all fair and shining in the sight of God, as nature and grace teach. But we are not afraid of this (except insofar as fear can assist us). Meekly we make our complaints to our most precious mother, Christ, and he will sprinkle us entirely with his precious blood and make our soul most soft, and completely mild, and will heal us most beautifully by the process of time, just as shall be the greatest glory to him and joy to us without end.

And he shall never stop or reduce the working of this sweet fire until all his most precious children are borne and brought forth. That he showed where he gave the understanding of his spiritual thirst; that is, the love-longing that shall last until Judgment Day.

Thus our life is grounded in our true mother, Jesus, in his own foreseeing wisdom from without beginning, with the noble might of the Father and the noble sovereign goodness of the Holy Spirit. In the taking on of our nature, he brought us to life, and in his blessed dying upon the cross he bore us into endless life. From that time, now and forever, as he shall until Judgment Day, he feeds us and fosters us just as the noble sovereign nature of motherhood wills and as the natural need of childhood asks. Fair and sweet is our heavenly mother in the sight of our soul. Precious and lovely are the children of grace in the sight of our heavenly mother, with mildness and meekness and all the fair virtues that belong to children by nature.

The child does not despair naturally of the mother's love; the child does not naturally presume upon itself; the child naturally loves the mother, and each loves the other naturally. These, with all the others that are like them, are the fair virtues by which our heavenly mother is served and pleased.

And I understand no status in this life to be more noble than childhood with its feebleness, and its failure of strength and intellect, until the time that our gracious mother has brought us up into our Father's bliss. There it shall be made known to us in truth what he meant in the sweet words where he says, "All shall be well, and you yourself shall see that all manner of things shall be well." And then shall the bliss of our mothering by Christ begin anew in the joys of our Father, God. This new beginning shall continue without end, beginning anew. Thus I understood that all his blessed children who have come out of him by nature shall be brought into him again by grace.

## Chapter 64

*The fifteenth revelation is as it was set down before; the absence of God in life is our greatest pain apart from other hard labor; but we shall suddenly be taken from all pains, since we have Jesus for our mother; our patient waiting is greatly pleasing to God; and God wills we take our discomfort lightly, for love, thinking we are always at the point of being delivered.*

Before this time I had had great longing and desire, by the gift of God, to be delivered from this world and from this life. For frequently I looked at the woe that is here, and the well-being and blessedness that being is there. And if there had been no pain in this life except the absence of our Lord, it seemed to me sometimes that that was more than I could bear. This made me mourn and long diligently. Also my own wretchedness, sloth, weakness and weariness made it displeasing to me to live and work hard, as it fell to me to do.

To all this our courteous Lord answered, for my comfort and patience, and said these words: "Suddenly you shall be taken from all your pain, from all your sickness, from all your discomfort, and from all your woe. You shall come up above and you shall have me for your reward. You shall be filled full of joy and bliss. You shall never again have any kind of pain, any kind of sickness, any kind of thing to displease you, or any defect in your will. You shall continually have joy and bliss without end. Why, then, should it distress you to suffer a while, since it is my will and for my glory?"

In the words "suddenly you shall be taken" I saw that God rewards man for the patience he has in awaiting God's will and his time, and that man extends his patience beyond his time of living because of his ignorance of the time of his passing. This is a great profit, for if a man knew when he was to die, he would not have patience beyond that time. Also, God wills that while the soul is in the body, it must seem to itself that it is continually at the point of being taken.

All this life and this languishing that we have here is only a point, and when we are suddenly taken out of our pain into bliss, then pain shall be nothing.

And at this time I saw a body lying on the earth. This body appeared heavy, ugly, frightening and without shape or form, as if it were a swollen bog of stinking mud. Suddenly out of this body sprang a most fair creature, a little child fully shaped and formed, swift and lively, and whiter than the lily, who sharply glided up into heaven. The swollenness of the body symbolizes the great wretchedness of our mortal flesh, and the smallness of the child symbolizes the cleanness and purity of our soul. And I thought that no fairness of the child stayed with this body, and that no foulness of the body dwelt in this child.

It is completely blissful for a man to be taken out of pain —more than for pain to be taken from a man. For if pain is taken away from us it can come back again. Therefore it is a sovereign comfort and a blissful vision in a longing soul to see that we shall be taken from pain. In this arrangement I saw the marvelous compassion that our Lord has for us in our woe, and a courteous promise of clean deliverance, for he wills that we be comforted in surpassing joy. That he showed in these words: "You shall come up above and you shall have

ne for your reward. You shall be completely filled with joy
and bliss."

It is God's will that we fix the point of our thought in this
blessed sight as frequently as we can, and that we keep ourselves in it for as long a time as we can with his grace. For
this is a blessed contemplation for the soul that is led by
God, and very much to his glory for the time that it lasts.

When we fall again into ourselves by heaviness and spiritual blindness, and feel spiritual and bodily pains through our
fragility, it is God's will that we know that he has not forgotten us. That is what he means in these words, saying them
for our comfort: "You shall never again have any kind of
pain, any kind of sickness, any kind of thing to displease you,
or any defect in your will. You shall continually have joy and
bliss without end. Why, then, should it distress you to suffer
a while, since it is my will and for my glory?"

It is God's will that we accept his arrangements and his
comforting as greatly and strongly as we can take them. Also,
he wills that we accept our periods of waiting and our dis-
comforts as lightly as we can take them, and that we should
count them as nothing. For the more lightly we take them
and the smaller the price we set on them, for love, the less
pain we shall have in the feeling of them and the greater the
thanks and reward we shall have for them.

## Chapter 65

*He who chooses God for love, with reverent meekness, is cer-
tain to be saved; this reverent meekness, says the Lord, is
marvelously great and the self is marvelously little; it is God's
will that we fear nothing but him; for the power of our
enemy is taken into the hand of our friend; and therefore all
that God does shall be a great delight to us.*

And thus I understood that any man or woman who deliberately chooses God in this life, for love, may be sure that he

is loved without end, with an endless love that works that grace in him. For he wills that we keep this trustfully: that we are as secure in our hope of the bliss of heaven while we are here, as we shall be in security when we are there. And always, the more delight and joy we take in this security, with reverence and meekness, the better it pleases him.

For, as it was shown, the reverence that I mean is a holy, courteous awe of our Lord, to which meekness is knitted. By it a creature sees the Lord as marvelously great and the self as marvelously small. These virtues are endlessly received by those loved by God.

This reverence can now be seen and felt in its measure by the gracious presence of the Lord, when he is present. This presence is most desired in all things, for it brings about that marvelous security in true faith and certain hope by the greatness of charity in an awe that is sweet and delectable.

It is God's will that I see myself as much bound to him in love as if he had done for me everything that he has done. And this is how every soul should think in regard to its lover; that is to say, the charity of God makes in us such a unity that, when it is truly seen, no man can separate himself from any other. And thus each soul ought to think that God has done for him all that he has done.

This he showed to make us love him and become like him and fear nothing but him. For it is his will that we know that all the power of our enemy is taken into our friend's hands. Therefore the soul that knows this certainly will fear nothing but him whom it loves. All our other fears it counts among passions, bodily sickness and imagination.

Therefore, though we are in so much pain, woe and discomfort that it seems to us we can think of absolutely nothing except the misery we are in or that we feel, as soon as we can we pass lightly over it and count it as nothing. And why? Because God wills to be known. For if we know him and love him and reverently stand in awe of him, we shall have patience and peace and dwell in great rest, and all that he does will be a great delight to us. This our Lord showed in these words: "Why, then, should it distress you to suffer a while, since it is my will and for my glory?"

Now I have told you about fifteen showings, as God had the graciousness to minister them to my mind, renewed by the illuminating and touching of the same Spirit (I hope), who showed them all. Of these fifteen showings, the first began early in the morning, at about the hour of four. The revelations, shown by a most beautiful process, each soberly following the other, lasted until past noon that day.

## Chapter 66

*The sixteenth revelation; it is a conclusion and confirmation of all the preceding fifteen; of her frailty and mourning in discomfort, after the great comfort of Jesus, in saying she had raved (which because of her great sickness was, I suppose, only a venial sin); but yet the devil, after that, had great power to vex her nearly to death.*

And after this, the good Lord showed the sixteenth revelation, on the following night, as I shall explain later. This sixteenth revelation was the conclusion to and confirmation of the preceding fifteen.

But first I must and ought to tell you about my feebleness, wretchedness and blindness. I said at the beginning, "And then, suddenly, all my pain was taken from me." I had no grief and no discomfort from this pain as long as the fifteen showings continued to be shown. At the end of them, everything was closed and I saw no more. Soon I felt that I would live and suffer longer, and immediately my sickness came back again, first in my head, with a sound and a din. Suddenly my entire body was completely filled with sickness, just as it had been before, and I was as barren and dry as if I had never had any comfort. As a wretch I mourned in depression on account of my feeling of bodily pains and the failure of spiritual and bodily comfort.

Then a religious person came to me and asked me how I was getting along. I said I had raved that day, and he laughed aloud and within himself. And I said that it seemed to me

that the cross that stood in front of me bled a great deal.
With that word, the person I was speaking to grew very serious, and marveled.

Immediately, I was very ashamed and astonished at my
recklessness. And I thought, "This man, who never saw any
of it himself, takes seriously the least word I can say." And
when I saw that he accepted it so seriously and with such
great reverence, I wept and grew most deeply ashamed at my
own unbelief. I wanted to be forgiven in confession, but at
that point I couldn't tell it to any priest, for I thought,
"How can a priest believe me when I do not believe our
Lord God (as I showed when I said, 'I raved')?"

Notwithstanding the fact that I believed him truly while I
saw him, and that my will and my intention then was to continue to do so forever, without end, nevertheless, like a fool,
I let it pass out of my mind. Ah! Look what a wretch I
was! This was a great sin and a most unnatural thing that
I, because of the trifle of feeling a little bodily pain, so un-
wisely abandoned, for the time, the comfort of all this blessed
showing from our Lord God.

Here you can see what I am of myself. But in this our
courteous Lord willed not to leave me. I lay still until night,
trusting in his mercy, and then I began to sleep.

In this sleep, at the beginning it seemed to me that the
devil set himself at my throat, putting forth his visage very
near my face. It was like a young man's, and it was long and
extremely lean. I never saw anything like it. Its color was red,
like a tilestone when it is newly fired, with black spots on it
like black freckles, filthier than a tilestone. His hair was red
as rust, uncut in front, with side locks hanging on the temples. He grinned at me with a shrewd look and showed me
white teeth—so much that I thought him even more ugly.
He had no shapely body or hands, but with his paws he
held me by the throat, and would have stopped my breath
and killed me, but he could not.

This ugly showing was given me while I was asleep, as no
other was. During all this time, I trusted to be saved and
preserved by the mercy of God. Our courteous Lord gave me
the grace of waking up, and I scarcely had any life left. The

people who were with me observed me and wet my temples, and my heart began to take comfort.

And at once a little smoke came in through the door with a great deal of heat and a foul stench. I said, "Bless the Lord! Everything here is on fire!" I imagined it was a physical fire that would burn us all to death. I asked those who were with me if they smelled any stench, and they said no, they smelled nothing. I said, "Blessed be God!" because then I understood clearly that it was the fiend, who had only come to tempt me. Immediately I recalled what our Lord had showed me that same day, with all the beliefs of holy Church, for I saw both as one. I fled to these two as to my comfort. At once everything vanished entirely, and I was brought to a great rest and peace, without sickness of body or dread of conscience.

## Chapter 67

*Of the glorious sight of the soul, which is so nobly created that it could not have been any better made; in it the Trinity rejoices everlastingly; the soul can have rest in nothing but God, who sits in it ruling all things.*

And then our good Lord opened my spiritual eye and showed me my soul in the middle of my heart. I saw the soul as large as if it were an endless world and also as if it were a blessed, blissful kingdom. By the conditions I saw in this, I understood that the soul is a glorious city.

In the middle of that city sits our Lord Jesus, true God and true man, a fair person, large in stature—the noblest bishop, the most solemn king, the lord most full of honor. And I saw him clothed solemnly. He sits in the soul in glory, completely tranquil in peace and rest, and he rules and saves heaven and earth and everything that exists. The manhood sits with the godhead at rest. The godhead rules, sustains and saves heaven and earth and all that exists, without any instrument or activity, and the soul is completely occupied with the godhead, which is sovereign might, sovereign wisdom and sovereign goodness.

The place that Jesus takes in our soul he shall never remove himself from, without end, as I see it. For in us is his most homelike home and his endless dwelling. This he showed in the delight he takes in the creation of man's soul. For as well as the Father could make a creature and as well as the Son could make a creature, so well did the Holy Spirit will that man's soul be made—and so was it done. Therefore the blessed Trinity rejoices without end in the creation of man's soul, for he saw without beginning what would please him without end.

Everything that he has made shows his lordship. An understanding of this was given me at the same time by the example of a creature that is led to see the great nobility and kingdoms belonging to a lord. When it had seen all the nobility beneath, then, marveling, it was stirred to seek up above to that high place where the lord dwelt, knowing by reason that his dwelling was in the worthiest place.

Thus I understood in truth that our soul can never have rest in things that are beneath itself. And when it comes above all creatures into itself, it still cannot dwell in this contemplation by its own strength, for all such contemplation is blissfully fixed in God, who is the maker dwelling within it. For man's soul is his true dwelling, and the most intense light and the brightest shining of the city is the glorious love of our Lord God, as I see it.

And what can make us rejoice in God more than to see in him that he rejoices in us, the noblest of his works? For I saw in the same showing that if the blessed Trinity could have made man's soul any better, any fairer, any nobler than he did make it, he would not have been fully pleased with the making of man's soul. But because he made man's soul as fair, as good and as precious as he could make a creature, therefore the blessed Trinity is completely pleased without end in the making of man's soul. And he wills that our hearts should be powerfully raised above the depths of the earth and all vain sorrows, and that they should rejoice in him.

## Chapter 68

*Of the knowing in truth that it is Jesus who showed all this and it was no hallucination; and how we ought to have secure trust during all our tribulations, that we shall not be overcome.*

This was a delectable sight and a restful showing that is this way without end. The contemplation of this while we are here is most pleasant to God and a very great profit for us. The soul that contemplates it this way makes itself like him who is contemplated, and joins itself to him in rest and peace by his grace.

It was a singular joy and bliss to me that I saw him sitting, for the security of sitting symbolizes endless dwelling. He gave me reassurance that, in truth, it was he who had showed me everything before this. When I had gazed at this with attention, our good Lord showed me words, most meekly, without voice and without the opening of lips, just as he had done before, and said most sweetly, "Now know well that it was no hallucination you saw today, but accept it, believe it, keep yourself in it, comfort yourself with it, and trust in it, and you will not be overcome."

These last words were said in order to teach that complete, real security that is our Lord Jesus, who showed me everything. Just as in the first word our good Lord said, "By this (meaning his blessed passion) is the fiend overcome," in exactly the same sense in the last word he said, with full, true faithfulness, "You (meaning all of us) will not be overcome." All this teaching and this true comfort are meant in general, for all my fellow Christians, as I have said before, and that is God's will.

The words "You will not be overcome" were said very sharply and very powerfully as a security and a comfort to be used in any tribulation that may come. He did not say, "You will not be troubled" or "You will not have bitter labor" or

"You will have no discomfort," but "You will not be overcome." God wills that we pay attention to this word and that we be ever strong in faithful trust, in well-being and woe. For he loves us and delights in us, and wills that, in the same way, we love him and delight in him and strongly trust in him—and all shall be well.

And soon all was closed, and I saw no more after this.

## Chapter 69

*Of the second long temptation of the devil to despair; but she strongly trusted in God and in the faith of holy Church, reciting the passion of Christ, by which she was delivered.*

After this the fiend came again with his heat and with his stench and kept me very busy, the stench was so vile and so painful, and the bodily heat was so dreadful and so like hard labor. I also heard bodily talking, as if there had been two people talking. As it seemed to me, both talked at once as if they were holding a parliament with much business, with everything softly muttered and whispered, and I did not understand what they said. All this was intended to stir me to despair, as I thought. It seemed to me they mockingly imitated a recitation of the rosary which is said boisterously with the mouth, lacking the devout intention and wise diligence we owe God in our prayers. And our Lord God gave me the grace strongly to trust in him and to comfort my soul with bodily speech, as I would have comforted another person who had endured bitter labor. It seemed to me that this busyness could not be compared with any bodily busyness.

I set my bodily eye on the same cross where I had received comfort before this time. I set my tongue to speak of Christ's passion and to recite the faith of holy Church. I set my heart to fasten itself onto God with all its trust and might. And I thought to myself something like this: "You are extremely busy now, keeping yourself in the faith, in order not to be captured by your enemies! Would that, from now on and evermore, you should be so busy keeping yourself from sin! This would be a good and sovereign occupation." For in truth, I thought that if I were safe from sin, I would be completely safe from all the fiends in hell and the enemies of my soul.

Thus he occupied me all that night and into the morning, until it was about prime [6 A.M.]. Immediately, then, they were gone and passed, and nothing was left behind there but the stench, which lasted for a while longer. I scorned him, and thus was I delivered from him by virtue of Christ's passion, for by it is the fiend overcome, as our Lord Jesus Christ had said before.

## Chapter 70

*In all tribulations we ought to be steadfast in the faith, trusting strongly in God; for if our faith had no enemies it would deserve no reward; and how all these showings are in the faith.*

In all this blessed showing our Lord gave me to understand that the seeing of them should pass. But the faith keeps this blessed showing with God's own good will and his grace. For he left with me neither a sign nor a token by which I could know it was real, but he left me with his own blessed word in true understanding, bidding me most powerfully to believe it —and I do so, blessed may he be!

I believe that he who showed it is our savior, and that it is in the faith that he showed it. Therefore I love it, ever rejoicing, and I am bound to it by everything he himself meant, together with the words that follow next: "Keep yourself in it, comfort yourself with it, and trust in it."

Thus I am bound to keep it in my faith. For on the same day that it was showed, when the seeing was past, like a

wretch I abandoned it and said aloud that I had been raving.
Then our Lord Jesus, of his mercy, willed not to let the revelation perish, but showed it all again within my soul, with
greater fulness and with the blessed light of his precious love,
saying these words most powerfully and most meekly: "Now
know well that it was no hallucination you saw today," as if
he had said, "Because the sight passed from you, you lost it
and could or might not keep it. But know it now," that is to
say, "now that you see it." This was said not only for that
time but also to be used as the ground of my faith, where he
says (immediately following), "but accept it, believe it, keep
yourself in it, comfort yourself with it and trust in it, and you
will not be overcome."

In the six commands that follow "take it," his intention is
to fasten it faithfully in our hearts, for he wills that it dwell
with us in faith until the end of our lives, and afterward in
the fulness of joy, willing that we have ever a sure trust in his
blissful commands and promises, knowing his goodness. For
our faith is opposed in various ways by our own blindness
and our spiritual enemy within and without. Therefore our
precious lover helps us with spiritual sight and light and true
teaching on different matters, interior and exterior, by which
we can know him.

And therefore, in whatever way he teaches us, he wills that
we perceive him wisely, receive him sweetly, and keep ourselves in him faithfully. For above the faith no goodness is
kept in this life, as I see it, and beneath the faith there is no
health of soul or help for it. But it is in the faith that our
Lord wills that we keep ourselves, for by his goodness and his
own working we are able to keep ourselves in the faith, and
by his permission, through spiritual enmity we are tested in
the faith and made strong. For if our faith did not face enmity, it would deserve no reward, as I understand what our
Lord means.

## Chapter 71

*Jesus wills that our souls look to him with a glad expression,
for he gives us a merry and loving look; how he shows us
three kinds of expression: of suffering, of compassion and of
complete bliss.*

Glad, merry and sweet is the blissful, lovely expression of
our Lord to our souls. For he sees us always living in love-
longing, and he wills that our souls look to him with a glad
expression, in order to give him his reward. And thus I hope,
by means of his grace, that he has drawn, and shall further
draw, the outer expression to the inner disposition, and will
make us entirely at one with him and with one another in
the true, lasting joy that is Jesus.

I have the meaning of three of our Lord's ways of looking.
The first is the expression of suffering, as He showed it while
he was with us in this life, dying. And though this sight is
mournful and full of sorrow, yet it is glad and merry, because
he is God.

The second way of looking is with pity, sorrow and compassion. This he shows with the certainty of preservation to
all his lovers, who have need of his mercy.

The third is the look full of bliss—as it shall be without
end. This was showed most often and continued longest.

Thus, in the time of our pain and our woe, he shows us
the look of his suffering and his cross, helping us to bear it by
his own blessed virtue. In the time of our sinning he shows
us the look of compassion and pity, mightily preserving us
and defending us against all our enemies.

These two are the common looks he shows us in this life,
mixing with them the third. That is his blessed look. It is
partly like what it will be in heaven, and it is shown us by
the gracious touching and sweet illumination of our spiritual

life. By it we are kept in true faith, hope and charity, with contrition, devotion and contemplation and all kinds of true joys, solace and sweet comforts. Our Lord God's look full of bliss accomplishes it in us by grace.

## Chapter 72

*Sin in the chosen souls is deadly for a time, but they are not dead in the sight of God; how we have here matter for joy and mourning, and that because of our blindness and the weight of our flesh; of the most comforting look of God; and why these showings were made.*

But now I must and ought to tell how I saw sin as deadly in the creatures who will not die on account of sin but who will live in the joy of God without end. I saw that two opposites cannot be together in one place. The greatest opposites there are, are the highest bliss and the deepest pain. The highest bliss there is, is to have God in the clarity of light and life, seeing him in truth, feeling him sweetly, having him absolutely perfectly and absolutely peacefully in the fulness of joy. Thus was the blissful expression of our Lord God showed, in part, in pity.

In this showing I saw that sin is the thing most opposite it, to the extent that, as long as we are tainted with any part of sin we shall never see clearly the blessed look of God. And the more horrible and grievous our sins are, the further away we are, for that time, from this blessed sight. And therefore, it frequently seems to us that we have been in peril of death and in hell's party, because of the sorrow and pain sin causes us. Thus, for the time, we are dead to the true sight of our blessed life.

But in all this I saw in truth that we are not dead in the sight of God, and that he never leaves us. But he will never have his full bliss in us until we have our full bliss in him,

seeing his fair, blissful expression in truth. For we are ordained for this by nature and brought to it by grace.

Thus I saw how sin is deadly for a short time in the
blessed creatures of endless life, and I saw ever the more
clearly that the soul sees God's blissful expression by grace of
loving, the more it longs to see it in fulness, that is to say, in
his own likeness.

For notwithstanding the facts that our Lord God dwells
within us, that he is here with us, that he calls us, that he encloses us for tender love so that he can never leave us, and
that he is nearer to us than tongue can tell or heart can
think, yet we may never stop mourning, nor weeping, nor
feeling, nor longing, until we see him clearly in his blissful
expression. For in that precious, blissful sight, no woe can
abide and no well-being can fail.

And in this I saw matter for mirth and matter for mourning. The matter for mirth is that our Lord, our maker, is so
near to us and that he is in us and we are in him by the sure
keeping of his great goodness. The matter for mourning is
that our spiritual eye is so blind and that we are so borne
down by the weight of our mortal flesh and the darkness of
sin that we cannot see our Lord God clearly in his fair expression of bliss. No, and because of this murkiness and darkness, we can scarcely believe and trust his great love and the
certainty of our preservation. That is why I say we can never
stop mourning, nor weeping.

This "weeping" does not have its whole meaning in the
pouring out of tears by our bodily eyes, but also leads to a
greater spiritual understanding. For the natural desire of the
soul is so great and so unmeasurable that if all the nobility
that God ever made, in heaven and on earth, were given to
us for our joy, solace and comfort and we did not see his fair
expression of bliss, we should still never stop mourning, nor
spiritually weeping (that is to say, longing painfully), until
we should see in truth our maker's fair expression of bliss.
And if we were experiencing all the pain the heart can think
or tongue can tell, and we could at that same time see his
blissful look, all this pain would not grieve us.

Thus does that blissful sight end all kinds of pain for loving, longing souls, and fulfill all kinds of joy and bliss. That he showed in the noble, marvelous words where he said: "I am that which is highest; I am that which is lowest. I am that which is all."

It is proper for us to have three kinds of knowing. The first is that we know our Lord God. The second is that we know ourselves—what we are by him in nature and in grace. The third is that we recognize meekly what our self is, as regards our sin and our feebleness. For these three kinds of knowing, this entire revelation was made, as I understand it.

## Chapter 73

*These revelations were showed three ways; of two spiritual sicknesses which God wills that we amend, remembering his passion and also knowing that he is All-love; for he wills that we have certainty and delight in love, and not entertain unskillful depression on account of our past sins.*

All this blessed teaching of our Lord God was showed in three ways, that is to say by bodily sight, by words formed in my understanding, and by spiritual insight.

As far as the bodily sight is concerned, I have said what I saw as accurately as I can. As far as the words are concerned, I have repeated them just as our Lord showed them to me. And as far as the spiritual insight is concerned, I have said something of it but I can never fully express it. Therefore I am stirred to say more about this spiritual insight, as God will give me grace.

God showed two kinds of sickness we have. The first is impatience or sloth, because of which we bear our hard labor and our pain with depression. The second is despair, or dread full of doubt, which I shall speak of later.

He showed sin in general as including everything, but he showed none but these two in particular, and these two are those which give us the most bitter labor and trouble us most, according to what our Lord showed me. Of these he wills that we be cured. (I speak of such men and women who, for God's love, hate sin and dispose themselves to do God's will.)

Then, by our spiritual blindness and bodily heaviness, we are most inclined to these two. Therefore it is God's will that they be known, and then we should reject them as we do other sins.

For complete help against these two, our Lord most meekly showed the patience that he had in his hard passion, and also the joy and delight that he has, for love, on account of that passion. This he showed by example so that we would gladly, wisely and easily bear our pains, for that is greatly pleasing to him and of endless profit to us. The reason why they cause us such bitter labor is our ignorance of love. (Though the Three Persons are all equal within the blessed Trinity itself, the soul received the greatest understanding of love.) Yes, and he wills that in all things we have our beholding and our rejoicing in love.

And we are most blind concerning this knowing. For some of us believe that God is Almighty and may do everything, and that he is All-wisdom and can do everything. But believing that he is All-love and wills to do everything—there we fail.

And it is this ignorance that most hinders God's lovers, as I see it. For when we begin to hate sin and amend our lives by the ordinance of holy Church, there still dwells in us a dread that holds us back, because of our seeing ourselves and the sins we have previously committed. And some of us are in fear because of our daily sins, for we do not hold to our promises or keep the cleanness that our Lord has set us in, but frequently fall into so much wretchedness that it is shameful to say it. And the contemplation of these things makes us so sorry and so depressed that with difficulty can we see any comfort. We sometimes mistake this fear for meekness, but it is a foul blindness and a wickedness. We cannot despise it as we do another sin that we recognize, for it comes from enmity and lack of true judgment, and is op-

posed to truth. For of all the properties of the blessed, bliss
ful Trinity, it is God's will that we have the greatest securit
and delight in love, for love makes might and wisdom mos
meek for us. For just as God, by his courtesy, forgets our si
when we repent of it, so he wills that we forget our sin as fa
as our unskillful depression and our doubt-filled dreads ar
concerned.

## Chapter 74

*There are four kinds of dread; but reverent dread is a lovely
true dread that is never separated from meek love; and ye
these are not both the same thing; and how we should pra
to God for reverent dread.*

I understood four kinds of dread. The first is the drea
from fright, which comes to a man suddenly by his frailty
This dread does good, for it helps to purge a man, as does
bodily sickness or any other such pain that is not sin. For al
such pains help man if they are patiently accepted.

The second is the dread from pain, by which man is stirre
and awakened from the sleep of sin. For a man who is fas
asleep in sin is not able, for that time, to receive the sof
comfort of the Holy Spirit until he has undergone this drea
from the pain of bodily death and of spiritual enemies, an
has an understanding of it. And this dread stirs us to see
comfort and mercy from God. Thus, this dread, serving as ar
entrance, helps us and enables us to have contrition by th
blessed touching of the Holy Spirit.

The third is the dread full of doubt. Insofar as doubt-fille
dread draws us to despair, God will have it transforme
within us into love, by the true knowing of love; that is to
say that the bitterness of doubt will be turned into the sweet
ness of natural love by grace. For it can never please ou
Lord that his servants doubt his goodness.

The fourth is reverent dread. There is no dread in us tha

fully pleases God except reverent dread. It is very soft, for the more it is possessed the less it is felt, because of the sweetness of love.

Love and dread are brothers. They are rooted in us by the goodness of our maker, and they shall never be taken away from us without end. We have the power to love from nature, and we have it from grace. We have the power to dread from nature, and we have it from grace. It is proper for us who are his servants and his children to dread him, on account of his lordship and his fatherhood, as it is proper for us to love him for his goodness.

Though this reverent dread and this love are not separated from one another, they are not both the same thing. They are two in their qualities and two in working, yet neither of them can be possessed without the other. Therefore I am sure that he who loves, dreads, though he scarcely feels it.

All dreads that are offered to us, other than reverent dread, though they come under color of holiness, are not so in truth. By this they can be told apart: the dread that makes us hastily flee from all that is no good and fall into our Lord's breast as a child into its mother's arms, with all our intent and all our mind, knowing our feebleness and our great need, knowing his everlasting goodness and his blessed, blissful love, only seeking within him for our salvation, cleaving to him with faithful, certain trust—the dread that draws us into doing these things—that dread is natural, gracious, good and true. All that is opposed to it is either wrong or mixed with wrong.

This, then, is the remedy: to know them both and to reject the wrong. For the natural profit that we have from dread in this life, by the gracious working of the Holy Spirit, shall be gentle, sweet and most delectable in heaven before God. Thus, in love we shall be friendly and near to God, and in dread we shall be gentle and courteous to God, and both will be exactly alike.

Then we should desire of our Lord God to dread him reverently, to love him meekly, and to trust in him strongly, for when we dread him reverently and love him meekly, our trust is never in vain. The more we trust and the more strongly we trust, the more we please and honor our Lord, in whom we trust. If we fail in this reverent dread and meek love (as, God forbid, we should do), our trust will soon be badly governed for that time. And therefore we greatly need to pray to our Lord that, by his grace we may have this reverent dread, and by his gift we may have this meek love in our hearts and in our work—for without this no man can please God.

## Chapter 75

*Love-longing and pity are necessary for us; of three kinds of longing in God that are in us; how on the Day of Judgment the joy of the blessed shall be increased as they see in truth the cause of all things that God has done; trembling with dread and thanking God for joy, they marvel at the greatness of God and the littleness of all that is made.*

I saw that God can supply all that is necessary for us, particularly these three things I shall speak of. We need: love, longing and pity. Pity, in love, preserves us in our time of need. Longing, in the same love, draws us into heaven, for the thirst of God is to have man in general within him. In this thirst, he has drawn his holy souls who are now in bliss. Getting his living members in the same way, he continually draws and drinks—and still he thirsts and longs.

I saw three kinds of longing in God, all directed to one end. We have the same three in us, of the same virtue and for the same end. The first is that he longs to teach us to know him and to love him ever more and more, as is suitable and profitable for us. The second is that he longs to have us up in bliss, as souls are when they are taken out of pain into heaven. The third is that he longs to fill us full of bliss, and that will be accomplished on the last day, to last forever.

For I saw, as is recognized in our faith, that the pain and

sorrow shall be ended for all who shall be saved, and not only shall we receive the same bliss that the souls before us have had in heaven, but we shall also receive a new bliss, which shall flow abundantly out of God into us and fill us full.

These are the good things he has ordained to give us from without beginning. These goods are treasured and hidden within himself, for until that time no creature is strong enough or worthy enough to receive them. In this we shall see in truth the cause of everything God has done, and evermore we shall see the cause of everything he has suffered. The bliss and the fulfillment shall be so deep and so high that, for wonder and astonishment at it, all creatures should have for God so great a reverent dread—surpassing anything that has ever been seen or felt before—that the pillars of heaven shall tremble and quake.

But this kind of trembling and dread shall have with it no kind of pain. It belongs to the worthy might and majesty of God to be looked at by his creatures this way—full of dread, trembling and quaking for the greatness of joy, marveling at the greatness of God the maker and at the littleness of all that is made. For the contemplation of this makes the creature marvelously meek and mild. Therefore God wills (and also, it is proper to us both in nature and grace) that we realize and know about this, desiring this sight and this working. For it commands us in the right way, keeps us in true life and makes us one with God.

As good as God is, so great is he, and as much as it is proper to his goodness to be loved, so much is it proper to his greatness to be dreaded. For this reverent dread is the fair courtesy that is in heaven before the face of God. And as greatly as the way he shall be known and loved then surpasses the way he is known and loved now, so greatly shall the way he shall be dreaded then surpass the way he is dreaded now. Therefore it must and ought to be that all heaven in truth shall tremble and quake when the pillars shall tremble and quake.

## Chapter 76

*A loving soul hates sin for its vileness more than for all the pain of hell; how the contemplation of other men's sins (unless it is done with compassion) hinders the contemplation of God; the devil, by reminding us of our wretchedness, would hinder us from the contemplation of God; and of our sloth.*

I speak very little about this reverent dread, because I hope it can be seen in the matter I have previously discussed. But I know well that our Lord showed me no souls but those that had dread for him.

I realized well that the soul that truly accepts the teaching of the Holy Spirit hates sin more, because of its vileness and its horribleness, than it hates all the pains that are in hell. For the soul that sees the kindness of our Lord Jesus hates no hell but sin, as I see it. Therefore it is God's will that we recognize sin, pray diligently, deliberately do bitter labor, and humbly seek teaching, that we may not fall blindly into it, and if we fall, that we may rise readily, for it is the greatest pain the soul can have to turn from God by sin any time.

The soul that will be in rest when other men's sins come to mind should flee from the thought as from the pain of hell, seeking a remedy for and help against it from God. For the contemplation of other men's sins creates, as it were, a thick mist before the eyes of the soul, and we cannot, for that time, see the fairness of God. This is true unless we contemplate them with contrition with the sinner, with compassion on him, and with holy desire for God on his behalf. Without this, such contemplation annoys, troubles, tempts and hinders the soul that engages in it.

For this I understood in the showing about compassion. In this blissful showing of our Lord, I have the understanding of two opposites. The one is the wisest thing any creature can do in this life, and the other is the greatest folly.

The wisest thing a creature can do is to act according to the will and the advice of his noblest sovereign friend. This friend is Jesus, and it is his will and counsel that we hold ourselves with him and fasten ourselves familiarly to him evermore, whatever the state we happen to be in. For whether we are dirty or clean, we are always the same in his loving. He wills that we never flee from him whether because of well-being or of woe.

But because of the changeability we dwell in, of ourselves, we often fall into sin. Then we have this difficulty from the stirring of our enemy and from our own folly and blindness. For they say thus: "You know well that you are a wretch and a sinner, and are also untrue, because you don't keep your promise. You have frequently promised our Lord that you will do better, and immediately afterward, you fall again into the same sins, specifically into sloth and the wasting of time." For that is the beginning of sin as I see it, especially for creatures who have given themselves to serve our Lord, with inward contemplation of his blessed goodness. And this makes us afraid to appear before our courteous Lord.

Then it is that our enemy will take us aback because of the pain with which he threatens us, by means of the false dread he gives us of our wretchedness. For it is his intention to make us so depressed and so sorry about this that we will allow the fair, blissful sight of our everlasting friend to slip out of our minds.

## Chapter 77

*Of the enmity of the devil, who loses more in our rising up than he wins by our falling, and therefore he is scorned; how the scourge of God should be endured with the spirit of his passion, because that is especially rewarded, more than pen-*

*ances we choose ourselves; and it is necessary that we have
woe, but courteous God is our leader, keeper and bliss.*

Our good Lord showed the enmity of the devil. By this I
understood that all that is opposed to love and to peace is
from the devil and from his party. Because of our feebleness
and our folly, it is ours to fall. Because of mercy and grace
from the Holy Spirit it is ours to rise to greater joy. If our
enemy wins anything from us by our falling (for that is his
delight), he loses very much more in our rising by charity
and meekness. This glorious rising is to him such great sorrow and pain because of the hatred he has for our soul, that
he burns continuously with envy.

In addition, the sorrow he would bring on us shall be
turned on himself, and it was for this that our Lord scorned
him and showed that he shall be scorned. And this is what
made me laugh loud and long.

This, then, is the remedy: that we be aware of our
wretchedness and flee to our Lord. For always, the more in
need we are the more profitable it is for us to draw near and
touch him. And this is what we say in our intentions: "I
know well I have a shrewd, deserved pain, but our Lord is Almighty and may punish me mightily, and he is All-wisdom
and can punish me skillfully. And he is All-goodness and
loves me most tenderly."

And it is profitable and necessary for us to rest in contemplating this, for it is the most lovely meekness of a sinful
soul, wrought by the mercy and grace of the Holy Spirit,
when we choose deliberately and gladly to accept the scourging and chastisement that our Lord himself wills to give us.
It will be very tender and very easy, if we will only hold ourselves satisfied with him and with all his works.

For the penance that a man takes upon himself was not
showed me (that is to say, it was not showed me specifically). But it was showed specifically, intensely and with a
completely lovely expression, that we should meekly and
patiently bear and suffer the penance that God himself gives
us with the spirit of his blessed passion. For when we have

the spirit of his blessed passion, with pity and love, then we suffer with him just as his friends who saw it did.

And this was shown in the thirteenth revelation almost at the beginning, where it speaks of pity. For he says, "Do not accuse yourself too much, judging that your tribulation and your woe are all your own fault. For I do not will that you be imprudently depressed or sorrowful. For I tell you, whatever you do, you will have woe. And therefore I will that you wisely recognize your penance, which you are in continually, and that you meekly accept it for your penance. Then you will truly see that all your living is profitable penance."

This place is a prison, this life is a penance, and he wills that we rejoice in the remedy. The remedy is that our Lord is with us, keeping us and leading us into the fulness of joy. For this, as our Lord intends it, is an endless joy for us: that he who will be our bliss when we are there is our preserver while we are here. Our way, and our heaven, are true love and secure trust. And of this he gave understanding in the whole revelation, specifically in the showing of his passion where he made me strongly choose him for my heaven.

If we flee to our Lord, we shall be comforted; if we touch him, we shall be made clean; if we cleave to him, we shall be secure and safe from all kinds of perils. For our courteous Lord wills that we be as familiar with him as heart can think or soul can desire.

But we must be careful that we do not take this familiarity so recklessly that we abandon courtesy. For our Lord himself is sovereign familiarity—and as familiar as he is, so courteous is he, for he is courtesy itself. And the blessed creatures who shall be in heaven with him without end, he wills to be like himself in everything. To be perfectly like our Lord is our true salvation and our complete bliss. If we do not know how we shall do so, let us desire all of it from our Lord, and he will teach us, for it is his own delight and his glory, blessed may he be!

## Chapter 78

*Our Lord wills we know four kinds of goodness that he does
for us; how we need the light of grace to know our sin and
feebleness; for we are nothing of ourselves but wretchedness;
we cannot know the horribleness of sin as it is; how our
enemy wishes we would never recognize our sins until our
last day; and therefore we are much bound to God, who
shows them to us now.*

Because of his mercy, our Lord shows us our sin and our
feebleness, by the sweet, gracious light of himself. For our sin
is so foul, so vile, and so horrible that he, because of his courtesy, does not will to show it to us except by the light of his
grace and mercy.

He wills that we have knowledge of four things. The first is
that he is the ground from whom we have our entire life and
our whole being. The second is that he keeps us powerfully
and mercifully while we are in our sins, among all our enemies, who are most deadly against us. And we are so much
the more in peril because we give them occasion to attack
and do not recognize our own need.

The third is how courteously he keeps us and causes us to
know that we go astray. The fourth is how steadfastly he
waits for us, and does not change his expression. For he wills
that we should be turned and joined to him in love as he is
to us.

And thus, by this grace-giving knowledge, we can profitably
see our sin without despairing. For, in truth, it is necessary
for us to see it. By the sight, we should be made ashamed of
ourselves, and our pride and presumption should be broken
down by it.

It is profitable for us to see, in truth, that, of ourselves, we
are absolutely nothing except sin and wretchedness. And thus
it is by the sight of this least, that our Lord shows us the
greater that is wasted, which we do not see. He, because of

his courtesy, measures the sight to our weakness, for it is so foul and so horrible that we could not stand to see it as it is.

And thus, by knowing this meekly, through contrition and grace we shall be broken away from everything that is not our Lord. Then our blessed savior will cure us perfectly and join us to himself. This breaking away and this curing, our Lord intends for men in general. For he who is highest and nearest to God can see himself as sinful and needy, with me, and I, who am the least and lowest of those who shall be saved, can be comforted with him who is highest. Our Lord has joined us in charity this way.

When he showed me that I would sin, and because of the joy I had in looking at him I did not readily pay attention to the showing, our courteous Lord stopped there and would teach me nothing further until he gave me the grace and will to pay attention. Thus was I taught that, though we are raised high into contemplation by the special gift of our Lord, still we must and ought to have with it the knowledge and sight of our sin and of our feebleness, for without this knowing we cannot have true humility—and without that we cannot be saved.

I also saw that we cannot have this knowledge of ourselves, nor from any of all our spiritual enemies, for they do not will us this much good! If they had their will, we would never see our sin and feebleness until the day of our death. Consequently, we are greatly bound to God, because he wills to show this to us himself, for love, in time for mercy and for grace.

## Chapter 79

*We are instructed about our own sin and not about our neighbors', except for their help; God wills that we know that whatever stirring we have contrary to this showing comes from our enemy; for the great love of God, we know that we should not be more reckless of falling; and if we fall we must hastily rise, or else we are most unnatural to God.*

I also had greater understanding in his showing me that I would sin. I took it nakedly as applying to my own, singular person, for I was moved no other way at the time. But by the lofty, gracious comfort of our Lord, which followed afterward, I saw that he intended it for man in general, that is to say all men who are sinful and will be so until the Last Day. I am, as I hope, a member of this "man," by the mercy of God, for the blessed comfort I saw is large enough for all of us.

And there I was taught that I should see my own sin and not other men's sin, unless it might be for the comfort or help of my fellow Christians.

I was also taught, in the same showing where I saw I would sin, to be full of dread because of my uncertainty of myself. For I did not know how I would fall, nor did I know the measure or the greatness of my sin. I wanted, full of dread, to know that, but I received no answer to that question.

Also at that same time, our courteous Lord showed most sweetly and strongly the endlessness and the unchangeability of his love, inwardly insuring by his great goodness and his grace that his love and our souls shall never be separated in two, without end.

And thus, in this dread I have matter for meekness that saves me from presumption, and in the blessed showing of love I have matter for true comfort and joy, which saves me from despair.

This whole friendly showing from our courteous Lord is a lovely lesson and a sweet, gracious teaching by himself to comfort our souls. For he wills that we know by the sweetness of his familiar love that all that we see or feel, interiorly or exteriorly, that is opposed to this, is from the enemy and not from God, like this, for instance.

If we are stirred to be more reckless in our living or in the guarding of our hearts because we have knowledge of this plenteous love, then it is greatly necessary for us to beware of this stirring. If it comes it is untrue, and we ought greatly to hate it, because it has absolutely no likeness to God's will.

And when we have fallen by frailty or blindness, then our

courteous Lord, touching us, stirs us, calls us and preserves us. Then he wills that we see our wretchedness and meekly acknowledge it, but he does not will that we brood on it or that we be too full of wretchedness toward ourselves.

But he wills that we hastily pay attention to him, for he stands all alone and waits for us, continuously, sorrowfully and mournfully, until we come and he makes haste to have us with him. For we are his joy and his delight, and he is our salvation and our life. (Where I say, "he stands all alone," I stop speaking about the blessed company of heaven and speak about his office and his working here on earth— as the condition of the showing demands.)

## Chapter 80

*By three things God is worshiped and we are saved; how what we know now is only an ABC; sweet Jesus does everything, waiting and mourning with us; but when we are in sin, Christ mourns alone; and then it is our place, because of nature and reverence, hastily to turn again to him.*

Man stands by means of three things in this life, and by these three things God is glorified and we are helped, preserved and saved.

The first is the use of man's natural reason. The second is the common teaching of holy Church. The third is the inward, gracious working of the Holy Spirit. These three are all from one God.

God is the ground of our natural reason, God is the teaching of holy Church, and God is the Holy Spirit.

All these are different gifts, for which he wills we have great regard and to which he wills we pay attention. For these continuously work in us all together, entirely for God, and they are great things.

God wills that we have knowledge of this greatness here, like that in an ABC. That is to say, we can have a little knowledge here of what we shall know in its fulness in heaven, and that is in order to help us.

We know in our faith that God alone took our nature, and none but he. Furthermore we know that Christ, and none but he, did all the great works that belong to our salvation. Just so, he alone now accomplishes the last end, that is to say, he dwells here in us, he rules us, he governs us in our living, and he brings us to his bliss. And thus shall he do as long as any soul that shall come to heaven is on earth, to such an extent that if there were only one such soul on earth, he would be with that soul all alone until he had brought it up to his bliss.

I believe and understand the ministration of the holy angels, as the clerks explain it, but that was not showed to me. For he himself is nearest and meekest, highest and lowest, and does everything—not only what is necessary for us but also everything that is full of honor, for our joy in heaven.

Where I say, "he waits for us sorrowfully and mournfully," I mean all the true feeling that we have within ourselves, in contrition and in compassion, and in all moaning and mourning because we are not made one with our Lord.

And all of this that is profitable is Christ in us. Though some of us feel it seldom, it never passes from Christ until he has brought us out of all our woe. For love never allows him to be without pity. When we fall into sin and abandon his mind and the keeping of our own soul, then Christ bears alone all the responsibility for us. That is why he stands "sorrowfully and mournfully."

It is our place, then, for reverence and on account of our own nature, to turn ourselves hastily back to our Lord and not leave him alone. He is here alone with us all; that is to say, only for us is he here. When I am a stranger to him by sin, despair or sloth, then I let my Lord stand alone, inasmuch as he is in me.

And so it goes with all of us who are sinners. But though it is true that we do this frequently, his goodness never allows us to be alone. Continuously he is with us, tenderly he excuses us, and always he shields us from blame in his sight.

## Chapter 81

*This blessed woman saw God in different ways; but she saw him take no resting place except in man's soul; he wills that we rejoice more in his love than sorrow for our frequent failings, remembering the everlasting reward and living gladly in penance; and why God allows sin.*

Our good Lord showed himself to his creature in different ways, both in heaven and on earth, but I saw him take no place except in man's soul. He showed himself on earth in the sweet Incarnation and his blessed passion. He showed himself in other ways on earth, as where I said, "I saw God in a point."

He showed himself in still another way on earth, as if it were a pilgrimage. That is to say, he is here with us, leading us, and shall be until he has brought us all to his bliss in heaven.

He showed himself at different times, reigning, as I have said before, but principally in man's soul. He has taken there his resting place and his glorious city. Out of this honorable seat, he shall never rise or remove himself, without end.

Marvelous and solemn is the place where the Lord dwells, and therefore he wills that we readily pay attention to his gracious touching, rejoicing more in his complete love than sorrowing in our frequent failings. For the greatest honor we can pay him of anything that we can do is to live gladly and merrily for his love, in our penance.

For he looks at us so tenderly that he sees all our living here as a penance. The natural longing in us for him is a lasting penance in us, which he works in us and mercifully helps us to bear.

His love makes him long, and his wisdom and his truth, with his rightfulness, make him suffer in us here. In this way he wills to see it in us, for this is our natural penance, and the highest kind, as I see it. For this penance will never leave us until the time we are filled full and have him for our reward. And therefore he wills that we set our hearts in that which surpasses—that is to say, that we move them from the pain that we feel into the bliss that we trust to receive.

## Chapter 82

*God sees the mourning of the soul with pity, and not with blame; yet we do nothing but sin, in which we are preserved in solace and in dread; for he wills we turn ourselves to him readily, cleaving to his love, seeing that he is our medicine; so we must love in longing and in rejoicing; and whatsoever is contrary to this is not of God but of enmity.*

But here our courteous Lord showed the moaning and the mourning of our souls, with this meaning: "I know well you will to live for my love, merrily and gladly suffering all the penance that may come to you. But inasmuch as you do not live without sin, therefore you are depressed and sorrowful. And if you could live without sin, you would suffer, for my love, all the woe, all the tribulation and all the discomfort that could come to you. And this is the truth. But don't be too much vexed with the sin that falls to you against your will."

And here I understood that the lord looked at the servant with pity and not with blame, for this passing life does not ask to be lived entirely without blame and sin. He loves us endlessly. We sin habitually, and he shows it to us most mildly. Then we sorrow and mourn prudently, turning ourselves inward to the contemplation of his mercy, cleaving to his love and to his goodness, seeing that he is our medicine, and recognizing that all we do is sin.

Thus by the meekness we acquire from the sight of our sins, we please him by faithfully being aware of his everlasting love, thanking and praising him.

"I love you and you love me, and our love will never be separated in two. And I suffer for your profit." All this was showed me in a spiritual understanding, in his saying of the blessed words "I keep you most securely."

And by the great desire I saw in our blessed Lord, that we shall live in this way—that is to say, in longing and rejoicing, as this entire lesson of love shows—I understood that everything that is contrary to this is not from him but from enmity. And he wills that we know it by the sweet, gracious light of his natural love. If there is any such lover living on earth who is continually kept from falling, I know it not. For it was not showed me.

But it was showed that in falling and in rising we are ever preciously kept in our love. For we do not fall in the contemplation of God, we do not stand in the contemplation of self —and both of these are true, as I see it. But the contemplation of our Lord God is the higher truth. Then we are much bound to God, because he wills, in this life, to show us this lofty truth.

And I understood that while we are in this life, it is most profitable for us that we see these both at once. For the noble contemplation keeps us in spiritual joy and true rejoicing in God. The other—that is, the lower contemplation— keeps us in dread and makes us ashamed of ourselves.

But our good Lord ever wills that we hold ourselves much more in the contemplation of the higher, while not abandoning the knowing of the lower, until the time we are brought up above, where we shall have our Lord Jesus for our reward and shall be filled full of joy and bliss without end.


## Chapter 83


*Of three properties in God: life, love and light; that our reason is brought into agreement with God, and it is the highest gift; how our faith is a light coming from the Father, measured out to us, and leading us in this night; at the end*

*of our woe, suddenly our eyes shall be opened in the com
plete light and clarity of sight that is our maker: the Fathe
and the Holy Spirit in Jesus our savior.*

I had in part touching, sight and feeling in the three quali
ties of God in which the strength and the effect of the entir
revelation stands. And these were seen in every showing, and
most specifically in the twelfth, where is says frequently, "I
am it."

The properties are these: life, love and light. In life there i
marvelous familiarity; in love there is gentle courtesy; in light
there is endless nature.

These three properties were seen in a single goodness. My
reason wanted to be joined to this goodness, cleaving to it
with all its might. I gazed with reverent dread, greatly mar
veling at the sight, and at feeling the sweet agreement that
our reason has in God, understanding that it is the highest
gift that we have received. It is grounded in nature.

Our faith is a light naturally coming from our endless day;
that is, our Father, God. In this light our mother, Christ,
and our good Lord the Holy Spirit lead us in this passing life.

This light is measured prudently, staying with us in the
night as we need it. The light is the cause of our life, and the
night is the cause of our pain and of all our woe. In this we
deserve reward and thanks from God, because we, with mercy
and grace, deliberately know and live our light, walking in it
wisely and mightily. And at the end of woe, suddenly our
eyes shall be opened, and in clarity of sight our light shall be
complete. This light is God, our maker, the Father and the
Holy Spirit in Christ Jesus, our savior. Thus I saw and under
stood that our faith is our light in our night. This light is
God, our endless day.

## Chapter 84

*Charity is this light; it is not so small as not to be necessary, with hard labor, for one to deserve the endless glorious thanks of God; for faith and hope lead us to charity, which is of three kinds.*

This light is charity. The measuring of this light is done profitably for us by the wisdom of God. For the light is neither so large that we can clearly see our blissful day, nor is it entirely shut off from us. It is a light such that we can live in it rewardingly, deserving, with hard labor, the glorious thanks of God. And this was seen in the sixth showing, where he says, "I thank you for your service and for your distressful labor." Thus charity keeps us in faith and hope, and faith and hope lead us in charity—and at the end all shall be charity.

I had three kinds of understanding about this light, charity. The first is uncreated charity. The second is created charity. The third is given charity. Uncreated charity is God. Created charity is our soul in God. Given charity is a virtue, and it is a gracious gift of the working by which we love God for himself, and ourselves in God, and all that God loves for God.

## Chapter 85

*God has loved his chosen ones from eternity, and he never allows them to be hurt in a way that might lessen their bliss; how secrets, now hidden in heaven, shall be known; therefore we shall bless our Lord that everything is so well ordained.*

And I marveled greatly at this sight. For notwithstanding our simple living and our blindness here, yet our courteous

Lord beholds us endlessly, rejoicing in this working. And of all things, we can please him best by believing it, wisely and truly, and by rejoicing with him and in him.

For as truly as we shall be in the bliss of God without end, praising him and thanking him, so truly have we been in the foresight of God, loved and known in his endless purpose from eternity. In this eternal love, he made us; in the same love he preserves us and never allows us to be hurt in any way by which our bliss might be lessened.

Therefore, when the judgment is given and we are all brought up above, then shall we clearly see, in God, the secrets that are now hidden to us. Then none of us shall be stirred to say about anything, "Lord, if it had been thus and so, it would have been completely well. . . ." But we shall all say with one voice, "Lord, blessed may you be! Because it is this way, it is well. And now we see in truth that everything is done as you ordained it before anything was made."

## Chapter 86

*The good Lord showed that this book should be completed in a way other than by the first writing; for his working he wills that we pray for this, thanking him, trusting him and rejoicing in him; how he made this showing because he wills to have it known; in this knowing he will give us grace to love him; for fifteen years afterward it was answered that the cause of the whole of the showing was love—the which may Jesus grant us! Amen!*

This book has been begun by God's gift and his grace, but it has not yet been completed, as I see it. We all pray together to God for charity, thanking, trusting and rejoicing by the working of God. This is how our good Lord wills that we pray to him, according to the understanding I drew from all of what he intended us to learn and from the sweet words he spoke most cheerfully, "I am the ground of your beseeching."

For I saw and understood truly from what our Lord intended that he showed it because he wills to have it known better than it is. In this knowing he wills to give us grace to love him and cleave to him. He beholds his heavenly treasure with such great love on earth that he wills to give us more light and solace in heavenly joy, drawing our hearts from the sorrow and darkness they are in.

From the time of the showing, I desired frequently to understand what our Lord's meaning was, and more than fifteen years afterward I was answered by a spiritual understanding that said, "Do you want to understand your Lord's meaning in this experience? Understand it well: love was his meaning. Who showed it to you? Love. What did he show you? Love. Why did he show it? For love. Hold yourself in this truth and you shall understand and know more in the same vein. And you will never know or understand anything else in it forever."

Thus was I taught that love is our Lord's meaning. And I saw most certainly in this and in everything that before God made us he loved us, and this love never slackened and never shall. In this love he has done all his works, in this love he has made all things profitable for us, and in this love our life is everlasting. In our creation we had a beginning, but the love by which he made us was in him from without beginning, and in this love we have our beginning. And all this we shall see in God without end.

# SCRIBAL ADDITIONS

Each of the manuscript versions of Juliana's *Revelations* ends with a kind of dismissal by the scribe, ranging from the brevity of the single Latin sentence of the 1413 manuscript to the several paragraphs of the scribe of Sloane 2499, faithfully copied by the scribe of Sloane 3705, who adds his own closing. Since each colophon adds something distinctive to the recorded manuscript, I have chosen to include all four in translation.

*1413* Thus ends Juliana of Norwich. (Latin)

*Paris* Thus is completed the book of the revelations of Juliana, an anchorite of Norwich, on whose soul may God have mercy. (Latin)

*Sloane 2499* Thus ends the revelation of love of the blessed Trinity showed by our savior Christ Jesus for our endless comfort and solace, and also that we might rejoice in him in the passing journey of this life. Amen, Jesus, amen.

I pray Almighty God that this book may come only to the hands of those who will be his faithful lovers, to those who will submit to the faith of holy Church and obey the wholesome understanding and teaching of the men who lead virtuous lives, are of serious age and are profound in learning. For this revelation is lofty divinity and high wisdom. Therefore it cannot dwell with him who is in slavery to sin and to the devil.

Beware that you do not accept one thing according to your desire and pleasure, and ignore another, for that is the behavior of a heretic. Accept everything with everything else, understanding it all truly. Everything is according to holy Scripture and is grounded in it, and Jesus our true love, light and truth will show that to all pure souls who perseveringly ask this wisdom of him with meekness.

And you to whom this book shall come, intensely and heartily thank our savior Christ Jesus for making these showings and revelations for you and to you from his endless love, mercy and goodness, for your and our safe guide and conduct to everlasting bliss. May Jesus grant us this! Amen. (English)

*Sloane* 3705 adds to this the following:

Here ends the sublime and wonderful revelations of the unutterable love of God in Jesus Christ, given to a dear lover of his and, in her, to all his dear friends and lovers, whose hearts, like hers, flame in the love of our dearest Jesus. (English)

# BIBLIOGRAPHY

In addition to the manuscripts described in the Introduction, I have used the following works in preparing this translation. Many of them contain bibliographies, more or less extensive, that will provide further information on specific related topics.

Butler-Bowdon, W., trans. *The Book of Margery Kempe*. New York: Devin-Adair Company, 1944.

Coleman, T. W. *English Mystics of the Fourteenth Century*. Westport, Conn.: Greenwood Press, 1971 (reprint; first published in London: Epworth Press, 1938).

Hodgson, Phyllis, ed. *Deonise Hid Diuinite and Other Treatises on Contemplative Prayer*. Early English Text Society No. 231. London: Oxford University Press, 1955.

Hudleston, Dom Roger, ed. *Revelations of Divine Love Shewed to a Devout Ankress, by Name, Julian of Norwich*. Westminster, Md.: Newman Press, 1952.

Johnston, William, S.J., trans. *The Cloud of Unknowing; and The Book of Privy Counseling*. Garden City, N.Y.: Doubleday Image Books, 1973.

Knowles, David. *The English Mystical Tradition*. New York: Harper & Brothers, 1961.

Meisel, Anthony C.; and del Mastro, M. L., trans. *The Rule of Saint Benedict*. Garden City, N.Y.: Doubleday Image Books, 1975.

Milosh, Joseph E. *"The Scale of Perfection" and the English Mystical Tradition*. Madison, Wis.: The University of Wisconsin Press, 1966.

Molinari, Paul, S.J. *Julian of Norwich: the Teaching of a 14th Century English Mystic*. New York: Longmans, Green & Co., 1958.

Ryan, John K., trans. *The Confessions of St. Augustine*. Garden City, N.Y.: Doubleday Image Books, 1960.

Sherley-Price, Leo, trans. *The Scale of Perfection*. St. Meinrad, Ind.: Abbey Press, 1975.

Sitwell, Dom Gerard, O.S.B. "Contemplation in 'The Scale of Perfection,'" *Downside Review*, 67 (Summer, 1949), 276–90; 68 (Winter, 1949–50), 21–34; 68 (Summer, 1950), 271–89.

————, trans. *The Scale of Perfection by Walter Hilton*. Westminster, Md.: Newman Press, 1953.

Stone, Robert Karl. *Middle English Prose Style*. The Hague: Mouton, 1970.

Walsh, James, S.J., ed. *Pre-Reformation English Spirituality*. New York: Fordham University Press, c. 1965 (no date given).

————, trans. *The Revelations of Divine Love of Julian of Norwich*. St. Meinrad, Ind.: Abbey Press, 1974.

Wolters, Clifton, trans. *The Cloud of Unknowing*. Baltimore, Md.: Penguin Books, 1961.

————, trans. *The Fire of Love by Richard Rolle*. Baltimore, Md.: Penguin Books, 1972.